D1034330

REVOLUTION

REVOLUTION

A HISTORY OF THE IDEA

Edited by David Close & Carl Bridge

BARNES & NOBLE BOOKS
Totowa, New Jersey

First published in the USA 1985 by
Barnes & Noble Books
81 Adams Drive
Totowa, New Jersey, 07512
Printed in Great Britain

Library of Congress Cataloging in Publication Data
Main entry under title:

Revolution: The history of an idea.

Includes index.
1. Revolutions – Addresses, Essays, Lectures.
2. Revolutions – Case Studies – Addresses, Essays, Lectures.
I. Close, D.H. (David H.) II. Bridge, C.R. (Carl R.)
JC491.R486 1985 321.09 84-28372
ISBN 0-389-20560-5

CONTENTS

PREFACE

David Close and Carl Bridge

This is a textbook for students written by staff of the History and Politics Disciplines of Flinders University, and was originally devised for a course which they have taught for several years. We have found no such work which combines the three elements of our course: an analysis of the concept of revolution, a historical survey of its use, and case-studies of attempts to realise it. We believe a historical approach to be valuable because aspects of the idea have engaged the attention of political theorists over many centuries. Before knowing what questions to ask about revolution, or how to answer them, we should try to learn from earlier theorists who have treated the concept. Our choice of case-studies is limited to the twentieth century because earlier revolutions can be seen in better perspective and so treated more conveniently as part of the history of the idea. The resulting bias of the book towards the twentieth century is justified by what we believe to be the unprecedented importance and diversity of the phenomenon of revolution in recent times.

We have not tried to reach agreement on our definition of an idea as contentious as this one, and, like Mao Zedong at one time, we have 'let a hundred flowers bloom'. However, among the few things that we do agree on is that a revolution includes an overthrow of the dominant value-system in a community. This view has led, in our case, to an emphasis on political events and ideas, although we have recognised contributions by disciplines other than ours, especially sociology.

We have not covered all major theorists or revolutions. In the space of a short book, a more comprehensive coverage would be too perfunctory to be useful. Our choice of subjects has been determined in part by our interests and by those of students.

We are grateful to Pauline Mulberry, Janet Pascoe, Joan Stephenson and Rae Tyler for producing the manuscript on the word processor.

CONTRIBUTORS

Carl Bridge is Lecturer in History at the University of New England, New South Wales, and formerly Tutor in History at the Flinders University of South Australia. He has written articles on the history of Australian and British conservative politics.

Bill Brugger is Professor of Politics at Flinders University. He has written four books, and edited two collections of articles, on contemporary China.

David Close is Senior Lecturer in History at Flinders University. He has written articles on British political history and is preparing a book on counter-revolution in modern Greece.

Richard DeAngelis is Senior Lecturer in Politics at Flinders University. He has written *Blue-Collar Workers and Politics: a French Paradox* (Croom Helm, 1982), and is writing a book on the Mitterrand government and its attempt at non-revolutionary structural reforms.

Cherry Gertzel is Reader in Politics at Flinders University. Her research interests focus primarily on the politics and administration of development in East and Central Africa. Her publications include *The Politics of Independent Kenya* (Heinemann, 1970); *Party and Locality in Northern Uganda* (Athlare Press, 1973); and, with Carolyn Baykes and Morris Szeftel, *The Dynamics of the One-Party State in Zambia* (Manchester University Press, forthcoming).

Kate Hannan is part-time Tutor in Politics at Flinders and Adelaide Universities. She is writing a thesis on the political implications of economic reforms in China and eastern Europe.

Peter A. Howell is Reader in History at Flinders University. He has written two books and thirty articles in the fields of the history of ideas or British imperial practice.

Norman Wintrop is Senior Lecturer in Politics at Flinders University, where he has taught several political theory courses, one of which was primarily a critical examination of the Marxist tradition. He is the editor and part-author of *Liberal Democratic Theory and its Critics* (Croom Helm, 1983).

PART I

A HISTORICAL SURVEY

Chapter One

THE MEANING OF REVOLUTION

David Close

'What a fine sight! It's the revolution' exclaimed Ernest Mandel, a leader of the Trotskyist Fourth International, during the street-fighting in Paris in May 1968.[1] The scene of destruction which he was admiring included his own car ablaze. For a contrasting view of revolution, more typical of generations of middle-class Europeans, take this imaginary description by Charles Dickens of a lynch-mob storming the Bastille:

> The sea of black and threatening waters, and of destructive upheaving of wave against wave, whose depths were yet unfathomed.... The remorseless sea of ... voices of vengeance, and faces hardened in the furnaces of suffering until the touch of pity could make no mark on them.[2]

Thus the idea of revolution has for a long time contained powerful and diverse associations. When trying to explain these associations by analysing the word, we find a puzzling variety of usage. The Oxford English Dictionary defines revolutions as 'a complete overthrow of the established government in any country or state by those who were previously subject to it: a forcible substitution of a new ruler or form of government.' Some contemporary theorists of revolution such as Peter Calvert accept this definition as enough in itself.[3] Its disadvantage is that it includes a broad category of events for which other terms are available: rebellions or coups, directed against individual holders of authority, but accepting the system through which they rule. There are numerous examples of these, for example, in the

1. P. Seale and M. McConville, Red Flag/Black Flag. French Revolution 1968 (G. P. Putnam's Sons, New York, 1968), p. 84 (my translation). The fellow-contributors to this book have made valuable comments on my chapters.

2. A Tale of Two Cities, 1859, Book 2, Ch. 21.

3. A Study of Revolution (Oxford University Press, London, 1970), p.5.

history of the Egyptian pharoahs, of imperial China and imperial Rome. Although violent and illegal they usually - perhaps always - left the system of government intact, and won retrospective legitimacy according to traditional norms. Thus they contain few of the qualities that are conventionally associated with revolution. Many writers nowadays dilute the term still more, so as to mean any large-scale process of change. The objection to this usage is that it blurs the vital distinction between revolution and reformist change, carried out in conformity to established norms and authorities. It is important to know when and why one occurs rather than another. At the other extreme are theorists like Samuel Huntington who confine the term, in effect, to a few fundamental upheavals of 'modern' times, i.e. the seventeenth century onwards.[4] The trouble here is that the 'great' revolutions which Huntington recognises, such as the English, the Mexican and Chinese, do not have much in common, while some of them, as we shall see, show similarities with earlier upheavals for which revolution seems the only adequate label. The definition of revolution which such theorists adopt tends to be arbitrarily exclusive. For Huntington the crucial ingredient is the demand for participation in a political system by social groups excluded from it; yet anyone can name revolutionary upheavals - such as the English of 1641-60 or the German of 1933-45 - where this was not apparently the main element.

The foregoing definitions surely miss the essential point about revolution, which is that it involves a change in a government's basis of legitimacy, that is in those principles, or norms, which determine its claims to its subjects' obedience, and the nature of its powers and responsibilities. In contemporary Britain or Australia, for example, such principles (in their ideal form) include government by consent and for the benefit of the governed, equality before the law, freedom of opinion and respect for private property. The word revolution has been associated with changes in government not only by long usage but also by logic, because it is only through a change of government that people can bring about a forcible, large-scale change in any sector of society. Strictly, therefore, the application of the word to non-political spheres (as in cultural, technological or economic revolution) is metaphorical: it can however be fruitful, so long as the word is confined to basic, normative change. The element of coercion or violence is also essential to revolution, because every political system rests ultimately on the sanction of force, and force is therefore needed to overthrow it. In theory the upholders of the old system may be so demoralised, and the champions of the new one may be so confident and united, that power is transferred peacefully. In practice these conditions never exist. There is a common belief that revolution must include some kind of social change; but this requirement is superfluous to the foregoing definition. A fundamental political change in any

---

4. Political Order in Changing Societies (Yale University Press, New Haven, 1968), p. 263.

society must in time affect many kinds of collective activity.[5] One needs to define the word revolution in subjective as well as objective terms in order to understand what exhilarated Mandel and horrified Dickens. The essential feel of revolution derives from its cataclysmic - sweeping, sudden and violent - quality. Cataclysmic change destroys people's security and unsettles their convictions. Hence the emotional extremism and intellectual effervescence that characterise those periods that intervene after old authorities have been shaken and before new ones have become established.

In trying to decide whether a movement is revolutionary, and if so, in what sense, it helps to bear in mind that revolution not only destroys a political system but also creates one in its place. How serious, and successful, was the movement concerned in furthering these two ends? If, like the English peasants' revolt of 1381, it produced some demands with revolutionary implications but did not try to replace the government, it cannot be called revolutionary. If it succeeded in replacing the government, but only for a time, it could usefully be called a partial revolution when some of its achievements endured - for example, the English revolution of 1641-60 - or a failed revolution when all its achievements were later reversed - for example the Nazi revolution of 1933-45.

A historical survey of the phenomenon of revolution will explain much about the present meaning of the word. Its current imprecision and diversity of usage can be accounted for by its tortuous etymology. Its meanings now and in different periods in the past have been coloured by association with certain phenomena with which the word has no essential connection. But we will find that the essential element in the idea, as defined above, has fascinated and stimulated political thinkers in many periods of the last 2,500 years.

Revolutions were not unusual events in the city-states of classical Greece, and then of medieval and Renaissance Italy. Changes of regime occurred in these city-states which sometimes affected the status-system within them, and to some extent the distribution of wealth.[6] The changes might be justified by appeals to political ideals, such as the permissive democracy of Periclean Athens, or the republican liberty of Renaissance Florence. These ideals were to a limited extent exportable. Athens encouraged democratic coups, and Sparta oligarchic ones, in other city-states during the Peloponnesian wars (431-404 B.C.). Siena adopted the Florentine cult of republican

5. Pace, I. Kramnick, 'Reflections on Revolution: Definition and Explanation in Recent Scholarship', History and Theory, vol.11, no.1 (January 1972), p. 30. But in other respects my definition follows Kramnick's closely.

6. N.G.L. Hammond, The Classical Age of Greece (Weidenfeld & Nicolson, London, 1975), pp. 149-154; B. Pullan, A History of Early Renaissance Italy (Allen Lane, London, 1973), pp. 124-5.

virtue in the early fifteenth century.[7] The use of terms by contemporary historians and theorists showed that they understood the concept of revolution. Aristotle spoke of stasis with metaboli politeias (a violent coup with a change of constitution). In fourteenth-century Italy, the word itself - rivoluzione - appears, and in its modern sense. Its first known use [8] was to describe an uprising in Siena in 1355, when an oligarchic regime was replaced by a popular one. Niccolo Machiavelli avoided the word - using such terms as 'mutazioni del stato' (changes in the state) instead - but was deeply interested in problems of political changes and stability, partly because he lived through two revolutions in quick succession (1494 and 1512) in Florence.

The differences between the revolutions in the city-states and those of the late eighteenth-century onwards were however as important as the similarities. The city-states differed sharply from modern nation-states in being intimate, face-to-face communities, where changes of government were usually if not invariably inspired by the greed, ambitions and resentments of small groups of people, however they might be justified subsequently in terms of political principle. More importantly, the protagonists in the dissensions within city-states invariably assumed that they would leave untouched most aspects of their social environment. Even in allegedly democratic states, they excluded, by tacit consent, the poorer majority of the population from political activity. Revolutions never changed radically the social structure, or the economic organisation, or the moral code, of the city-states concerned. This is certainly not because of prejudice against government interference in these matters. It was because the status quo in these matters was assumed to be natural, or God-given, so that the duty of government - any government - was to intervene (in such matters as food prices, social status, or moral behaviour) in order to maintain it. Ideologies were retrospective rationalisations of the status quo rather than programmes of radical change. In any case, before the diffusion of printing in the fifteenth century, those important prerequisites of the formation of ideology - the articulation and circulation of conflicting ideas - were difficult. The significance of revolution in any city-state was further limited by the fact that each was but a fragment of a recognised national community - classical Greece or medieval Italy - that was bound together by manifest ties of culture, language and religion. For these reasons it seems misleading to compare - as Nicholas Hammond does - the ideological competition of Athens and Sparta in the fifth century B.C. with the recent Cold War between the USA and the USSR.[9]

The idea of revolution as applied by contemporaries to the city-

---

7. H. Baron, The Crisis of the Early Italian Renaissance (Princeton University Press, New Jersey, 1955), p. 361.

8. A. Hatto, ' "Revolution": an Enquiry into the Usefulness of an Historical Term', Mind, vol.58, no.232 (October 1949), p.502.

9. P. 190.

states differed in another great respect from its modern counterpart. Far from being seen as the beginning of a new order, revolutions were seen by contemporaries as phases in a sequence of changes which might well include return to an earlier order. This assumption was realistic. The political volatility of the city-states was combined with an underlying continuity of political culture and social structure. Plato in The Republic saw a pattern to the changes in the city-states, his ideal state degenerating into timocracy (e.g. rule by the brave), which led to oligarchy (e.g. rule by the rich few) which led to democracy (rule by the many poor) which led to tyranny (rule by the arbitrary one).[10] His notion that extreme democracy tends to change into tyranny has remained influential until the present, partly because it seemed to have been vindicated by the outcome of the French and Russian revolutions. The historian Polybius turned Plato's succession into a cycle, labelling it by a Greek term 'anakiklosis'[11] - an exact counterpart of revolution, which itself derives from the same Latin origin as the word 'revolve'. The cyclical idea was borrowed from the astronomical one of the supposed orbit (or revolutions in a now archaic sense) of the stars, the force behind the cycle being the supernatural one of Fortune. The idea of revolution as part of a cycle governed by supernatural forces survived into modern times, being used for example by the English historian Lord Clarendon in the seventeenth century. A specific application of the idea was to label as revolutions those upheavals which were believed to restore an old system. This was the meaning of the famous Glorious Revolution of 1688 in England; and at the time this was a conventional use of the word.[12] The influence of the cyclical connotation tells us two things about theories of revolution before the eighteenth century. They lacked a notion of rectilinear (as opposed to cyclical) development such as progress, and they recognised little freedom in humans to change permanently their political environment.

Another type of revolution in medieval and Renaissance Europe was inspired wholly or partly by religion. Christianity, like Judaism, has tended to produce millennarian movements, which are characterised by the belief that existing society is fundamentally evil, and that a community of believers can, with divine aid, overthrow it and establish an ideal one.[13] Like modern revolutionary movements, millennarian ones have flourished in conditions of collective anxiety

---

10. Book 8.

11. Cited in Hatto, p. 499.

12. Hatto, p. 505; V.F. Snow, 'The Concept of Revolution in Seventeenth-Century England', Historical Journal vol.5, no.2 (March 1962), pp. 167-190.

13. N. Cohn, 'Medieval Millenarianism: its Bearing on the Comparative Study of Millenarian Movements', in S. Thrupp (ed.), 'Millenial Dreams in Action - Essays in Comparative Study', Comparative Studies in Society and History Supplement II (Mouton, The Hague, 1962), pp. 31-43.

and upheaval. Most such movements have accepted existing governments, while awaiting Christ's second coming. But some have anticipated this event by trying to establish free communities of the godly which - in the case of movements appealing to the poor - have been revolutionary in their egalitarianism. Such was the Anabaptist regime in the independent German city of Munster (1534-5), whose leaders imposed communal ownership of goods and a reign of terror on the inhabitants.[14] Anabaptism thereafter won a European-wide reputation similar to that of communism or anarchism earlier in this century. The movement led by Girolamo Savonarola in Florence in 1494-8 was a form of patriotic millennarianism that appealed to the political and moral beliefs of the socially privileged as well as the humble, and contributed to a radical democratisation of the regime.[15] Because the technique of printing was now available for the circulation of ideas, we can more easily speak of revolutions as inspired by ideology, in something like its full sense of a political programme derived from a Weltanschauung or philosophical view of the world. But millennarian movements have never known how to win power on more than a local scale, and even then have been so provocative in their radicalism as to suffer speedy suppression.

Other forms of Christianity have proved politically radical when forced to revolt against governments by being refused tolerance; and the cases of such disagreement between subject and ruler multiplied with the Reformation. When religious dissent fused with other discontents, the result could be revolution, as in the case of the Dutch revolt against the Spanish monarch in the late sixteenth century, and the parliamentary revolt against the English monarch in the mid-seventeenth century. These were broader in scope than previous revolutions in Western history, because they were national in scale, and inspired by religious as well as political aims. Neither can be called a social revolution, although the English one had social consequences, in that governments were thenceforth more considerate towards commercial interests, while the political influence of the peerage was temporarily weakened.[16] Radical social change in either country was precluded by the fact that the revolutions were controlled by established elites, particularly landowning gentry or aristocracy. These continued to deny any political voice to the poor majority of the population, and suppressed those, like the Digger communities in England, who tried to engage in social revolution. The ideas of the democratic Levellers and the communist Diggers are examples of the intellectual effervescence which makes revolutions fascinating as

14. Cohn, The Pursuit of the Millennium 2nd edn (Oxford University Press, New York, 1970), pp. 261-280.

15. D. Weinstein, 'Millenarianism in a Civic Setting: the Savonarola Movement in Florence', in Thrupp, pp. 187-203.

16. G.E. Aylmer, The Struggle for the Constitution in England in the Seventeenth Century, 4th edn (Blandford Press, London, 1975), pp. 141, 173-4.

political laboratories. But such influence as they had lay mainly in the future.[17] There was moreover a technical barrier to radical revolution in this period, which was the limited scope of national government. Even in those nations which were politically united - such as Spain, France and England - central government was weak, being conducted through a small body of royal servants. Most of the routine work of government - such as the maintenance of religion and order, the provision of poor relief and of roads - lay in the hands of local notables, whose powers and composition were difficult to change from the centre. In their attitude to the past, the Dutch and English revolutions were ambivalent. Their initial aim was a backward-looking defence of old although vigorous institutions: the states-generals and local liberties in the Netherlands, parliament and the rule of law in England. Only with reluctance, and through force of circumstances, did their leaders take such radical steps as the abolition of monarchy. But other kinds of appeal to the past were radical. Such was the Calvinists' reinterpretation of the Bible in both countries. Such also was the invocation of a mythical golden age, Saxon England, by the Levellers.

The concept of revolution acquired much of its modern power and associations during the French revolution of 1789. Underlying the declarations of the revolutionary leaders were two particularly radical assumptions. The first was that they could renovate society completely, by reference to abstract principles, not to precedent. This assumption has since tended to characterise revolutions. The appeal to the 'normative past'[18] survived in the late eighteenth century only in references to a mythologised, remote society, particularly that of republican Rome. Essentially revolutionaries now looked to posterity, not to tradition, for justification. This fundamental reorientation of radical thought had been brought about by the philosophers of the Enlightenment - that is by political thinkers of diverse interests and nationalities (although chiefly French) during the previous century. They popularised the idea that human reason was an objective instrument by which all customs and institutions could be tested and reformed, so that societies could be progressively improved on principles that were universally applicable. Inheriting the Christian belief that the universe was planned and harmonious, they went on to assume that its laws were manifest in the world of nature, of which

---

17. C. Hill, The World Turned Upside Down. Radical Ideas during the English Revolution (Temple Smith, London, 1972), pp. 86-120; A. Lloyd-Moote, 'The Preconditions of Revolution in Early Modern Europe: Did they Really Exist?' Canadian Journal of History, vol.7, no.3 (September 1972), p. 225.

18. P. Zagorin, 'Prolegomena to the Comparative Study of Revolution in Early Modern Europe' Comparative Studies in Society and History, vol.18, no.2 (March 1976), p. 171.

human society was part.[19] Through their reason, humans could understand these laws, and turn this understanding to their own advantage by improvements both in material well-being, and in the organisation of society. This process of improvement was widely evident in the Western world, but painfully slow, when considered in relation to the misery and injustice that the philosophers saw everywhere. Their belief that these evils were curable was new. Hitherto poverty and oppression had normally been seen as the natural condition of the majority of mankind. The philosophers possessed a crusading zeal to overcome them; and their disciples, the revolutionary politicians of France (commonly termed Jacobins, after one of their parties) expressed this zeal in sweeping reforms in 1789-1793. Their bold reconstruction, along more rational lines, of parliament, law courts, local government, ecclesiastical and administrative boundaries, weights and measures, proved enduring achievements. Yet for all their practical concentration on improving the world below, the Jacobins resembled the millenarians in their dogmatism and utopianism. Like the millenarians, they reserved their ideal society for a unanimous body of true believers, while condemning their opponents as degenerate products of the old order. Here lay the totalitarian tendencies henceforth common in revolutionary thought.[20] The revolution, like Christ's second coming, was the end of an old era and the prelude to a new one. The belief (which in retrospect seems pathetically deluded[21]) that they were creating a new society has since characterised revolutionaries in the Western world.

The revolutionaries' second great assumption was that there existed universal human rights which were derived from natural law. The onus of justification now lay on apologists for man-made constraints and inequalities, including especially the privileges of monarchs, priests and aristocrats. The fact that human rights were claimed to be self-evident by the revolutionaries, and widely accepted as such in other countries, was a tribute to the educational achievement of the Enlightenment. Indeed the concept possessed a greater power than the revolutionary politicians were aware of. The logical conclusion that there existed no natural right to private property was drawn in the 1790s by an extremist fringe of Jacobins under Gracchus Babeuf and they founded a body of socialist thought which was to expand steadily. The immediate liberal corollary of natural rights theory - that government should be based on popular consent - combined with the influence of romantic theorists of the cultural unity of peoples such as Johann Herder to arouse nationalist feeling throughout Europe. This was stimulated at the same time by reaction to the outburst of French nationalism which was deliberately

19. C.L. Becker, The Heavenly City of the Eighteenth-Century Philosophers (Yale University Press, New Haven, 1960), p. 43.

20. J.L. Talmon, Political Messianism. The Romantic Phase (F.A. Praeger, New York, 1960), p. 20.

21. H. Arendt, On Revolution (Faber, London, 1963), p. 39.

encouraged by revolutionary governments in order to secure mass support within France. (By nationalism, of course, is meant not mere patriotism, but the political theory that there exists such an entity as a nation, with recognisable boundaries, which forms the sole proper basis of a state.) Nationalism provided an emotional bond between social classes for which there was no substitute in revolutions before the late eighteenth century, and has proved important to the success of perhaps all revolutions since then.

The diversity of appeal of the revolution's ideas was another novel feature. Revolutions before the eighteenth century had little appeal outside their home country, and even there were of interest mainly to a propertied minority of the population. The fascination of the French Revolution for contemporaries was reinforced by the fact that it occurred in what was then the leading power and cultural heart of Europe. It had a profound impact on the political consciousness of radicals and conservatives, have-nots and haves throughout Western civilisation. Henceforth 'the dumb savage discontent of the have-nots changed into a realisation of rights and into a Messianic expectation, the dread of riot of the haves into a never receding fear of some total upheaval'.[22] The revolution shaped the thought-world of the nineteenth century, and until well into the twentieth it appeared to be the model which successors were thought likely to follow.

After the general restoration of the old monarchical and aristocractic order in 1815, the ideas of the French revolution lived on in the activities of radical thinkers and politicians in many countries. Some were socialist, some liberal, some nationalist: all were united for the time being by the bond of a common enemy and by the millenarian vision bequeathed by the Enlightenment.[23] The years 1815-1850 were punctuated by fairly frequent revolts which were interpreted, accurately, as a continuation of the French Revolution. Thus the professional revolutionary became - and has hitherto remained - a prominent figure in Western society. Highly articulate, ideologically inspired and communicating with fellow believers in other countries, he worked for revolution as a long-term goal. But his creed could no longer be the same as that of the Jacobins. As Jacob Talmon pointed out, the experience of the French revolution, the Napoleonic wars and still more the industrial revolution stimulated a greater awareness of the extent to which men were moulded by social groups, with complex interrelationships, and of the extent to which these groups were moulded by history. Thinkers became particularly interested in identifying the underlying forces of historical development - forces which seemed to have swept the actors in the French revolution to unexpected ends - and which could be turned into allies if they were understood.[24]

---

22. Talmon, p. 27.
23. Ibid., pp. 29-30.
24. Ibid., pp. 22-3; Arendt, p. 45.

In this environment Karl Marx developed ideas which appeared in 1848 and have since tended increasingly to dominate revolutionary thought. He offered socialist revolutionaries the potent conviction that the forces of history were on their side. He identified such forces by undertaking an analysis of contemporary industrial society that was so observant of its damage to human relationships, yet so sympathetic to its potential benefits to human well-being, that it has remained influential to this day. He dedicated himself to the task of preparing for a proletarian revolution, and he saw (at least at one stage) the need for a party which would doggedly pursue this end, even while fighting the same enemies as middle-class liberals.[25] Largely because of Marx's influence, revolution in most people's minds in the twentieth century has been associated with class conflict.

The idea of revolution acquired important new meanings with the seizure of power in Russia by the Bolsheviks in 1917. For the first time revolution became institutionalised. This was the achievement of the party which V.I. Lenin built up from 1903. Tightly disciplined, with professional leaders and a potential for mass expansion, it was a phenomenon outside the experience of Karl Marx's world of 1850. From 1917 it drew in millions of Russians, and set up an apparatus of government which eventually controlled all sectors of society. The furtherance of revolution was now whatever the Bolshevik leaders decided to do. For a generation in fact, the Kremlin was the centre of world revolution, because the Russian party dominated international Communism. With institutionalisation however came an agonising contradiction which has afflicted other revolutionary parties since 1917. Institutionalisation enabled the revolutionary regime to survive - in the Soviet Union's case against great odds - but the survival of the institution became an end in itself, and in the process the ideals of the revolution were distorted out of recognition. A particularly striking example of this distortion was the official justification of inequality by Josef Stalin in the 1930s. There was a corresponding change in personnel. Those who made the revolution tended to be idealistic, argumentative and in a way egalitarian. They were replaced under Stalin by pragmatic, conformist and status-conscious bureaucrats.

The Bolshevik revolution was new also in scope: no previous revolutionaries had dreamt of undertaking a complete reconstruction of the economy and society, as well as of government. The eighteenth-century revolutionaries believed that the renovation of society would result simply from the destruction and replacement of pernicious forms of authority. The forces of economic progress - the human faculties and the technological processes - were already in existence, and needed merely to be unshackled. Marx thought primarily of changing their ownership. The Bolsheviks went much further in undertaking

25. 'Address to the Communist League' (March 1850), in D.McLellan (ed.), Karl Marx. Selected Writings (Oxford University Press, London, 1977), pp. 280-5.

from the start to create the forces of progress: to start new industries, change methods of production, educate and train an illiterate population. They undertook literally to transform every citizen's conditions of existence. So began the first developmental revolution, in which economic development became a major aim of the new regime. The Bolsheviks showed the mentality of later revolutionaries in underdeveloped countries, in that they wanted to catch up economically with the West, and to free their country from economic dependence on it. Indeed, because economic development seemed vital to the survival of the Bolsheviks' rule, it has effectively eclipsed their other original aim of creating an egalitarian community. In later independent Communist revolutions, the latter has received somewhat more attention, but is still subordinate. The success of the longer-established Communist regimes (the Soviet Union, China, Yugoslavia) in developing their countries economically and ending their subservience to the West has been remarkable and fully advertised.

Since 1917, the interdependent aims of development and independence have been a common concern of revolutions. Development has meant primarily the adoption of Western technology, which has been sought as a basis of military power, and as a means of raising people's living standards. Adoption of new technology by a backward country inevitably entails far-reaching changes in its social and political systems. The importance of Marxism-Leninism to this process has been, not its socialism, but its special (though not unique) interest in economic growth of a kind compatible with national independence, and its special ability to provide strong government through the instrument of the centralised party. The fact that Marxist-Leninist parties that win power usually overthrow old elites like landlords and hereditary rulers is of special importance, because this overthrow, as Willem Wertheim argues persuasively, may be a necessary prerequisite for economic advance for the majority of the world's population that lives in countries conventionally considered as underdeveloped.[26] Understandably, the interest of Marxist and other revolutionaries has tended to shift from the industrial proletariat of advanced societies (who have generally been unresponsive to revolutionary appeals), to the rural masses of the third world. This transfer of attention from the centres of civilisation to the peripheries has been a historically new development in revolutionary thought.

The desire for development as a path to national independence has been especially strong in countries dominated by the West, whether through territorial encroachment and infiltration of government (as in the Ottoman empire and imperial China), or through primarily economic ties (as in Cuba in the 1950s), or through formal possession (as in most colonies, including much of Africa as late as the 1970s). In such countries nationalism has provided revolutionary leaders with a vital means of winning popular support and unifying their countries.

---

26. Evolution and Revolution. The Rising Waves of Emancipation (Penguin, London, 1974), p. 295.

For these reasons revolutions in modernising countries tend to be intensely nationalist (including Marxist-Leninist ones, despite their theoretical disapproval of nationalism).

A result of these trends has been a form of revolution known as the people's war.[27] Lenin's work Imperialism of 1917 pointed the way intellectually, and the Chinese Communists provided the prototype in the 1930s.[28] The Chinese example was followed independently by the Communist parties of Yugoslavia, Greece and Vietnam in the 1940s, and then by non-Communist but socialist revolutionaries in Algeria in the 1950s, and in Guinea-Bissau, Angola and Mozambique in the 1960s. Being denied access to the cities by their foreign (and sometimes also domestic) enemies, these revolutionaries have turned to the peasants, and appealed to their national feeling as well as their material interests. They have educated them to participate in broad-based organs of local government controlled by themselves - an achievement made possible by shared hatred of the foreign enemy. This political organisation has supported their guerrilla campaigns, through which they have built up a military force capable of conquering the urban centres of power. Having formed a government, they have then faced immense economic problems - at first of reconstruction and later of development - with little expertise. The resulting disillusionment among them has been intensified by the usual corruption of power. The counterparts of people's wars in Latin America - of which the most important so far have been those in Cuba in the 1950s, Nicaragua in the 1970s and El Salvador at present - differ in being waged primarily against a domestic enemy, and in that the guerrillas have relied less on their own political organisation and more on those of a broad range of allies in city and country. The leaders of the Cuban revolution, and influential sympathisers like Regis Debray,[29] exaggerated the importance of the guerrillas as a nucleus (or foco) of mass revolt, and publicised in the 1960s a strategy of revolution based on them. So far all the guerrilla-led revolutions have been, in varying degrees, supported by Communist regimes and opposed by capitalist ones, a fact which has influenced the ideological directions of some. Those who deride the contrast between the promises and performance of such revolutions may be overlooking their achievement of creating political order where little or none existed. Like the Bolsheviks, they have created governments capable of commanding their citizens' respect and loyalty, maintaining order among them, showing practical concern for their welfare, and defending them (militarily, and perhaps economically) from foreign powers.

Another use which revolutionary leaders have made of nationalist appeals has been to lessen the conflict between modernisation and

---

27. See B. Davidson, The People's Cause. A History of Guerrillas in Africa (Longman, London, 1981), Ch. 14.

28. See below, Chs. 6 and 9.

29. Revolution in the Revolution? Armed Struggle and Political Struggle in Latin America (Pelican, London, 1968), pp. 22-5.

traditional loyalties. This conflict seems to be especially acute in Islamic societies, presumably because Islam as a religion has broad political claims. In Turkey (the heartland of the former Ottoman empire) Kemal Ataturk carried out a sweeping secularisation of the political, educational and legal systems, believing that national survival in face of the West after the First World War demanded drastic modernisation on Western lines. In Iran, modernisation carried out in a dictatorial and politically clumsy way by the late Shah provoked, in 1978, a revolution led by Ayatollah Khomeini and other mullahs (who are the rough equivalent of clergy among Shiah Muslims). The regime that has resulted is intensely nationalist, and dedicated to a restoration of Islamic values and a repudiation of Western culture. It is theocratic in giving supreme power to the Ayatollah and seeking to base all laws on Islamic principles; radical in nationalising much of the press and the economy; populist in providing for elections on a broad suffrage and sweeping expropriations of wealth; and tyrannical towards a wide range of dissidents.

This phenomenon ought to end the old-fashioned tendency to identify revolution with left-wing ideals, which can be summarised by the Jacobin slogan 'liberty, equality, fraternity', usually combined with faith in the power of reason to achieve progress. This view of revolution dates from the Enlightenment, and has recently been justified in new and varying ways by Arendt, Huntington and Wertheim.[30] Yet since the 1930s the word revolution has been claimed by a wide variety of regimes. Some, like Franco's in Spain (1939-75), 'the junta' in Greece (1967-74) and several recent military dictatorships in Latin America, such as those in Brazil since 1968 and in Chile since 1973, have shown themselves in practice to be narrowly conservative and politically sterile. For them the term counter-revolution as defined by Wertheim (as opposing emancipation and defending old elites) has much value.[31] There have been other movements - undeniably right-wing in their exaltation as ultimate values of authority, inequality, conflict and the irrational, as well as their denial of progress - which can claim to be revolutionary in a more radical sense. Hitler's Germany - a monstrous descendant of the romantic nationalism described earlier - is an outstanding example. There are however revolutions to which the terms left and right seem irrelevant - Ataturk's for example, or Khomeini's.

What seems significant is the diversity of forms which revolution can take, and the unprecedented prestige of the word today. In recent decades the cult of revolution has flourished and diversified. The word has been adopted by a wide variety of governments, partly to justify their departure from legality, but also to claim originality and importance for their achievements. Such usage reflects the ambitious, interventionist role generally assumed nowadays by national governments, especially in the management or development of their

30. Arendt, p. 21; Huntington, pp. 274-5; Wertheim, p. 128.
31. Wertheim, pp. 133-4.

economies. Revolutionary governments are the most ambitious of all in that, as John Dunn observed, they offer an image of control and purpose in conditions of frightening uncertainty.[32] In Western countries the word revolution has passed into everyday usage - among writers, for example, merely to stress the importance of what they are describing, or among advertisers to suggest the novelty of what they are selling. The attitude underlying this popularity seems to be a high regard for change in itself, especially in the form of technological progress. The word has also been adopted by youth movements in the West to convey vitality, spontaneity, and opposition to authority generally. Movements of this kind were prominent in the 1960s, examples being the attempts by students to democratise universities, and opposition to the USA's military intervention in Vietnam.[33] Another youth-movement of the late 1960s - but of a more puritanical cast - was the Cultural Revolution stimulated in China by Mao Zedong, as an expression of his creed of continuous (and effectively eternal) revolution.[34] In both kinds of youth-movement, revolution ceased to be a specific goal, and became instead an idealised way of life.[35]

The contemporary interest in revolution can be partly explained in technical terms. Because of development in communications, the ideas and techniques of revolution circulate further and more freely than ever, as do those of counter-revolution. Neither has necessarily become any easier, but each is assured of a wider audience than ever before, and each can derive stimulus and instruction from remote parts of the world.[36] Advances in communications, together with the international spread of political ideas, have caused the idea of revolution to impinge more widely on ordinary people's consciousness. Today, in all but the most primitive societies, every politically conscious person is likely to be aware that there exist, somewhere, potentially revolutionary challenges to his or her form of government, be they communist, capitalist, dictatorial, secularising, theocratic, or whatever. This situation is new. Among most societies for most of human history, revolution was unknown because no alternative form of government was conceivable.[37] Now that knowledge of alternative political systems has become general, so has interest in revolution.

---

32. Modern Revolutions. An Introduction to the Analysis of a Political Phenomenon (Cambridge University Press, London, 1972), p.294.

33. Free (Abbie Hoffmann), Revolution for the Hell of It (Dial Press, New York, 1968), pp. 157-8, 218-9.

34. G. Young & D. Woodward, 'From Contradiction among the People to Class Struggle: the Theories of Uninterrupted Revolution and Continuous Revolution', Asian Survey, vol.18, no.9 (September 1978), pp. 917-9.

35. Calvert, Revolution (Macmillan, London, 1970), p. 109.

36. See Calvert, Study, p. 173.

37. As Dr Howell illustrates below, p. 34.

Chapter Two

THE GREEK EXPERIENCE AND ARISTOTLE'S ANALYSIS OF REVOLUTION

P.A. Howell

The first general analysis of revolutionary phenomena was made by the ancient Greek philosopher, Aristotle (384-322 B.C.). Political and constitutional instability, serious enough to make revolution a common occurrence, was the most urgent and difficult question in the political life of ancient Greece. Many thought the problem could never be solved. To the historian, Thucydides, for example, writing at the end of the fifth century B.C., it seemed that disease is as inseparable from the human character as it is from the human body, and so people would always have to contend with tensions leading to political disorder and the disruption of the state.[1] Nevertheless, the limitations and deficiencies of Greek political life prompted philosophers to investigate the subject and propose remedies.

The wide range of the Greeks' political experience arose from the fact that the Hellenic world consisted of a multitude of city-states. Most major valleys, peninsulas and islands were the seats of separate towns or cities. As each had its own fields, pastures, forests, quarries and water supplies, and nearly all had access to the sea, they were long able to be, to a very large extent, economically self-sufficient. Each was self-governing, and jealous to preserve its independence. And while all acknowledged ties of brotherhood to the other Hellenic cities, each claimed the right to engage in diplomatic intercourse and to make war and peace.

Most of these city-states experienced a similar political evolution. Founded by tribes or clans, they began as monarchies. In the course of the eighth century B.C., landed wealth became concentrated in comparatively few hands, and the kings were replaced by the nobles, who called their form of government 'aristocracy', literally 'government by the best'. Aristocracy proved no more permanent than monarchy. An increasing scarcity of agricultural land prompted the Greeks to expand all over the Mediterranean area, founding settlement colonies in places that were thinly populated. As a result, trade and industry grew in importance. The urban populations of the city-states

---

1. Thucydides, The Peloponnesian War, trans. R. Warner (Penguin, London, 1956), pp. 203-12.

increased, and wealth assumed new forms. During the seventh century B.C., in one city after another, the new merchant class joined with dispossessed farmers in an attack on the landholding nobles, and 'tyrants' seized control. By promising relief from chaos, ambitious individuals won enough popular support to enable them to ride into power in defiance of constitutions and laws. The Greek word tyrannos meant a usurper, one who ruled without any legal right. Not all the tyrants ruled oppressively; a few could be styled benevolent despots. Ultimately, however, the increasing economic power and political consciousness of the ordinary citizens led to dissatisfaction with the tyrants, even the able and enlightened ones, and the establishment of a new form of government, democracy. In some cases the wealthy seized power and set up more or less liberal oligarchies. However, few cities ever enjoyed the luxury of long-term constitutional stability. Revolutions continued to occur as democratic and oligarchic factions contended for power, and in several cases demagogues were able to establish new tyrannies for a time. The ascendancy of one party usually led to the exclusion of the other from political life. The losers often were banished, and sometimes they were massacred.

While the Greeks invented the word demokratia, literally meaning 'rule by the people', it has to be remembered that the most democratic of their communities were, by modern standards, oligarchies. On one hand, women had no political status. On the other hand, slavery was always regarded as an essential feature of ancient Greek civilisation. Thus, even as far as the male portion of a city-state's population was concerned, the citizens were generally outnumbered by the slaves, serfs and resident aliens. Moreover, while the Greeks had the form of democracy (even if their definition of citizenship seems unacceptably narrow), they never had the substance of democracy as it is now understood in the Western world. There were no legal or constitutional rules to protect minorities, let alone individuals or non-citizens. There was no machinery for making assemblies accountable for their decisions, nor any appeal from the judgments of the courts. An individual had no rights against the state.[2]

Through all their internal upheavals, the Greeks' particularism kept the cities apart, except in the face of extreme danger. Early in the fifth century B.C. they came together to repulse the Persian invaders, Darius and Xerxes, at Marathon, Salamis and Plataea, but resumed their quarrels when the danger had passed. Finally, after twenty-seven years of fighting one another in the Second Peloponnesian War, they were left weak, spiritless and drained of their resources. This made them an easy prey for new invaders, from Macedon, who defeated them at Chaeronea in 338 B.C. From that date the city-states never again enjoyed real independence, but the Macedonians and, later, the Romans allowed them to continue as the units of political organization for most of the Greek-speaking world.

---

2. J.F. Costanzo, 'The Graeco-Roman politeia - the city of men', Fordham Law Review, vol. 20, no. 2 (June 1951), p. 131.

When Thucydides diagnosed political instability as the principal disease of the Hellenic bodies politic, he did no more than describe and deplore its symptoms. He blamed it for promoting a decline in honesty and all decent feeling, and producing situations in which the stupid acted without thinking while the clever were too frightened to act. The atrocities associated with revolution led to a general reversal of values. Recklessness was mistaken for courage; prudent delay and any attempts to understand a question from all sides were ridiculed as cowardice; moderation was regarded as the disguise of unmanly weakness. Fanaticism and violence were held to be the marks of a real man, and the seal of good faith was neither law nor justice but fellowship in crime.[3]

The philosopher, Plato (428-347 B.C.), offered a cure. In his dialogue, The Republic, he presented a blueprint for a city founded totally on justice, but governed by true aristocrats - his 'guardians' or 'philosopher-kings' - wielding a monopoly of force. Plato was an idealist, impatient with men's weaknesses and limitations. Convinced of the validity of his principles, he took the position that if reality did not conform to them it ought to be changed. If people did not suit his ideal city they must be dehumanised.[4]

Plato's most brilliant pupil, Aristotle, was not so interested in ideal politics. He achieved fame as the founder of the science of logic, and as the author of extraordinarily influential works on subjects as diverse as metaphysics, anatomy, ethics, physiology, economics, biology, aesthetics and physics. It has been well said of him that 'there is probably no parallel in history' to the vastness of his intellectual achievement.[5] Because of his early scientific training and his fascination with what actually happens in the real world, he gathered facts, and deduced his principles from them. He applied the same method to the study of politics. He did have his own ideal state, giving an unfinished sketch of it in the last two books of his work entitled The Politics. Yet he knew that what ought to be was not always realisable. He saw that there were possibilities for good in imperfect things, and that good things may have imperfections. He 'understood the necessity of adaptation, adjustment, compromise' and regarded virtue as a 'mean between two extremes.'[6]

---

3. The Peloponnesian War, pp. 209-11.

4. To build a state where wisdom reigns, Plato would have resorted to inhuman means. For example, he advocated an intolerable regulation of the sex-lives of the ruling classes, a system of eugenic breeding, and the abolition of family life: a mother was to have nothing to do with the rearing of her own child, and would never know it. Plato, The Republic, trans. H.D.P. Lee, 2nd edn (Penguin, London, 1974), pp. 237-252.

5. M.B. Foster, 'Aristotle', in Masters of Political Thought, ed. E.M. Sait (3 vols., Harrap, London, 1942-59), vol. 1, p. 121.

6. J.A. Abbo, Political thought: men and ideas (Newman Pr., Westminster, Md, 1960), pp. 46-7.

In the years 334-323 B.C., Aristotle was asked to draw up new constitutions for more than forty of the Greek city-states. In doing so, he and his pupils in the Lyceum, the school he had founded in Athens, studied some 158 old or existing constitutions. Thus Aristotle's approach to political matters had a practical object. Moreover, his investigations had the special aim of guiding Greek statesmen and lawmakers, in the drafting and administration of various kinds of constitutions, so as to promote political stability. He considered that radical constitutional change should be avoided. Why? Like earlier writers, he saw that political and social change went hand in hand in ancient Greece, and that constitutional change usually meant social revolution. He believed that the benefits that were sometimes obtained through this process were outweighed by the disasters which accompanied or followed it. Political disorder bred vindictiveness, threatening the lives and possessions of individuals. It was therefore bad. In addition, he observed that the wise and virtuous people in any community, who were morally best entitled to rebel, seldom participated in revolutions. This was because the citizens of outstanding merit were always in a minority, and they recognized that fact. Consequently they had been restrained from initiating or joining attempts to oust unjust governments by the practical consideration that they had not got the numbers to ensure that the bad governments, if overthrown, would be replaced by something better.[7]

The principal extant results of Aristotle's investigation of revolutionary phenomena are to be found in Book V of The Politics, a work prepared for study and discussion by his pupils in the Lyceum. One aspect of it has led some scholars to give Aristotle's contribution to our subject less attention than it deserves. While the ancient Greeks invented words to identify many political concepts and institutions, they did not have one exactly corresponding to our term 'revolution'. In writing about revolutionary tendencies and events they used the word *stasis*. Some English-speaking translators and commentators have rendered this as 'revolution'.[8] However, others have argued that this is misleading. It now seems clear that the essential feature of *stasis* is the formation of a group of people who are prepared to use violence and illegal methods to seize power. *Stasis* had been common in the history of the Greeks simply because they had had nothing resembling a modern party-political system and the associated constitutional machinery which enables a dissatisfied faction or class to seek power by peaceful means. Indeed, it can even be regarded as having been a

---

7. Aristotle, *The Politics*, trans. T.A. Sinclair (Penguin, London, 1962), pp. 190 and 199. Unless otherwise indicated, this edition is used for subsequent references to *The Politics*.

8. Translators of *The Politics* who have done this include: B. Jowett (Clarendon Pr., Oxford, 1885); W.D. Ross (Clarendon Pr., Oxford, 1921); F. Susemihl & R.D. Hicks (Macmillan, London, 1894); and Sinclair (1962). Most of the translators of Thucydides have rendered *stasis* as 'revolution'.

normal instrument for effecting major change. Suggestions for a shorthand means of expressing what is involved in stasis have included 'civil disturbance', 'sedition', 'political instability', 'political and social confusion' and even 'economic and social class-struggle'.[9] The point is that Aristotle distinguished between stasis and metaboli politeias - constitutional change. It was obvious that political disorder does not necessarily lead to or involve constitutional change. The rebels may not succeed, or they may stage a coup without overthrowing the constitution. Likewise, constitutional change may take place gradually, hand in hand with social and economic change, without any violent upheaval. It is only those events which include both political disorder and constitutional change that we now call revolutions. As stasis and constitutional change normally did go together in the Greek experience, it was logical for Aristotle to treat them together; and in every case in which both elements were present it is reasonable to use our word 'revolution'. There is also sound sense in the present-day view that Aristotle's analysis benefited from his side-glances at non-revolutionary constitutional change, and at examples of stasis which had led to a change in the governing body without major constitutional change, because these episodes do throw light on essential phases of the phenomenon of revolution.[10]

In presenting his findings on the causes of revolution, Aristotle devoted four chapters to causes which had operated in all kinds of constitutional situations. He considered that the fundamental cause was a sense of injustice arising from inequality. He was convinced that there is a close connexion between an individual's social and economic status and his political principles. As different people have different conceptions of justice and equality, they differ about the distribution of goods and political power. Democracy is based on the notion that those who are equal in one respect are equal in all respects: as all citizens are equally free-born they should be equal in everything. Similarly, oligarchy is based on the opinion that those who are unequal in wealth should be unequal absolutely.[11] Both democrats and oligarchs therefore resort to revolution if they do not enjoy the share of political privileges which accords with their idea of what is just:

---

9. W.L. Newman, The Politics of Aristotle (4 vols., Clarendon Pr., Oxford, 1887-1902), vol. 1, p. 522; The Politics of Aristotle, trans. and ed. E. Barker (Clarendon Pr., Oxford, 1948), p. 204n.; R.G. Mulgan, Aristotle's Political Theory (Clarendon Pr., Oxford, 1977), p. 118; M. Wheeler, 'Aristotle's analysis of the nature of political struggle', American Journal of Philology, vol. 72, no. 286 (April 1951), p. 151; M. Lerner's 'Introduction' to Aristotle's Politics (The Modern Library, New York, 1943), pp. 24-5.

10. Mulgan, pp. 118-9.

11. Aristotle reiterated this in Book V, ch. 12: 'the extremely wealthy do not think it right that those who are not possessed of any property should participate in the state on equal terms with those who are'. The Politics, p. 234.

'The lesser rebel in order to be equal, the equal in order to be greater'.[12] In other words, revolutions are most commonly the product of class-war arising from feelings of injustice.

A second cause of revolution which, according to Aristotle, applies in all cases is that the dissatisfied have some specific goal to aim at. They become revolutionaries because they hope to win profit (economic advantage) and honour (including political power), or else because their object is 'to avoid loss of money and loss of status'.[13]

Aristotle then discussed at some length the various factors which initiate the desire for equality or superiority in profit and honour. These deserved study as additional causes of stasis leading to constitutional change. In the first place there are what we might call psychological factors - things which create an emotional response in the minds of the citizens. Thus the people in power may provoke envy by the extravagant manner in which they use their political privileges and wealth. Thoughts of revolution may also spring from indignation which will develop if the rulers treat their subordinates cruelly and oppressively. Fear is something which initiates sedition among two groups: evildoers, who are afraid of being punished for their crimes, and citizens who are afraid they will suffer some wrong - Aristotle instanced an oligarchic revolution which had occurred in Rhodes earlier in the fourth century B.C. when the wealthy had taken alarm at the number of law-suits being initiated against them.[14] Another psychological factor is contempt. In oligarchies, the democratic majority may become contemptuous of the rulers if public affairs are mismanaged. There had also been cases in which the propertied classes had become contemptuous of the disorder and inefficiency of democratic regimes, and had overthrown them.

Social factors can also trigger the growth of a disposition towards revolution. The first Aristotle identified is 'excessive power' ('pre-eminence' or 'superiority' in some translations). This becomes significant when a demagogue or a group acquires so much power that the opportunity to establish a dictatorship or dynastic oligarchy is perceived. Over-mighty subjects have appeared in all sorts of societies. Aristotle observed that cities such as Argos and Athens had found a remedy in the practice of ostracism: the citizens could, by vote, impose a sentence of banishment for five or ten years on any individual who had become dangerously powerful. Characteristically, he added: 'But it is much better to look ahead and prevent the rise of such outstandingly powerful men than to let things slide and look for a remedy afterwards.'[15]

Much more common and important as a cause of revolution, in Aristotle's opinion, is what he called the 'disproportionate aggrandisement' of one social class in the state. If one class increases

12. Ibid., p. 192.
13. Ibid., pp. 192-3.
14. Ibid., p. 194. Newman, vol. 4, p. 299.
15. The Politics, p. 194 n.

in size in relation to the others, the constitution will no longer suit the community's social composition. For example, if there is a considerable rise in the proportion of people living in poverty, they may stage a revolution. A change of this kind may be the consequence of different birth-rates in the different classes, or of a decline in the general level of prosperity. Aristotle also saw that it may come about accidentally and unexpectedly, as had happened in several cities after a high proportion of their upper-class citizens had been killed in wars with neighbouring states. In each of these cases, the underprivileged had seized the chance to overthrow the polity (Aristotle's name for constitutional democracy) and substitute extreme democracy - rule by the lowest class of citizens for their own benefit, with no respect for law. Likewise, a rise in the prosperity of a democracy could produce a dramatic increase in the proportion of wealthy people and thus be the occasion of an oligarchic revolution. It is obvious that Aristotle recognised the significance of economic forces as a cause of social changes and revolutions.[16]

A third social factor which leads to civil disturbances is dissimilarity of the elements which make up the state. The phrase Aristotle used in describing one kind of dissimilarity is sometimes translated as 'difference of race', which suggests a situation like the one we see in Zimbabwe. However the Hellenes regarded all non-Greeks as barbarians who could never be granted full citizenship save in exceptional circumstances, and then only in small numbers. The differences Aristotle had in mind were not even as great as the differences between ethnic groups in modern Belgium, Yugoslavia, Cyprus or Canada. As examples he mentioned six relatively young city-states, each of which had attracted large bodies of emigrants from two older Greek cities (whereas most Hellenic states originating as settlement colonies had a preponderance of citizens drawn from a single older city). In half of these cases both groups of citizens were descendants of the same tribe, the Ionians. They therefore spoke the same dialect and shared the same literary heritage and many customs.[17] Yet each group's jealous loyalty to the traditions peculiar to its mother-city was strong enough to prevent it uniting harmoniously with its rivals for civic purposes. Conflicts between factions of this kind could be as bitter as the conflicts between social classes in other city-states, and in all the cases Aristotle cited the weaker group was eventually driven into exile.

Aristotle then noted that geography may give rise to dissimilarity

---

16. Ibid., pp. 194-5, and 199.

17. Newman, vol. 4, p. 309. In this passage Aristotle did not need to point out that the Zancleans, Samians, Amphipolitans etc. were of Ionic extraction, as this would have been well-understood by the readers of his original manuscript - just as every educated Hellene would have known that the citizens of Tenedos, Lesbos etc. were of Aeolian extraction, while Melos, Cos, Rhodes etc. had been peopled by Dorians.

of elements. The territory of several Greek states embraced an island as well as part of the adjacent mainland.[18] The island-dwellers' interests were generally at variance with those of the main part of the population and this could lead to internal strife. Modern history offers further examples. The relations between the component states of the Federation of Malaysia in the 1960s, or between the component states of the West Indian Federation in the 1970s, might well have been better if those nations had not been severed by the sea. Yet Aristotle observed that there did not have to be a water barrier: distance itself could result in division. In Athens, the inhabitants of its port, the Piraeus, were much more democratically inclined than the more prosperous citizens who lived near the acropolis, seven kilometres away. This had been significant in the overthrow of the thirty oligarchs who ruled the city in 404-403 B.C., though Aristotle did not mention that revolution. He did add that the outstandingly important dissimilarity of elements within a state was the division between the public-spirited citizens and those who were solely preoccupied with promoting their own selfish interests. Next in importance was the division between rich and poor.[19]

In the fourth chapter of Book V, Aristotle observed that while the issues at stake in revolutions are generally great, the occasions of it may be small. Incidents or situations which are in themselves quite trifling may be significant when they concern the rulers. Greek history furnished many examples. Thus, revolutions had occurred when prominent individuals, who had been cuckolded, or deprived of an inheritance, or fined by a son-in-law, or frustrated in their matrimonial plans, vented their spleen by enlisting the support of one or more social classes who had had no share in the constitution. Similar incidents were to trigger revolutions in the city-states of medieval Europe. For example, in thirteenth-century Florence, the Guelphic oligarchy was overthrown and its leaders expelled after one of their number, Buondelmonte dei Buondelmonti, had jilted a girl of the 'honourable and noble' Amidei family.[20] The moral to be drawn from such phenomena, in Aristotle's opinion, is that private feuds between leading members of the ruling class, under any kind of constitution, ought to be settled at once.[21]

---

18. Aristotle mentioned Clazomenae. Other examples were Cnidus, Apollonia, Aradus and Tyre. Newman, vol. 4, p. 316.

19. The Politics, pp. 196-7.

20. N. Machiavelli, History of Florence, trans. anon. (Dunne, Washington, 1901), pp. 49-51; Villani's Chronicle, trans. R.E. Selfe, rev. edn (Constable, London, 1906), pp. 121-3, 141-6; P. Villari, The first two Centuries of Florentine History, trans. L. Villari, 2nd edn (Fisher Unwin, London, 1901), pp. 173-5. This affair is best known because of its treatment by Dante, in The Divine Comedy, especially in Paradise, Canto XVI. See K. Mackenzie's translation (Folio, London, 1979), pp. 117, 380-1, 489 and 540.

21. The Politics, pp. 197-8.

At the end of his examination of the causes and occasions which can lead to revolutions of all types, Aristotle paused to consider the methods used by revolutionaries and noted that force and trickery are both used. Violence may be employed either from the beginning (as was usual in democratic revolutions) or at a later stage, when it becomes essential if the rebels are to keep control. Trickery also may be used initially or at a later stage. Revolutions which begin in deceit are not just a twentieth century phenomenon. For example, to establish his first tyranny, in Athens in 560 B.C., Peisistratos began by assuming leadership of the lower classes, posing as the champion of those seeking equality of political privileges. Then, when he seized power with the aid of a carefully chosen band of followers, prompting the oligarchic elements to flee the city, he was able to achieve his real object fairly easily, even though he had to use force to maintain his despotic regime. Similarly in the Athenian revolution of 411 B.C., the Four Hundred first tricked the people into accepting oligarchy by spreading the false rumour that the Persian king would provide money for the war against Sparta.

Aristotle added that sometimes constitutional change results from an initial act of persuasion followed by a similar policy so that the new rulers keep control with general acceptance by the citizens. This has led a recent writer to assert that 'Aristotle did not regard force as being essential to the act of revolution.'[22] However, it seems quite clear that, in the passage relied on for this statement, Aristotle was once again distinguishing non-violent constitutional change from events in which stasis and constitutional change went hand in hand; and as has been mentioned, it is only in connection with the latter class of events that we may rightly use our modern word 'revolution' if we are to interpret him correctly. Aristotle had offered three examples of non-violent constitutional change in the third chapter of Book V. They are: changes resulting from lobbying and election intrigues - in which category we can place Britain's Great Reform Bill of 1832, and the federation of the Australian colonies at the end of the nineteenth century; changes resulting from letting people who are not dedicated supporters of the constitutional status quo hold high office - which looks like a foreshadowing of Lord Derby's re-appointment of Disraeli to the Chancellorship of the Exchequer in Britain in 1866, or the Americans' election of the Roosevelt Administration in 1932; and, finally, gradual and imperceptible change, which happens in every society - Aristotle instanced Ambracia, where the small property-qualification required for citizenship 'was gradually reduced and became so low that it might as well have been abolished altogether'.[23] There is no element of stasis in changes effected by persuasion and other lawful means, where there is neither use of force

22. P. Calvert, Revolution (Macmillan, London, 1970), p. 35. See also p. 41.

23. The Politics, pp. 195 and 199. See also Barker's translation, pp. 210 and 214.

nor an actual and perceived threat of violence at any stage.

Yet we should not lose sight of the significance of Aristotle's point that fraud deserves study as a technique used by those who seek root-and-branch change. His example of the assumption of power by the Four Hundred in Athens is an interesting one. If we momentarily leave aside the consideration that they had to use force to retain the power they won, can it be said that the establishment of their oligarchy was a revolutionary act? It is arguable that it was. The city was experiencing stasis, and the essence of the fraud was that the Four Hundred deluded the people with the prospect of relief from current violence which had every appearance of becoming worse. As Lenin and his Bolsheviks realized, and as the behaviour of the bulk of the Russian army in the last months of 1917 demonstrated, the promise of deliverance from present and impending violence can be as real an inducement to passive acceptance of constitutional and social change as is the threat that non-compliance or resistance will receive violent treatment.

In subsequent chapters, Aristotle proceeded to identify causes of stasis and constitutional change which operate in particular constitutional situations. Here his treatment became much less systematic as he offered a great number of historical examples to demonstrate the richness of the subject. His method contrasts with that of modern social scientists, who strive to quantify their data. He sought to include every piece of evidence that might have relevance, and often left it to his readers to draw their own conclusions about the relative significance of individual elements in the resulting kaleidoscope of examples. Nevertheless, he had no difficulty in identifying the outstanding factors promoting the overthrow of each kind of constitution.

He found that the most common cause of revolution in democracies had been unprincipled behaviour by the popular leaders. To curry favour with the mass of the people, demagogues oppressed the rich with capital levies which forced them to break up their estates, income taxes which crippled their revenues, and even prosecutions based on false accusations, launched with a view to confiscating their possessions entirely. Such conduct had often driven the property-owners to join forces (because common fear unites even the bitterest of enemies) to overthrow a democracy and establish an oligarchy. In the case of oligarchies, the evidence showed that the two most potent causes of revolution had been discontent, resulting from oppression of the classes excluded from power, and dissension within the ruling clique - for oligarchs are prone to quarrel with each other.[24]

States enjoying mixed constitutions were generally better governed and so tended to be the most stable. In this category Aristotle included both polities and aristocracies. Given the social conditions of the Greek city-states of his day, Aristotle favoured constitutional democracy, because it could reconcile the two warring

24. The Politics, pp. 200-5.

classes by allowing scope for the wealth and honour prized by the rich, as well as for the liberty and equality prized by the poor. 'The better mixed a constitution is, the longer it will last.' Moreover, the backbone of such a polity is the middle class. Comfortable enough not to envy the rich, not wealthy enough to be envied by the poor, it had virtues of its own. Its members were moderate and law abiding; they had the capacity to rule and to obey; they did not go in for scheming as long as they had some share in power.[25] As a middle-class person himself, by birth as well as occupation, Aristotle's prejudice was natural enough. As he used the term, 'aristocracy' was the rule, not of a wealthy hereditary caste (he regarded that as an extreme oligarchy, a very undesirable form of government little better than tyranny), but of the outstanding citizens, duly appointed to exercise power with the consent and for the best interests of the community. Our word 'meritocracy' fits his conception well. The main difference from a polity is in the attitude to law. In a polity, such as Solon's Athens, the law, once promulgated, is supreme. In an aristocracy, if the exercise of power is really confined to those of outstanding ability, they can deal with each problem on its merits, without being fettered by constitutional rules and conventions. Yet even mixed constitutions may be overthrown. This had usually occurred because of failure to secure the right admixture of democratic and oligarchic elements to ensure that benefits and privileges were distributed solely on merit, or because those who were not so well off became convinced that they were being unfairly treated. Aristocracies had a tendency to be over-indulgent towards the rich, and that was often their downfall.[26]

Monarchies are most likely to be threatened when the officials who share in the royal power quarrel amongst themselves, or when the subjects find the king becoming unduly oppressive. Aristotle had a rosy view of kingship. He accepted the traditional Hellenic assumption that a king held office by the consent of his subjects, which was accorded him so long as he ruled for the common good, standing between the rich and poor and seeing that neither class suffered wrong from the other. Tyranny was the antithesis of kingship. The tyrant regards the common good only so far as it promotes his own. Thus he tends to plunder rather than benefit his subjects. Tyrants are hated for their oppressive rule, and because the mismanagement and inefficiency that so often characterise their regimes breed contempt.[27]

At the end of Chapter 7, Aristotle introduced another factor which could well have been mentioned earlier in his list of general causes of revolution, namely, the influence of foreign states. He referred to the conduct of Athens and Sparta, which had long been the strongest city-states in the Hellenic world. The generally democratic

25. Ibid., pp. 172-6.

26. Ibid., pp. 206-8. For his use of 'aristocracy', see pp. 131 and 151-2, and also his Ethics, trans. J.A.K. Thomson, rev. edn (Penguin, London, 1976), pp. 178 and 275-6.

27. Ibid., pp. 217-24. For his treatment of kingship see pp. 135-47.

Athenians had everywhere put down oligarchies. Their rivals, the Spartans, had overturned popular governments. A city as powerful as either of these could influence internal affairs even in distant states. This phenomenon has reappeared in modern times. In Chapter 10 Aristotle added that any kind of constitution can be undermined by external pressures, but tyrannies seem especially susceptible to being overthrown by hostile neighbours.[28] Perhaps it is symptomatic of our age that in the last half century it has been, in most cases, popular governments that have been overturned by foreign intervention, most notably in Europe between 1939 and 1948. However, external force also caused the collapse of the Nazi dictatorship in Germany and the Fascist dictatorship in Italy.

The remainder of Book V of The Politics is devoted to a consideration of the means of preventing revolutionary change, and this topic is further examined in Book VI. Aristotle believed that the best method of preserving stability is for rulers to pursue a policy of moderation, so that the citizens loyal to the constitution are stronger than those who are disloyal. The most successful way of ensuring the greatest possible consent to any regime is to treat the subjects fairly. People who have little or no share in power will be much more likely to tolerate the status quo if the fundamental source of conflict, the division between the wealthy and the poor, can be reduced. Constant vigilance can forestall conduct which could induce a class to develop feelings of envy, contempt and so on. As some people are unable to 'master the intoxication of success', the exaggerated increase of any individual should be prevented. Legislation controlling inheritances can help keep any one citizen from becoming excessively influential. If that fails, the over-powerful individual should be banished.

Aristotle declared that of all the methods of ensuring stability, the most important, in every type of constitutional situation, is education. There is no point in having a perfectly appropriate system of laws if the rising generation of citizens has not been attuned by teaching and the force of habit to the spirit of their particular society. Aristotle found that this consideration was singularly neglected in his own day. Thus in oligarchies, the children of the rulers were brought up to enjoy ease and comfort, a very bad preparation for assuming office, while the children of the poor were accustomed to and toughened by labour, and so were more inclined and better able to start a revolution. Democracies make a comparable mistake. The great attraction of democracy is that it maximises individual freedom. But the other essential feature is the principle of the sovereignty of the majority, and democrats foolishly neglect this in the education of their children. Thus the young grow up believing that each may do whatever he likes, according to his fancy for the moment. Such unrestrained licence paves the way for the emergence of forces hostile to the continuation of democracy. To live according to the rules made by the majority should not be considered a denial of liberty, but rather 'self-

28. Ibid., pp. 208 and 222.

preservation'.[29] Aristotle's warning about the vital role of education has often been ignored. The British Empire supplies the most spectacular example in modern times. There was a fundamental contradiction in keeping millions of people in subjection while providing them with thousands of schools which taught children to read Shelley and Byron, and permitting the establishment of universities in which students were encouraged to read Locke on the right of rebellion, Bentham on the principle of utility, Mill on liberty and representative government, and so on. Thus, from the first decades of the nineteenth century, when they were still creating their Empire, the British unwittingly but unceasingly sowed the seeds of its destruction.

Turning to special techniques to be applied in each kind of constitution, Aristotle reiterated that all rulers should avoid extremes. Oligarchies should, like aristocracies, be willing to allow deserving individuals to join them in office, and they should never permit oppression of the poor. The oligarchs themselves should undertake the most onerous public duties without payment. They should also provide public entertainments and make generous contributions towards the cost of adorning their city with monuments and fine public buildings, so that those who are excluded from power will more readily tolerate them for having to pay a high price for the privilege of ruling. Democracies should not plunder the rich to the extent that they fear annihilation: taxes should be moderate. In mixed constitutions, the tenure of office should be for strictly limited periods, so that as many people as possible have a chance to share in the exercise of power. Such communities should also enact legislation to control the rivalries and ambitions of the rich. Disproportionate increase should be dealt with promptly by gradual alterations in the balance of power. Intrigue, and quarrels within the ruling class arising from insults, personal spite or love affairs, cannot be prevented, but they must be nipped in the bud. Monarchies may collapse if there is no really competent person available to succeed to the throne. This problem can be reduced, as was done at Sparta, by limiting the power of the king, so that the ability of one individual is not of such great moment. In short, there is some way of handling most of the causes of revolution.[30]

Many of Aristotle's readers have been surprised that his discussion extended to the preservation of tyrannies. He regarded tyranny as the most pernicious form of government because it was rule based wholly on force, exercised over unwilling subjects, and was maintained by the use of mercenaries paid from the proceeds of heavy taxes which brought suffering to the poor as well as the rich. Thus defined, a

---

29. Ibid., p. 216. This anticipated by 2,000 years the doctrine of the English liberal philosopher, Locke, that the purpose of law 'is not to abolish or restrain, but to preserve and enlarge Freedom'. J. Locke, Two Treatises of Government, ed. P. Laslett (Mentor, New York, 1965), p. 348.

30. The Politics, pp. 209-18, 224-5, and 235-49.

tyrant and his subjects live in a constant condition of stasis. Why then should Aristotle seek to prop up tyrannies?[31] The answer is that he did not have that intention. It was rather that, having set himself the task of studying the maintenance of political stability, his passion for comprehensiveness compelled him to examine the problem in all types of government. No one could have written more critically of what he called the 'traditional' methods of maintaining a tyranny. These aimed to make the subjects unable to revolt. They included doing everything possible to prevent the people getting to know and trust each other, by employing spies, promoting hostility between individuals, setting class against class, and generally humbling everyone, because broken spirits are incapable of conspiracy. Tyrants never cease their attacks on citizens of consequence, periodically assassinating some, secretly or openly, or banishing them. Similarly, they are perpetually finding excuses for wars with foreign states, to keep the masses occupied and always in need of a leader - a technique adopted by some modern despots, such as Mussolini and Sukarno. Aristotle regarded all such methods as equally immoral and contemptible; in Barker's translation: 'the arts of the tyrant ... plumb the depths of wrongdoing'.[32] Besides, they do not work, save for a time. The history of the Greeks showed that of all forms of government none had had so short a life-span as tyranny.[33]

However, there had been a handful of tyrants who had pursued a different method: they had behaved, or had appeared to behave, more like kings. Thus they had not aroused their subjects' indignation by squandering tax-revenues on lavish gifts to their mistresses and other favourites. On the contrary, a couple had published accounts, which gave them the image of prudent administrators rather than tyrants. The tyrants in this group were never known to rape anyone, and took pains to curb the excesses and insolence of their entourages. If disposed to other vices, like gluttony or drunkenness, they likewise kept them concealed. They made a show of rewarding talent and meritorious conduct, and of acting fairly. They adorned their cities as if they were the people's trustees, and seemed to be zealous in the performance of their religious duties. By inspiring respect rather than fear, they had made a significant proportion of their subjects unwilling to revolt.[34]

Some scholars, reading the eleventh chapter of Book V too narrowly, have interpreted these passages as 'counsel' or 'advice' to

---

31. Recent writers who imply that he did so, or who at least charge him with inconsistency on this score, include Abbo, Political Thought, pp. 42-3, Calvert, Revolution, p. 38, Mulgan, Aristotle's Political Theory, p. 136.

32. p. 246.

33. The Politics, pp. 225-7 and 231-2.

34. Ibid., pp. 228-31.

tyrants.[35] Machiavelli certainly rewrote them with that object in The Prince, but in the process he perverted the subject. Nothing could be more misleading than to contemplate Aristotle through Machiavelli's jaundiced eyes. Aristotle's profound moral sense, and his abiding concern for individuals, could never have permitted him to approve of Machiavelli's doctrines that a ruler is 'often obliged, in order to maintain the state, to act against faith, against charity, against humanity', and that he must 'as the variations of fortune dictate ... be able to do evil'.[36] Again, Mulgan has observed that if a tyrant really behaves in a kingly fashion, the character of his rule will have altered so much that he can no longer be considered a tyrant.[37] Yet if chapters 11 and 12 are taken together, it seems arguable that Aristotle's object here was description rather than prescription. The particular tyrants he identified as having ruled moderately had always been regarded as tyrants, and each had retained the capacity to compel the obedience of the many who never consented to their rule. Moreover, Aristotle warned that, as there is no really effective way of killing the spirit of freedom in men, even the least obnoxious tyrannies are doomed to be overthrown eventually.[38] In other words, the preservation of tyranny is a lost cause.

The brilliance of Aristotle's observations on revolutionary phenomena has been acknowledged by virtually all his readers. He was right to emphasise the fact that men rebel because they are convinced, first, that the existing distribution of power in their society is unjust, and secondly, that they can remedy their economic and social grievances by seizing power for themselves. He well understood the class-basis of revolutionary movements. He was right to see the importance of psychological factors as well as social and economic conditions as causes of revolution, and right to see that stasis and constitutional change can also be the result of ethnic and similar divisions within a state, or pressure from foreign powers. In distinguishing the underlying causes of revolution from the particular and sometimes trivial incidents which can trigger the outbreak of revolutionary violence, he discovered a truth which modern historians keep stressing.[39] It is likewise to his credit that he noticed that many revolutionaries employ trickery and deception as well as force to achieve their aims. His understanding of the ruthless behaviour of successful rebels towards the class they have defeated fully

---

35. E.g., Newman, vol. 4, p. 279; T.A. Sinclair, A History of Greek Political Thought, 2nd edn (Routledge, London, 1967), p. 230; G.H. Sabine, A History of Political Theory, 3rd edn (Harrap, London, 1951), p. 109.

36. N. Machiavelli, The Prince and The Discourses, trans. L. Ricci (Modern Library, New York, 1940), p. 65.

37. Mulgan, pp. 135-6.

38. The Politics, pp. 228-32.

39. E.g., C. Brinton, The Anatomy of Revolution, rev. edn (Vintage Books, New York, 1965), pp. 69-78.

foreshadows the 'reign of terror' phase of modern revolutions. His observations that political disorder can often be prevented from developing if rulers are moderate in their behaviour, vigilant in spotting and remedying grievances, willing to adapt the constitution by degrees so that it corresponds to changing social and economic conditions, and sensible in superintending the quality of education offered to the young, further illustrate his wisdom. They also anticipate the policies advocated by many later enlightened conservatives - witness Edmund Burke's dictum that 'A state without the means of some change is without the means of its conservation.'[40]

Of course, Aristotle was not omniscient, and we can supplement and refine his discoveries. For example, when explaining how rich and powerful states can promote revolutions in their neighbours, he did not recall that their attempts to assert hegemony could sometimes have anything but the desired result. As W.L. Newman noted, in several cases Greek states had given supreme power to the class which was least likely to betray them to their external foes. Thus, one reason why oligarchs won and retained control of Corinth was that its dreaded neighbour, Argos, was democratically governed; and a reason why democracy long held sway in Argos was that its principal enemy, Sparta, was the very opposite in its political structures.[41] Similar considerations have contributed to the unpopularity of the Communist Parties in modern Greece and West Germany. Again, the rise of nation-states, since the fifteenth century, has created some new considerations Aristotle could not have foreseen. Thus the anonymity of most individuals in states whose population is numbered by the million instead of by the thousand has meant that the relative potency of impersonal forces, especially economic conditions, has increased. Consequently, students of modern revolutions must give these factors much more searching attention than Aristotle accorded them. Meanwhile, colonisation by conquest (instead of by settlement) as practised by the Portuguese, Spaniards, Dutch, French, British, Russians and others, has created communities with internal racial and religious divisions - and thus a potential for violence - of a savagery and scale the ancient Greeks could never have imagined. Futhermore, the size and complexity of nation-states, and the enormous power wielded by their rulers, have meant that most modern revolutions have ended in power being exercised by a dictator of one sort or another: Napoleon I, Napoleon III, Stalin, Franco, Pol Pot and so on. Even democratic revolutions now tend to have this fate. But to point to considerations such as these is merely to add footnotes to Aristotle's analysis. Besides, he had the great merit of being free from the modern conceit that the only revolutions worth studying are those which take their nations on a step to the left. Aristotle was more than a pioneer observer of the process of violent political change. His

---

40. E. Burke, Reflections on the Revolution in France, ed. C.C. O'Brien (Penguin, London, 1968), p. 106.

41. Newman, vol. 4, pp. 277-8.

industry and insight enabled him to be a great one. Indeed, no modern social scientist has gone beyond him in establishing a framework for understanding the causes of revolution. All later students of the subject stand in his debt.

Chapter Three

THE TRANSITION FROM CLASSICAL TO MODERN TIMES

P.A. Howell

The ancient Greek philosophers' opinion that revolution was bad and should be prevented had a very long run, and it still has many adherents. It was reinforced in the second century B.C. by Polybius, the Greek-born historian of Rome's rapid rise to Mediterranean hegemony. Polybius declared, more directly than any earlier writer, that each of the common forms of government is subject to corruption, and that this happens according to a cyclical process. Monarchy degenerates into tyranny. Tyranny becomes intolerable, and its abolition is followed by aristocracy, which degenerates into oligarchy. The injustice of oligarchic rule provokes the people to establish a democracy, but it in turn degenerates into mob rule. The people eventually accept a new monarch in hopes of deliverance from civil strife, and the sorry pattern of violent political change repeats itself. The cycle, he claimed, is natural and inevitable.[1]

How, then, had the Roman Republic survived so long? Polybius thought the answer was to be found in the Romans' adoption of a mixed constitution, blending authoritarian, elitist and popular principles of government in a system of mutual checks and balances: power was distributed between the consuls, representing the monarchical principle, the aristocratic senate, and the assemblies of the people. All was 'accurately adjusted and in exact equilibrium', and it was 'impossible to find a better political system'. In reality, the history of the Roman Republic had been fraught with strife between the patricians and the plebeians and the tribunate of Tiberius Gracchus brought a renewal of political chaos in Polybius's own lifetime. Besides, as Polybius's analysis of the structure of the republic took no account of the tribunes of the people (elected magistrates who had authority to veto the decrees of the senate and even to imprison consuls) or of the dictators (appointed by the consuls and senators, from 501 B.C. onwards, to exercise absolute power in times of military or civil crisis), it was as idealised as his account of the 'cycle' of

1. Polybius, The Histories, trans. W.R. Paton (6 vols., Heinemann, London, 1922-27), vol. 3, pp. 275-89.

constitutional change. Nevertheless, after presenting his flattering description of Rome's constitution as it had appeared at the time of the Second Punic War (218-201 B.C.), he warned that 'all existing things are subject to decay and change', and that a time would come when the populace would

> no longer consent to obey or even to be the equals of the ruling caste, but will demand the lion's share for themselves. When this happens, the state will change its name to the finest sounding of all, freedom and democracy, but will change its nature to the worst thing of all, mob-rule.

That is, he feared that even the best organised state would ultimately experience the evils of revolution.[2]

Not until the seventeenth century of the Christian era was a radically new approach proclaimed. In 1649, defending the execution of Charles I, John Milton, poet, and a secretary to the English Commonwealth's Council of State, suggested that revolution could be a _good_ thing because it is the right of every people to give itself the kind of government it thinks best.[3] How did this more favourable attitude towards revolution arise, and why did it take so long to develop?

The second of these questions can be answered quite simply. The last of the dictators of ancient Rome, Julius Caesar, effectively ended republican government in the years 49-44 B.C., and his heir, Octavian, later called Augustus, the first Roman Emperor, ushered in a new era of stability. Thus monarchy, which for several centuries had been derided by many southern Europeans as an archaic form of government, became respectable once more, for all enjoyed the benefits of the _Pax Romana_: by the beginning of the second century A.D., the Empire was providing an orderly administration of justice and internal peace from Britain to Egypt, and from Lusitania and Mauretania on the Atlantic to Assyria and Mesopotamia on the Tigris. However, from the third century to the fifteenth century inclusive, war was the dominant feature of life in Europe. Initially this was a consequence of a long succession of barbarian invasions, by the Goths, Franks, Alemanni, Visigoths, Huns, Alans, Sueves, Burgundians, Ostrogoths, Lombards, Angles, Jutes and Saxons, followed immediately by the Viking invasions of the ninth to the eleventh centuries, and accompanied, from the eighth century, by almost equally formidable Islamic invasions. Then, while the new masters were becoming more civilised, they were constantly resorting to war with one another to avenge real or imagined wrongs. Throughout this era, the first requirement for a ruler was the capacity to lead his people to victory in battle. So for Europe, as for the rest of the world, monarchy was

---

2. Ibid., vol. 3, pp. 293-311 and 397-9.

3. J. Milton, _Tenure of Kings and Magistrates_, republished in _Works of John Milton_, ed. F.A. Patterson _et al._ (18 vols. in 21, Columbia U.Pr., New York, 1931-38), vol. 5, pp. 1-59.

accepted as the necessary form of government. Only a few city-states, and some isolated primitive tribesmen, such as the Bushmen and the Australian Aborigines, were able to pursue different arrangements. As long as people believed that monarchy was the only possible form of government, revolution was impossible, and writers did not venture to speculate about it.

Yet, from the advent of the Caesars until the rise of the modern nation-states, subjects dissatisfied with a monarch who ruled oppressively did not necessarily lack prospects of relief. They could either hope for conquest by a better king, or else they could rebel and invite someone else to ascend the throne. Less risk was attached to the latter remedy. Thus the middle ages saw the beginnings of debate about what circumstances, if any, would justify the use of force to overthrow a tyrannical king. Ultimately, these debates were to contribute much towards the shape of modern thinking about revolution. In the short term, they were greatly influenced by the spread of the teachings of Christianity.

Christianity is not a political theory: it is a doctrine of personal sanctification and salvation. Nevertheless it has always had the capacity to change people's lives in their social and political aspects, as well as in their religious aspects. In his teaching, Christ presented a distinctive view of what it means to be human. This was that all people are children of God. Each person is a free spirit, sacred and inviolable, capable of and called to perfection. God's kingdom is a kingdom whose membership is open to all. Thus every human being matters. It is not enough to value the good for being good, the wise for being wise, the brave for being brave. People of both sexes, of all races and conditions, and even the most vicious members of the species have a value that no one can deny them because each is made in God's image, because each has an immortal spirit, and because Christ died to save everyone. As St Paul put it, in his Letter to the Galatians:

> there are no more distinctions between Jew and Greek, slave and free, male and female, for you are all one in Christ Jesus.[4]

The early Christians found it extremely difficult to persuade people to accept this teaching, for it was contrary to all previous traditions. Even that great thinker, Aristotle, had written about slaves as if they were sub-human.[5] Plato had been still more contemptuous of the lower classes, and had seen no value at all in humans simply as humans. Thus he had recommended that diseased individuals and illegitimate children should not be kept alive.[6] Besides being at variance with mankind's ancient prejudices, the new doctrine faced the further difficulty that so many people seem to be a denial of the principle that each is valuable, because they have been damaged by misfortune, their own

4. Gal. 3:28.
5. The Politics, trans. Sinclair, pp. 30-7, 40, and 52-3.
6. E.g., The Republic, trans. Lee, rev. edn, pp. 241-3.

wickedness, or the injustice of others. However, Christ had kept reiterating the truth that even the individuals who were most mutilated by disease or evil living still had an essential dignity because of their humanity, and that every instinct should call for their restoration and salvation.[7]

This doctrine had an important corollary: as all men and women are children of God, they are all brothers and sisters. Here was another challenge to racial and class barriers, and in particular it gave a new meaning to the old Pentateuchal precept commanding the people of Israel to love their neighbours as themselves.[8] For the Jews, a neighbour was a relative, a friend or a fellow-Israelite, but not a stranger or an enemy.[9] Christ, by contrast, taught His followers to have a loving, selfless concern for everyone, because all are children of God.[10] This led to a new conception of social justice. Christianity tempered the Greek philosophers' maxim that every individual was entitled to his due with the notion that each should be dealt with liberally and generously in a spirit of charity.[11]

Furthermore, Christ's teaching led to a secularisation of government. Cultic practices divorced from the state had become common in the Levant, but Christ made the first principled distinction between religion and politics, proclaiming: 'Render to Caesar the things that are Caesar's, and to God the things that are God's.'[12] The state should not claim people's allegiance in the things that are not Caesar's. No longer was the state to determine what is morally right and wrong: 'Gone is the union, in the person of Caesar, of the royal and priestly power. Religion is no longer under the control of the state. Obedience to Caesar is no longer obedience to God. It might happen that disobedience to Caesar is obedience to God.'[13] Thus spiritual liberty became compatible with social order. Thenceforth the state was competent only in temporal matters. For people's spiritual needs, Christ established His Church, a society intended to help Christians attain their final and most important end, eternal salvation. That is, each person's first duty is not to the state, but to God, and to himself.

The idea that there are limits to the state's legitimate authority, like the doctrines of the intrinsic value and brotherhood of all people, has borne striking fruit in the present century in the lives of those Christian revolutionaries who have been active in various parts of

---

7. E.g., Matt. 8:1-4, 9:27-33; Mark 2:1-12, 5:21-43; Luke 5:17-26, 7:36-50, 15:1-7 and 11-32, 17:11-19; John 8:1-11.

8. Lev. 19:18.

9. H. Ringgren, Israelite Religion, trans. D. Green (S.P.C.K., London, 1969), p. 34; The Dead Sea Scrolls in English, trans. and ed. G. Vermes, rev. edn (Penguin, London, 1968), p. 72. C.H. Dodd, The Founder of Christianity (Fontana, London, 1973), pp. 77-8.

10. Luke 10:25-37.

11. E.g., 1 Cor. 13:4-7.

12. Matt. 22:21.

13. Abbo, Political Thought, p. 64.

the Third World. An extreme example was the Rev. Camilo Torres Restrepo, a priest who joined Marxist guerilla groups fighting in Colombia and who was killed by government forces in 1966. But Christianity's capacity to provide a revolutionary dynamic emerged extremely slowly and is still much debated, because most theologians have always taught that the Christian's primary duty is to establish the kingdom of God in his own heart. Besides, as Christ offered no political program, on most questions of practical politics different Christians have adopted different views.

Right at the beginning, a certain tension sprang from the apparently conflicting advice offered by Christ's first interpreters, Saints Peter and Paul. When Peter was arrested on a charge of disturbing the peace of Jerusalem by his preaching, he maintained, as his guiding principle: 'We must obey God rather than men.'[14] Yet Paul wrote to his Roman converts: 'Let every person be subject to the governing authorities. For there is no authority except from God, and those that exist have been instituted by God.'[15] This seems to suggest a counsel of passive acceptance of whatever a ruler decrees. Yet it has to be understood in its context. The immediately preceding sentence reads: 'Resist evil and conquer it with good'; and a few lines further on appears the maxim: 'If you love your neighbour you have carried out all your obligations.' So early Christian writers, notably the North African theologians Tertullian and Origen, and the Syrian, St John Chrysostom, interpreting this Pauline passage, stressed that the authority of civil rulers is limited, and that they can command obedience only insofar as their power is exercised lawfully and for the common good.[16] At the beginning of the fifth century, St Augustine, Bishop of Hippo, put it still more strongly in his aphorisms: 'Without justice, what is sovereignty but organised brigandage?', and 'Where there is no justice, there is no true state'.[17]

An initial theoretical obstacle to Christian participation in violent political change was the belief of most of the early Christians that the obligation of charity precluded them from taking up arms. In the Sermon on the Mount, Christ had extolled as virtues peacemaking, and the enduring of political and social persecution. The Christian should love his enemies: 'Do good to those who hate you, pray for those

---

14. Acts 5:29.

15. Rom. 13:1.

16. The Ante-Nicene Christian Library, ed. A. Roberts & J. Donaldson (24 vols., Clark, Edinburgh, 1867-72), vol. 10, pp. 400-2, vol. 11, pp. 110-2 and vol. 23, pp. 90-1, 483-7 and 558; C.H. McIlwain, The Growth of Political Thought in the West (Macmillan, London, 1932), pp. 152-3; W. Parsons, 'The influence of Romans XIII on Christian political thought', Theological Studies, vol. 1, no. 4 (December 1940), pp. 337-64 and vol. 2, no. 3 (September 1941), pp. 325-46.

17. St Augustine, De Civitate Dei (The City of God), ed. G.E. McCracken & W.M. Green (7 vols., Heinemann, London, 1957-72), vol. 2, p. 16 and vol. 6, p. 206. My translations.

who insult you'. Moreover, 'if anyone strikes you on the right cheek, turn the other to him also'.[18] Consequently, in the second century, when the Church was suffering savage persecution, Tertullian observed that although 'a single night with a torch or two could achieve an ample vengeance', Christians should never have recourse to violence, because they were forbidden to repay evil with evil.[19] On the same ground, in the first three centuries of the Christian era, churchmen tended to condemn warfare. Even self-defence seemed unlawful. Most Christians rejected military service, and suffered the resultant penalties.[20]

However others thought the issue was not clear-cut. Christ had used 'a whip of cords' to drive the merchants and money-changers from the Temple, and He had told His disciples: 'Do not think that I have come to bring peace to the earth; I have not come to bring peace but a sword.'[21] These incidents corresponded better with the lessons of the Old Testament, according to which God had often commanded the Israelites to wage wars, either to preserve their faith or to conquer territories He had promised them. They received more attention in the fourth century, when the Pax Romana was disintegrating before the onslaughts of the barbarians. The Church's bishops and theologians subjected the Sermon on the Mount to radical reinterpretation and began to develop a theory of the 'just' war. It was argued that just as a loving parent should rebuke and if necessary punish a perverse child, the obligation to love one's enemies could require a state to resist and punish aggression from a neighbouring state. The trend accelerated after 381, when Christianity became the official religion of the Empire, and still more after the barbarians forced the abdication of the last Western Emperor in 476. In a period of chaos, the good life is impossible: a tranquil environment and a sufficiency of material goods are imperative if every individual is to have the opportunity of behaving virtuously. Warfare aimed at restoring peace and stability came to be considered necessary rather than evil. Thus in the sixth century, when the civil powers failed to act in the face of the Lombard invasion of Italy, Pope Gregory I, appalled at the prospect of further anarchy, took the initiative and successfully organised the defence of Rome and other cities. Later Churchmen were to call for holy wars or crusades

---

18. Matt. 5: 9-11, 39 and 44.

19. The Ante-Nicene Christian Library, vol. 11, p. 116.

20. E.A. Ryan, 'The rejection of military service by the early Christians', Theological Studies, vol. 13, no. 1 (March 1952), pp. 1-32; S. Windass & J. Newman, 'The early Christian attitude to war', Irish Theological Quarterly, vol. 29, no. 3 (July 1962), pp. 235-48; P. Ramsey, War and the Christian Conscience (Duke U. Pr., Durham, N.C., 1961), pp. xv-xvi.

21. John 2:14-15; Matt. 10:34.

to defend Christianity against heretics and infidels.[22]

The spread of the belief that Christians may lawfully kill their fellow-men when waging war for a just cause was a necessary prelude to the development of theories that Christian subjects may forcibly resist and rid themselves of unjust rulers. But meanwhile, a further theoretical difficulty had arisen. The lawyers of the Roman Republic had maintained that sovereignty belongs to the people. They had insisted that the powers exercised by all magistrates and other officials had been delegated by the people, and defined law as that which the populus command and have established. These central principles of the old Roman constitution had persisted under the pagan emperors. Law was now promulgated and enforced by the emperor, but the Lex regia de imperio declared that the emperor derived his power from the people and was their delegate. Professor Ullmann has styled this theory 'the ascending conception of government', and has shown that it was also held by a number of the Teutonic and Scandinavian tribes living beyond the boundaries of the Empire.[23] However, after the Christianisation of the Empire and the subsequent gradual conversion of the chieftains of the tribes which overran and destroyed it, monarchs seized upon the Pauline maxim about all authority coming from God and insisted on the acceptance of a 'descending' thesis of government, integral to which was the notion that a monarch was above the law of the land. This did not receive its most extreme formulation until the seventeenth century, when the Protestant Kings James I of England and Frederick III of Denmark postulated their 'divine right of kings' theory. Yet, in the meantime, theologians applied to Christian kings the Old Testament idea of the king being 'the Lord's annointed', and they developed coronation rites emphasizing that each monarch - regardless of whether he had been designated king by election or hereditary succession - was 'King by the Grace of God'.[24]

No theoretical justification of regicide was possible while the descending conception of government was generally accepted. But here too the march of events prompted fresh thinking. The rise of feudalism, from the eighth century onwards, provided one environment for the regeneration of ascending or populist notions. Faced with the chaos brought by the barbarian invasions, men took oaths of allegiance to powerful individuals, theoretically surrendering absolute ownership of their land as a surety for their loyalty in return for protection. The oaths of fealty barons made (as tenants-in-chief) to their king (as overlord) constituted contracts requiring the king to govern by

---

22. R.H. Bainton, Christian Attitudes to War and Peace (Abingdon Pr., New York, 1960), pp. 85-116; F.H. Russell, The Just War in the Middle Ages (C.U.P., Cambridge, 1975), pp. 12 ff; J.D. Tooke, The Just War in Aquinas and Grotius (S.P.C.K., London, 1965), pp. 10-25.

23. W. Ullmann, Principles of Government and Politics in the Middle Ages (Methuen, London, 1961), pp. 20-22.

24. Ibid., pp. 23-5.

consultation and agreement. This meant he was compelled to include at least some of his tenants-in-chief in the council of his advisers - the body in which he promulgated laws and dispensed justice. Thus the development of feudal institutions provided a challenge to the notion that God was the sole source of a king's authority.[25]

Again, after the First Crusade had reopened the Mediterranean to European traders, at the end of the eleventh century, towns and cities grew rapidly in size and wealth. Groups of merchants, manufacturers and master-craftsmen established guilds to act as benefit societies and to regulate their own particular industries; and as a new social group, the middle class, they soon won acknowledgment as a significant element in society, alongside the clergy and nobility. The guilds' early success in organising public works, such as the erection of city walls, commanded respect and helped towns and cities to obtain charters of self-government. Guilds and town councils were additional incubators for populist ideas about government.

Thirdly, there was the impact of conflicts between Church and state, which loomed large on the stage of medieval history. In theory, the Church existed to promote people's spiritual well-being, temporal rulers to promote their temporal well-being. This distinction had been re-emphasized in 494 by Pope Gelasius I, in his doctrine of the 'Two Powers', declaring that the Church should not meddle with worldly affairs, while secular authorities should not interfere with spiritual matters.[26] In practice, however, a harmony between two independent powers is always difficult to maintain. Some monarchs attempted to intervene in doctrinal disputes. Many quarrelled with the papacy over questions of jurisdiction, the appointment and investiture of bishops, the taxation of Church property and so forth. On their part, popes claimed that their office was superior in point of value and dignity, becaused it was concerned with man's final end, and that they had a right to pass judgement on a ruler's performance of his duties towards, and as a member of, the Church, which therefore entitled them to comment on his fitness for office. These disputes intensified after 800, when Pope Leo III crowned Charlemagne Emperor, and they became still more spectacular after Pope John XII restored the imperial dignity in 962. The Holy Roman Empire, which survived until 1806, was essentially a German empire; but some emperors dreamt of exerting a kind of overlordship of the whole Christian world. This led to various attempts to subjugate the papacy, and when that failed emperors helped to set up anti-popes (rival claimants to the See of Rome) on more than a dozen occasions. Popes responded by issuing excommunications and interdicts, instigating wars against recalcitrant rulers, and even arranging for the election of anti-emperors.

---

25. W. Ullmann, A History of Political Thought: the Middle Ages (Penguin, London, 1965), pp. 146-8.

26. Church and State through the Centuries, ed. S.Z. Ehler & J.B. Morrall (Newman Pr., Westminster, Md, 1954), p. 11; Abbo, Political Thought, p. 88.

A papal bull of excommunication could pose a serious threat to a medieval monarch. It declared him deprived of his title to his country's crown, absolved from their oaths all who had sworn allegiance to him, and charged 'all and singular', the nobles and people of his realm, that they must cease to obey the orders, mandates and laws of the deposed emperor or king on pain of incurring the like sentence of excommunication. Furthermore, these bulls generally ordered the rulers and people of other Christian states to take steps to reduce the condemned monarch, by force, to obedience to the papacy. The interdict, used to discipline civil rulers who were non-believers and therefore indifferent to ecclesiastical censure, was a more potent weapon still, because it affected all members of the laity in the kingdom concerned. It debarred them from attending Mass and other liturgical rites, which _inter alia_ meant that they could not receive Christian burial, or the Church's blessing on their marriages. It also commanded everyone in the rest of Christendom to terminate all trade and commerce with the country concerned, which placed a special burden on the vocal middle class. In an age of faith the interdict proved an effective way of forcing a refractory monarch's subjects to put pressure on him to come to some agreement with the papacy. By the thirteenth century, the succession of Church-state conflicts had diminished the mystique attached to monarchy and had made ordinary folk more aware that a king's power was at least to some extent dependent upon their consent to his rule.

A fourth challenge to monarchical power came from the revival of natural law doctrines. The lawyers of ancient Rome had developed the notion, implicit in much Greek philosophy,[27] that law ought to correspond to nature. That is, the laws promulgated in any nation (its positive law) ought to conform to objective moral rules (natural law), which we can discover by the use of reason - through a study of human nature, and by applying right reasoning to action. Its proponents maintained that the law of nature carries its own sanction. Anyone who disobeys it is abandoning his better self, denying his own nature, and becoming less than human. On the other hand, it has its own reward. It can lead every individual to virtue, and all mankind to unity, happiness and peace. Any legislation which departs from the natural law is _ipso facto_ unreasonable and unjust, and therefore not binding on the citizens, because no ruler can make wrong right, or right wrong. As Cicero (106-43 B.C.) put it:

> It is never morally right to alter this law, nor is it allowable to attempt to suppress any part of it, and it is impossible to annul it entirely. We cannot be freed from its obligations by the senate or the people, and we need not look outside ourselves for an expounder or interpreter of it.[28]

---

27. L. Strauss, _Natural Right and History_ (Phoenix, Chicago, 1965), pp. 120-64.

28. Cicero, _De re publica, De legibus_, ed. E.H. Warmington _et al._ (Heinemann, London, 1928), pp. 210-1.

These ideas had great appeal for the jurists at the University of Bologna, who, in the eleventh century, revived the study of Roman law. They were taken up by the civil and canon lawyers in twelfth century Paris. They were equally attractive to the English common lawyers, heirs to the quite different Saxon traditions that the fundamental law of the realm is customary law - the laws observed from time immemorial - and that the king, like all his subjects, is obliged to obey the law. In the thirteenth century the concept was also adopted by St Thomas Aquinas, the greatest of the medieval philosophers and theologians, who synthesised many different strands of learning and sought to show that the philosophy of Aristotle could be reconciled with Christianity and become more rational within it. For Aquinas, natural law ceased to be merely an abstract rule of reason. He saw it as a manifestation of a provident God's concern for His beloved children. Our rational nature allows us to have a share of the Divine Reason. So, for Aquinas, natural law is a practical reflection in us of God's wisdom, providing us with objective, universal rules of action. In its basic precept, it commands us to do good and avoid evil; that is, we should rationally follow our natural inclinations so as to attain our proper natural end, namely happiness.[29]

The vital implication of this teaching, in the present context, is that belief in natural law necessarily implied that there is a body of rules above the state and its government, and prior to them, by which anyone who uses his reason can judge the legitimacy of the state and the laws it enforces. From Gregory I to Gregory VII, Innocent III and Boniface VIII, popes had claimed the right to rebuke kings and emperors who infringed the laws God had revealed to His Church. The revival and development of the idea of natural law now encouraged a wide range of laymen to assess the justice of their rulers' conduct. It also had another implication, which became equally significant in the long run. As Cicero and the Roman lawyers had pointed out, it reduced the Greeks' debates about the merits of government by one man, a few, or the whole populace to secondary importance. Any form of government could be good so long as law was sovereign. This notion ran so counter to the entrenched medieval prejudice in favour of monarchy that it won general acceptance only very slowly. Yet at the University of Paris, Aquinas took it up in his Summa Theologica, and went so far as to declare that a 'mixed government', in which law is enacted 'by the common consent of the people', is the best.[30] In this way, discussion about the possibility of constitutional change was resumed.

The reign of King John in England illustrates the changing temper of the times, for in the years 1207-1215 there surfaced in his kingdom all four of these emerging challenges to arbitrary rule: barons asserting their feudal rights as tenants-in-chief, urban populism, papal

---

29. Aquinas, Selected Political Writings, ed., A.P. D'Entreves, trans. J.G. Dawson (Blackwell, Oxford, 1959), pp. 113-5 and 123-7.

30. Ibid., pp. 131-3 and 149.

intervention, and the growing tendency of the discontented to raise the cry of injustice and demand constitutional change. In 1207, after the election and consecration of an exceptionally well-qualified individual, Stephen Langton, as Archbishop of Canterbury, John, piqued because he had not been permitted to select the new Primate, refused to let him enter his diocese. When clerics demanded that the King keep out of Church matters, he only became more stubborn. Consequently, in 1208 the Pope placed England under an interdict, at a time when it was annually exporting several million pounds of wool to the great textile centres in Flanders and Italy. All the English cities possessing charters of self-government supported Langton. John fancied himself surrounded by conspiracies, and a suspected plot to kill him finally induced him to make peace with the papacy in 1213. By that stage his use of writs to withdraw large numbers of lawsuits from the jurisdiction of local courts had aroused deep resentment, as had his repeated demands for more revenue than feudal custom allowed. He made matters worse by a disastrous military expedition in France in 1214. This left him with no funds to employ mercenaries, while the feudal magnates were still a warrior class: 'they all had chain-armour and war-horses, some had been to the Crusades, and many lived in a state of chronic skirmishing with their Welsh and Scottish neighbours'.[31] Fed up with royal despotism, the barons rose in armed rebellion early in 1215, and with the support of Archbishop Langton (still backed by the cities) they forced upon John the negotiations which led to the issue of Magna Carta. This had a dramatic impact on English constitutional development. It specified that general taxes required the consent of a baronial council, that freemen should be tried by their equals according to the law of the land, and it guaranteed the liberty of the Church. As a whole, it embodied the principle that the king was under, not superior to, the law, and that he must recognise certain legal rights of his subjects.[32]

While these events pointed more to the future than the past, they were manifestations of the changing climate of opinion which made it possible for Christians to begin to defend tyrannicide. The first writer known to have attempted this was another Englishman, John Petit, generally known as John of Salisbury, a theologian and classical scholar who became Bishop of Chartres in 1176. His main work, the *Policraticus*,[33] is a comprehensive political treatise covering such subjects as the nature and functions of the state, the concept of a

31. G.M. Trevelyan, *History of England*, 3rd edn revised (Longmans, London, 1958), p. 167.

32. A.L. Poole, *From Domesday Book to Magna Carta*, 2nd edn (Clarendon Pr., Oxford, 1955), pp. 445-77; J.C. Holt, *Magna Carta* (C.U.P., Cambridge, 1965), espec. pp. 130-200.

33. The standard modern edition is the one edited by C.C.J. Webb (Clarendon Pr., Oxford, 1909). J. Dickinson's translation of selections from the *Policraticus* was published as *The Statesman's Book of John of Salisbury* (Knopf, New York, 1927).

'higher' law to which all man-made legislation was obliged to conform, and the powers and duties of kings. On the ever-topical question of Church-state relations, John defended the extreme view that the papacy has the right to depose a secular ruler who violates the law of God and disregards the Church's teaching. In the eighth book of the Policraticus he defined tyranny as oppressive rule based on force, and contrasted it with rule exercised in accordance with law. But here he had a problem, because of the influence of the descending thesis of government. His concept of government did not recognize any agency by which the ruled could judge the lawfulness of a ruler's actions, nor any secular constitutional machinery for correcting or deposing a bad king. However, a prince who became a tyrant might rule so oppressively as to become unbearable. So John drew on the Old Testament, at some length, to show that the killing of a tyrant is not unlawful, and that the tyrant's killer could be seen as an agent of God. He also saw the hand of God in the violent deaths of European tyrants like the Emperor Julian and King Sweyn, the Danish conqueror of England. Thus he justified tyrannicide, not in terms of human law, but in terms of inescapable justice and God's will. In resisting and killing the tyrant, no violation of the law is being committed, for it is the tyrant who has disarmed the law by enslaving it to his arbitrary whims, and it was fitting that justice should arm herself against him.

John of Salisbury did not rest content with a cautious declaration that tyrannicide is not unlawful. He took the further step of suggesting that it is 'generally' right and just to kill a tyrant, for in reducing his people to slavery, the tyrant is assailing the grace of God. When a ruler pursues a course of evil, 'it is God himself who in a sense is challenged to battle':

> The origin of tyranny is iniquity, and springing from a poisonous root, it is a tree which grows and sprouts into a baleful pestilent growth, and to which the axe must by all means be laid.[34]

In a subsequent passage, the descending conception of government reappeared: John admitted that it was widely held that the killing of a tyrant should not be undertaken by anyone who is bound to him by an oath or by the obligation of fealty, 'since sureties for good behaviour are justly given even to a tyrant'. This barrier to action would of course be removed if the Church excommunicated the tyrant. Till that was done, the most useful and the safest course for the oppressed was 'to pray devoutly that the scourge wherewith they are afflicted may be turned aside from them'. Nevertheless, he added that tyrants deserve to be destroyed, and that the person who slays a tyrant is acting as an instrument of God. Thus the principle remains: the slaying of a tyrant can be lawful.[35]

34. The Statesman's Book, p. 336.
35. Ibid., pp. 367-375.

St Thomas Aquinas (1225-74) called this a 'dangerous' doctrine, because it could lead to rash action by individuals acting on their private judgement, and because it might encourage 'evildoers' to think they had a licence to assassinate a ruler all honest people thought good. However, his reading of Aristotle and history led him to affirm that tyranny is the worst of all forms of government, and that 'the overthrowing of such government is not strictly sedition'. Although he was writing less than a century after John of Salisbury's death, his ideas sound much more modern. For example, he held that the power of the state, the essential principle of authority, resides in the people. He declared that 'the law must have as its proper object the well-being of the whole community'. Again, government and the promulgation of law are the 'task' and the 'business' of the whole community, or whoever represents it.[36] For Aquinas, all authority is in the nature of a trust. When a ruler uses it despotically, he forfeits the power entrusted to him: in spreading discord and strife among the people, he is himself guilty of sedition. Moreover, Thomas rejected John of Salisbury's quibble about the obligation of fealty in the case of a feudal ruler turned tyrant. He maintained:

> Nor should the community be accused of disloyalty for ... deposing a tyrant, even after a previous promise of constant fealty; for the tyrant lays himself open to such treatment by his failure to discharge the duties of office as governor of the community, and in consequence his subjects are no longer bound by their oath to him.[37]

In the same spirit, he was the first writer since ancient times to argue that democracy was a good form of government, far better than oligarchy let alone tyranny, and that a mixed constitution was superior to rule by one man alone.[38] Thus, in Aquinas's writings on political matters we can see a substantial revival of the ascending conception of government, and the source of several ideas that were to be influential in the English, American and French Revolutions.

When Aquinas left the area of principles and addressed himself to the question of techniques, he was much more cautious. He shared Aristotle's dislike of violent constitutional change in general, and of rebellions against tyranny in particular, on the ground that they can set in motion an unforeseen chain of reactions, worse than the evils the rebels wish to remedy. So he declared:

> If the tyranny be not excessive it is certainly wiser to tolerate it in limited measure, at least for a time, rather than to run the risk of

36. Aquinas, Selected Political Writings, trans. J.G. Dawson, pp. 31, 111 and 161. See also Aquinas, Summa Theologiae, ed. & trans. T. Gilby et al. (60 vols., Eyre & Spottiswoode, London, 1963-81), vol. 28, p. 15.

37. Sel. Pol. Writings, pp. 33 and 161.

38. Ibid., pp. 131-3 and 149.

> even greater perils by opposing it. For those who take action against a tyrant may fail in their object, and only succeed in rousing the tyrant to greater savagery.[39]

At the same time he justified civil disobedience, on the ground that people are only bound to obey rulers 'to the extent that the order of justice requires'. This was a distinct advance on the teaching of the early 'fathers' of the Church, who had held that a subject was obliged to obey civil rulers except in matters where the ruler commanded something contrary to the laws of God and his Church. Aquinas insisted that all authority has to be properly constituted, and that any legislation which is unreasonable or not for the common good 'is no longer legal, but rather a corruption of law'.

> For this reason if rulers have no just title to power, but have usurped it, or if they command things to be done which are unjust, their subjects are not obliged to obey them.[40]

Aquinas's political writings imply that people generally have the government they deserve. If they really want to, and if they use their power intelligently, they can control their government. Thus, while monarchy was the overwhelmingly dominant form of government in the middle ages, Thomas strongly recommended that monarchy should be elective, to give the people a chance to choose the best candidate and to impose limits on his power. Moreover, royal power should be tempered by blending it with aristocratic and democratic elements. Like Aristotle he saw merit in letting one man command, but the subjects should participate in government according to their abilities. A distribution of power would make it more difficult for good government to degenerate into tyranny. Then, if such preventative measures fail and the executive does become tyrannical, the task of disciplining or getting rid of tyrants is not left to private initiative, for the constitution will contain some public authority, a senate or popular assembly, which can put matters aright in an orderly fashion. Failing that, the subjects of a tyrannical king could ask the emperor to intervene. The case histories Aquinas offered to illustrate his recommendations are interesting. Thus:

> So the Romans deposed Tarquin the proud, whom they had previously accepted as king, because of his and his children's tyranny, and substituted the lesser or consular power instead. So also Domitian ... was slain by the Roman Senate because of his tyranny: and all the injustices which he had brought upon the Romans were legally and wisely revoked and made void by decree of the Senate.[41]

These examples show that, while urging that everything possible should be done to prevent grounds for revolution developing, Aquinas was

39. Ibid., p. 29.
40. Ibid., pp. 109-13, 129 and 179.
41. Ibid., pp. 29-33, 131-3 and 149-51.

clearly of the opinion that in certain circumstances violent political and constitutional change was legitimate. In the long run, this was to prove a more important breakthrough than John of Salisbury's defence of tyrannicide.

A temporary collapse of the Holy Roman Empire in the second half of the thirteenth century released the cities of northern Italy from the imperial yoke. As fully-independent city-states, they were frequently at war with each other and, as Dr Close has mentioned,[42] they continued to be so bedevilled by internal upheavals that the word rivoluzione was first coined there. Nevertheless, enriched by commerce, they became centres of high culture, and the outstanding political theorists of the 250-year period following Aquinas's death were, like him, Italians. But given the traumatic upheavals they lived through, it is not surprising that the main object of these writers was to discover the best means of creating order and stability. Two were Florentines: the poet, Dante Alighieri (1265-1321), and the bureaucrat, Niccolo Machiavelli (1469-1527). Both were freedom-lovers at heart, but both had to endure periods of banishment from their native city. They enunciated counter-revolutionary doctrines because they were convinced that a period of firm dictatorship was the only way to restore Italy to political health.[43]

There was greater novelty in the ideas of a third writer, Marsilius of Padua (c.1275-1342), who also had some experience of the life of a fugitive until he found refuge in the court of an excommunicated monarch, Louis of Bavaria. Marsilius's main work, the Defensor pacis (The Defender of Peace) is essentially an anti-clerical tract, inspired by an intense hatred of the papacy, which he regarded as the chief disturber of the peace of Italy. He denounced as a 'pestilence' the long-accepted idea that each Christian is subject to two authorities, the spiritual and the temporal, and alleged that it had brought about permanent anarchy. He advocated the complete subjection of the Church to the state, so that secular rulers and laymen would appoint bishops and priests, control Church property, and settle doctrinal disputes.[44] However, like Aquinas, he recommended that a monarch should be elected, and he considerably developed Aquinas's notion that the power of the state resides in the people - so much so that he is widely regarded as the first writer to have stated clearly the doctrine that sovereignty in every state is vested in the supreme legislator, consisting of 'the whole body of citizens, or the weightier

42. See Ch. 1, 'The meaning of revolution', p. 4.

43. Dante, On World-Government (De Monarchia), trans. H.W. Schneider, introd. by D. Biogongiari, 2nd edn (Bobbs-Merrill, Indianapolis, 1957), pp. 8-17; M. Lerner, 'Introduction', in Machiavelli, The Prince and The Discourses (Modern Library, New York, 1950), pp. xxxv-xlv; F. Chabod, Machiavelli and the Renaissance, trans. D. Moore (Harper Torchbooks, New York, 1965), pp. 61-78.

44. The Defender of Peace, trans. & ed. A. Gewirth (Harper Torchbooks, New York, 1967), pp. 261, 266, 282 and 286-70.

part thereof'. He added that by the 'weightier part' he meant to take into consideration not just a majority but the 'quality' of the citizens, and he commended a chapter of The Politics in which Aristotle had suggested that the best democracies are those giving a property-owner's vote the same value as the combined votes of five poor citizens.[45] So he was not what we would call a democrat. Yet he was the first medieval thinker to assert that only the citizens had the right to make laws, and that as the sovereign legislator they controlled the person they appointed to rule, that is, to execute the law.[46]

Marsilius was also the father of modern legal positivism - the doctrine that law is what law enforcers enforce. He defined law as 'an ordinance made by political prudence, concerning matters of justice and benefit and their opposites, and having coercive force'. This was a complete break with the view of medieval jurists and philosophers that law is an ordinance of reason, founded on and compatible with justice. For Marsilius, the essence of law consists in coerciveness: its morality is irrelevant. He claimed that even when a legislator's commands are based on 'false cognitions of the just and the beneficial', those ordinances are still law.[47] Conversely, every command which either lacks the coercive element, or whose coerciveness involves merely spiritual punishment or punishment in eternity, is not worthy of the name 'law'. Divine law (revealed in the Ten Commandments and the teaching of Christ), natural law, and the laws made by the Church are not true laws, because coercive power here on earth belongs exclusively to the state.[48] Thus Marsilius sought to promote peace by depriving would-be revolutionaries of any external standard for assessing the legitimacy of a particular government's structure, policies and actions. In addition, he held that 'prudence' can sometimes permit rulers to act illegally. Executing conspirators without trial, for example, he thought could be justified on the ground that it was intended to prevent rebellion.[49]

These notions helped Machiavelli to construct his defence of an amoral, pitiless dictatorship, and they have served the cause of counter-revolution everywhere. For example, when a majority of the common lawyers of England finally adopted positivist doctrines in the second half of the nineteenth century, it led to a completely different interpretation of the old maxim that 'an Act of Parliament can do no wrong'. Formerly, save on those occasions when they were suborned by exceptionally strong-willed monarchs such as Henry VIII and James I, the English judiciary had held the maxim to mean that if a statute violated the fundamental principles of English law, it was null and void to the extent that it did so. From 1871, the judges have held that whatever an Act of Parliament decrees is law and must be enforced.

45. Ibid., pp. 45-6.
46. Ibid., pp. 72-80 and 88-9.
47. Ibid., p. 36.
48. Ibid., pp. 37, 165.
49. Ibid., pp. 56-7.

Thus the courts have not even interfered with legislation like Northern Ireland's Preventive Detention Act of 1929 and related ordinances, authorising the executive to imprison people indefinitely, not only without trial, but without any charges being preferred against them, and further authorising the prohibition of any inquest should such people die while in custody - which means that allegations about the use of torture in the six counties can be neither proved nor satisfactorily disproved.

On the other hand, disciples of Marsilius's positivist teaching have denied that anyone has the right to question the legitimacy of what the state does during the 'reign of terror' stage of a revolution. Both Robespierre and Lenin received their legal training in institutions dominated by the positivist school of jurisprudence. It was this doctrine which allowed Lenin to claim that as the Bolsheviks must reject any morality based on 'God's commandments' or universal, 'extra-class' concepts, they were entitled to use the power of the state to impose a radically new code of 'ethics and morality':

> We say: morality is what serves to destroy the old exploiting society .... Communist morality is the morality which serves the class struggle, which unites the toilers ... against small property; for small property puts into the hands of one person what has been created by the labour of the whole of society.[50]

Thus ideas propounded by Marsilius have been used by revolutionaries as much as by counter-revolutionaries.

In the shorter term, it was his subordination of the Church to the state that attracted most interest. He defined the Church as the whole body of the faithful: it is the human legislator at prayer. It is not a reality distinct from the state, but simply the religious aspect of the state. So it is up to the whole body of the faithful to determine religious doctrine and discipline, and it is up to the secular ruler to exact obedience and grant dispensations. In the same vein, he took pains to argue that 'all bishops, and generally all persons now called clergymen, must be subject to the coercive judgment or rulership of him who governs by the authority of the human legislator'. Bishops and priests should live in poverty, and the state should have power to expropriate any surplus they receive through gifts or legacies. The sole functions left to the clergy are teaching the Gospel and administering the sacraments. Only the civil ruler has authority to excommunicate an individual for heresy or for giving scandal by persisting in public sin.[51] Marsilius's stout denials of the primacy of the Bishop of Rome and his authority to make laws for the Church's members were branded

50. The Tasks of the Youth Leagues (1920), trans. J. Katzer, reprinted in V.I. Lenin, Collected Works, 4th edn (45 vols., Lawrence & Wishart, London, 1963-70), vol. 31, p. 293.

51. The Defender of Peace, pp. 66, 113-26, 151, 161, 177-8, 262, 264-5, 296-7 and 428-30.

heretical.[52] Consequently his writings had a limited and secret circulation until they were first openly published by Swiss Protestants in 1521.

Prior to that, Marsilius's advocacy of republicanism in religion appealed to some of the English Lollards, and still more to the leaders of late medieval millenarian movements, notably the Taborite wing of the Hussites in Bohemia.[53] Though these heretical groups were generally short-lived, they did encourage some diffusion of ideas that social as well as religious revolution was a legitimate goal, which in turn produced a number of savagely repressed peasant revolts.[54]

Notions Marsilius had first propounded undoubtedly influenced leaders of the great sixteenth century religious revolution, the Reformation. Martin Luther was rightly charged with propagating Marsilian ideas,[55] and his supporters published a German translation of the second and third discourses of The Defender of Peace, advocating subordination of the Church to the state. Thomas Cromwell, Henry VIII's chief minister in the 1530s, had an English translation published 'with the King's most gracious privilege', and he constantly borrowed Marsilius's arguments to persuade the King that Parliament should reject all papal claims to jurisdiction over the Church in England, establish the royal supremacy, dissolve the monasteries, regulate the clergy and promulgate the doctrines which it, as legislator, approved.[56]

The success or failure of the Reformation in each country largely depended upon whether its rulers accepted or rejected the new ideas, for the preceding century had seen a dramatic growth in the

---

52. After Pope John XXII pronounced Marsilius and his protector heretics, in 1327, Louis invaded Italy and, on reaching Rome, declared the Pope deposed, appointed an anti-pope, had himself crowned Emperor by Sciarra Colonna (designated the people's 'representative'), and appointed Marsilius (a layman) 'Spiritual Vicar' of the Eternal City. This brief attempt to implement Marsilius's ideas was disastrous: the people of Rome rebelled, and Louis and Marsilius beat a hasty retreat to Nuremberg.

53. Gewirth's 'Introduction' to his edition of The Defender of Peace, p. xix.

54. N.R.C. Cohn, The Pursuit of the Millennium, rev. edn (O.U.P., New York, 1970), pp. 198-222.

55. A. Gewirth, Marsilius of Padua (2 vols., Columbia U.P., New York, 1956), vol. 1. p. 302.

56. Significantly, in the translation of The Defender of Peace published in London in 1535, the thirty-three sections insisting that the people should elect the ruler and correct and if necessary depose him were omitted. A reference to the people's legislative power was allowed to remain with the insertion of a note explaining that in this passage Marsilius 'speaketh not of the rascall multytude, but of the parlyament'! Fo. 28v in the British Library's copy. G.R. Elton, Studies in Tudor and Stuart Politics and Government (2 vols., C.U.P., Cambridge, 1974), vol. 2, pp. 151-2, 228-30.

power of governments. The military aspect of feudalism had declined because constant warfare had destroyed a large proportion of the nobility and produced impossible confusions of loyalty. This, plus the introduction of gunpowder and the development of cannon, had permitted rulers to centralise power in strong administrations backed by mercenary soldiers. In Continental Europe, representative assemblies were summoned much less frequently - in France, the Estates-General did not meet between 1484 and 1560 - as kings found they could levy taxes without that kind of consultation. The accession of wealth from newly discovered overseas colonies further aided the rise of absolutism. The liberty of individual subjects reached a new low.

The Protestant reformers, Luther and Calvin, did not lament this trend, and indeed it enabled them to find safe refuges. Luther (1483-1536) preached the duty of passively accepting the established social and political order. In a work entitled Temporal Authority: to what Extent it should be Obeyed (1523), he declared that monarchs are usually 'the biggest fools or the worst scoundrels on earth'. Nevertheless he insisted that even those whose rule is unjust or cruel must be obeyed because the world is wicked and does not deserve virtuous rulers.[57] Two years later, when the growing power of the princes and the effects of inflation had provoked the series of uprisings known as the Peasants' War, he replied to the rebels' demands with an Admonition to Peace in which he expanded on the theme that 'the wickedness and injustice of authority are no warrant for revolt'. This was followed by his notorious pamphlet Against the Robbing and Murdering Hordes of Peasants, denigrating the rebels as 'mad dogs'.[58]

In the self-governing city of Geneva, Calvin (1509-64) established a theocracy in which 'no aspect of private or public behavior was immune from his supervision'.[59] He admitted in theory that in exceptional cases, there was a right of resisting tyrannical rulers, if the resistance was organised by the magistrates or the legislature. But if the latter did not take the initiative, obedience and respect must characterise the people's attitude towards despots. Moreover, he suggested that any rebellion is likely to be displeasing to God, and that it is better to 'suffer anything rather than deviate from piety'.[60]

Absolutism was to find defenders, not only amongst new proponents of the descending thesis of government, like Luther and

57. Trans. J.J. Schindel, in Luther's Works, ed. J. Pelikan et al. (54 vols., various publishers, 1958-75), vol. 45 (Muhlenberg Pr., Philadelphia, 1962), pp. 85-114.

58. Trans. C.M. Jacobs, in Luther's Works, vol. 46 (Fortress Pr., Philadelphia, 1967), pp. 17-43 and 49-55.

59. V.H.H. Green, Renaissance and Reformation (Edward Arnold, London, 1952), pp. 173-6.

60. J. Calvin, Institutes of the Christian Religion (1536), trans. F.L. Battles, ed. J.T. McNeill (Westminster Pr., Philadelphia, 1960), pp. 1509-21.

James I, but also in the ranks of some subscribers to the ascending thesis. Thus the French political writer, Jean Bodin (1530-1596), thought it could be argued that in the case of kingdoms such as France, England, Spain, Scotland, Ethiopia, Turkey, Persia and Russia, the people had reposed absolute sovereignty in the hands of the monarch. Therefore, in no circumstances were they entitled to rebel against him. If he became tyrannical, their only hope was that the ruler of a neighbouring state would intervene, and, if necessary, take up arms to overthrow the oppressor.[61] The influential Dutch Protestant writer, Hugo Grotius, and the English political theorist, Thomas Hobbes, were to advance similar doctrines in the seventeenth century.[62]

As the Reformation developed, the intensity of religious controversy prompted several fresh defences of tyrannicide. The arguments of John of Salisbury were revived and bettered by Catholic writers such as Jean Boucher, a Parisian priest, Guillaume Rose, Bishop of the French diocese of Senlis, and Juan de Mariana, a Spanish Jesuit who was subsequently imprisoned for his outspoken criticisms of King Phillip III's fiscal policies. Mariana, for example, took as his main ground the principle that the people are sovereign. Any power exercised by kings is simply executive power, not legislative, and it is granted subject to strict limitations and conditions. He maintained it was properly the province of the legislature, an assembly of the people, to deal with a king who turns tyrant. But a tyrannical ruler is likely to prevent the assembly from meeting or acting, and in such an event any private citizen is justified in killing him at the citizen's own discretion. Mariana answered Aquinas's objection about the dangers of accepting such a doctrine by arguing that it would in practice be hard to find an individual who was prepared to take the risks involved in attempting to kill a king, and 'it is therefore a salutary restraint upon princes to inculcate the belief that the right to assassinate them if they become oppressive belongs to every one, and that the authority of the people is above their authority.'[63]

Meanwhile, many of the Calvinists living outside the community of saints at Geneva found themselves in environments hostile to their creed, and thus began to doubt the wisdom of Calvin's advice that they should remain submissive, repent, and pray. In the Netherlands, Calvinism became associated with the successful patriotic movement to win independence from Spanish rule. In Scotland, Queen Mary (Stuart)'s abortive scheme to revive Catholicism led the Calvinist

---

61. J. Bodin, The Six Bookes of a Commonweale, trans. R. Knolles, ed. K.D. McRae (Harvard U.P., Cambridge, Mass., 1962), pp. 222-5.

62. H. Grotius, The Law of War and Peace, trans. F.W. Kelsey (Bobbs-Merrill, Indianapolis, 1962), pp. 115 and 149-50; T. Hobbes, Leviathan, ed. M. Oakeshott (Blackwell, Oxford, 1947), pp. 114-6.

63. De rege et regis institutione (On Kingship), published 1599, quoted in W.A. Dunning, A History of Political Theories from Luther to Montesquieu (Macmillan, New York, 1947), pp. 70-2.

George Buchanan (tutor to James VI in the years 1570-78 while Mary was being detained in England without trial) to publish a treatise against absolutism, in which he defended the doctrine of tyrannicide.[64] But it was the Huguenots, as the French Calvinists were called, who had most to complain about. The Queen Mother, Catherine de Medici, attempting to rule France from 1559 to 1589, during the reigns of her feeble and neurotic sons, Francis II, Charles IX and Henry III, was appalled by the civil disturbances which accompanied and followed the Huguenots' desecration of hundreds of churches and convents, and tried to use the power of the state to impose uniformity of belief, even if it meant compelling both sides to make concessions. This only enraged all those Catholics and Protestants who valued principle more than a quiet life. It seems the Huguenots were never more than seven per cent of the population. However, they won the allegiance of many of the wealthier townsmen - who found religious dissent a focus for resistance to interference with their towns' privileges by the officials of the central government. They also gained the moral support of two-fifths of the nobility - many of whom hoped that if France became Protestant they could share in the dispersal of monastic and other Church property, as their counterparts in Germany and Britain had done. The upshot was the series of bloody struggles known as the French Wars of Religion, 1562-93.[65]

Several Huguenot writers assumed the task of rewriting Calvin's political theory to justify those who had been resisting the Crown. One of their brethren, Francois Hotman (1524-1590), a jurist and historian, prepared the groundwork in his Francogallia (1573), which attempted to show that France was never, in its constitutional origins,an absolute monarchy. He identified the precedents which suggested that succession to the throne had always been based on popular consent and that the Estates-General retained the right to resist a bad king.[66] This argument was extended by Theodore Beza (1519-1605), a biblical scholar who had been acknowledged as the Huguenots' spiritual leader since Calvin's death in 1564. In 1574 Beza published a pamphlet, The Right of Magistrates, urging that if a king becomes a 'clearly flagrant' tyrant who 'endures no remonstrances', all members of the aristocracy, lords of castles, and elected (as distinct from royal) officials, such as mayors, aldermen, provosts, consuls and sheriffs, are released from their oaths of loyalty and become entitled to refuse to obey any

---

64. First printed in 1579 in Latin, as De jure regni apud Scottos, trans C.F. Arrowood as The Powers of the Crown in Scotland (Univ. of Texas Pr., Austin, 1949). See also Q. Skinner, The Foundations of Modern Political Thought (2 vols., C.U.P., Cambridge, 1978), vol. 2, pp. 343-5.

65. R.S. Dunn, The Age of Religious Wars, 1559-1689 (Norton, New York, 1970), pp. 20-31.

66. Trans. & ed. J.H. Franklin, in his Constitutionalism and Resistance in the Sixteenth Century (Pegasus, New York, 1971), pp. 53-96.

commands threatening the welfare of the realm, as the latter was of over-riding importance. Beza still insisted that only the Estates-General had the right to punish such a king. If the tyrant refused to summon the Estates, private individuals were not forbidden to voice demands that he change his mind, nor to insist that their local officials do likewise. Apart from that, 'they have no other remedy but penitence and patience joined with prayers'.[67]

As the Estates-General had not passed judgement on the monarchy's conduct, Beza's pamphlet was not enough to justify the thousands who had taken up arms, nor did it justify the Huguenots' inviting English and German troops to come to their aid. However, many laymen took up their pens with gusto. The Vindiciae contra tyrannos (A Defence of Liberty against Tyrants) became by far the best-known of these efforts because it first propagated the notion that constitutional arrangements are the product of a contract between God, king and people.[68] This was pure phantasy, but it had an immediate appeal to Protestants throughout Europe and, later, its overseas colonies because their studies of the Old Testament accounts of the Covenant between God and his Chosen People, the Israelites, made it easy for them to jump to the conclusion that covenants or contracts - the most solemn obligations known to man - ought to be, and therefore somehow must have been, the foundation of all authority. Everyone seemed to forget that Aristotle and countless other philosophers had argued, persuasively, that human beings are by their very nature social and political creatures. In politics, however, the popularity of an idea is of greater practical import than whether or not it makes anthropological or historical sense. This one spread as the Vindiciae appeared in many editions and translations. It was often invoked during the English Revolutions of the seventeenth century and, secularised by Rousseau and Jefferson, it played its part in the American and French Revolutions; for to say that a ruler has broken the contract to which he owes his position and lawful power is the most convenient and comforting of all the arguments that can be invoked to justify rebellion.

The Vindiciae was first published under the pseudonym 'Stephen Junius Brutus' in 1579. After four centuries, historians and linguists are still arguing about the identity of the author, but it seems probable that it was written by Philippe Duplessis Mornay (1549-1623), a soldier and diplomat.[69]

The second key idea running through the Vindiciae is the notion that kings are trustees for the people they govern: whatever authority has been given to a ruler is to be exercised, not for his personal benefit, but for the benefit of those on whose behalf he acts. If a trustee violates or abuses his trust, he forfeits the position. Even in the case of a hereditary monarchy, the fact that a particular king has

67. Trans. & ed. J.H. Franklin, in ibid., pp. 110-2, 123-4, 129-30.
68. Trans. & ed. J.H. Franklin, in ibid., pp. 143-5, 146-51, 158-61.
69. Ibid., pp. 138-40.

been allowed to succeed to the throne is a sign that he holds his sovereignty from the people, and from the moment of accession his 'first obligation' is 'to be the guardian, minister, and protector' of the nation and its laws.[70] As we have seen, this was a notion that had been developed by St Thomas Aquinas. The Vindiciae transmitted it to Europe's Protestant communities, and in England, for example, it was taken up by Whiggish political theorists as disparate as Locke, in the 1680s, and Burke, in the 1790s.

When it comes down to practical questions about how to deal with a monarch who oppresses the people by arbitrary violations of the law or by persecuting 'true' religion, the Vindiciae is, like Calvinist Church government, aristocratic rather than democratic. Mornay repeatedly stressed that it is the function of the Estates-General, or failing it, the nobility and the elected officials, to act to rebuke, discipline and, if necessary, depose and kill a tyrannical king.[71] Moreover, they were quite entitled to seek aid from foreign governments, and the latter would be wicked to refuse it:

> A neighbouring prince, furthermore, should be at least as willing to help an oppressed people ... as to come to the aid of a king, if his people should become seditious. Indeed, he should be even more willing in the first case where there are a great many victims, not just one.[72]

This was a reflection of the basic Christian principle that every human being has a value. That also emerged in a passage in which Mornay conceded that in the theoretical case of a usurper who gains a kingdom by violence and then rules tyrannically, anyone, 'including private individuals', could be justified in assassinating him.[73]

The most important aspect of the attempts to construct doctrines of tyrannicide is that they had led to insistence on the idea that the authority of rulers is limited because their sovereignty is conferred on them by the people, and because power in any state must be shared between various groups and institutions. Later generations were to demand that the share allotted to those other institutions should be significantly increased.

Nevertheless, prior to the seventeenth century, all writers who sought to justify any kind of rebellion or violent constitutional change did so with some reluctance. Even when there was no other solution, it was at best a regrettable necessity, for all scholars were legatees of the Greeks' dislike of the killing and destruction that are inevitably associated with violent change. The sixteenth century monarchomacs, as the Catholic and Calvinist defenders of tyrannicide were called,

---

70. Ibid., p. 169.

71. E.g., ibid., 151-6 and 161-7.

72. Ibid., pp. 198-9.

73. Ibid., p. 188. For a fuller rendering of this passage see the translation of 1689, in A Defence of Liberty against tyrants, introd. by H.J. Laski (Geo. Bell, London, 1924), p. 191.

conformed to this tradition of exhorting people to endure indignities, oppression and even persecution as long as they were sufferable, and to risk the probably greater evils of rebellion only as a last resort. Yet the demands of Luther, Calvin and other religious reformers for freedom to follow their own consciences, plus similar demands from those, such as the English Jesuit, Robert Parsons,[74] who dissented from the creed that became dominant in their nation, led increasing numbers of people to stress liberty rather than authority. So in the seventeenth century, writers began to take a more positive approach to political and constitutional change, and to suggest that it was worth initiating a revolution, with all its perils, in order to secure a freer way of life.

The English republican propagandist, John Milton (1608-1674), signalled the advent of the new attitude in his pamphlet, The Tenure of Kings and Magistrates (1649). This appeared soon after Oliver Cromwell and his supporters had eliminated the English monarchy, abolished the House of Lords, and established an oligarchic republic. Cromwell had considered 'the principles of Mariana and Buchanan' sufficient to establish the lawfulness of executing Charles I.[75] Milton went further. His pamphlet was at once the last of the tracts on the right of resisting a tyrant and a first joyful affirmation of a right of revolution. The link between these two themes was Milton's claim that freedom is mankind's 'natural birthright'. After adding this to the monarchomac doctrine that sovereignty always 'remains fundamentally' with the people and cannot be taken from them, he proceeded:

> It follows lastly, that since the King or Magistrate holds his autoritie of the people, both originaly and naturally for their good in the first place, and not his own, then may the people as oft as they shall judge it for the best, either choose him or reject him, retaine him or depose him though no Tyrant, meerly by the liberty and right of free born Men to be govern'd as seems to them best.

Milton insisted that this doctrine was defensible 'with plain reason', but immediately introduced a flurry of biblical quotations to show that 'the right of choosing, yea of changing their own Government is by the grant of God himself in the People'.[76] Professor Friedrich's comment on the passage is apt:

> It is no longer a question of whether the ruler is tyrannical or not, whether he is unlawful or not. It is simply a question of what the people want. If the people no longer like what they have in the way of government, or political order, they can do away with it and put another in its place.[77]

---

74. C. Morris, Political Thought in England: Tyndale to Hooker (O.U.P., London, 1953), pp. 135-7.

75. Skinner, Foundations, vol. 2, p. 348.

76. Republished in Milton's Works, vol. 5, pp. 8, 10 and 14-18.

77. C.J. Friedrich, An Introduction to Political Theory (Harper & Row, New York, 1967), p. 41.

Milton stood at the threshold of a new era in the history of writing about revolution. Like the medieval and early modern theorists, he was religious in outlook. More recent writers by and large made man the centre and measure of all things and, in their search for truth and norms of action, recognised reason and experience as their only guides. Milton was still concerned about the will of God, and about man's duties towards his Maker and his fellow men. Yet, like many of his contemporaries in England in the 1640s, and like later publicists, he placed strong emphasis on the will of the people and on the people's rights of changing their government. He saw no conflict in the pursuit of these various ends. But the full import of this novel notion of the people's 'rights' - something quite different from feudal rights, which had simply been the rights of the several parties to a contract, and equally distinct from any legal rights that might have been conceded by the state, either by legislation or by judicial decisions - emerged only after Milton's death, and it must be examined in the next chapter.

Chapter Four

LIBERAL THOUGHT ABOUT REVOLUTION FROM LOCKE TO MAZZINI

P.A. Howell

The seventeenth and eighteenth centuries witnessed the rise of liberalism, a political creed which began by advocating the maximisation of individual freedom and ended by adopting programmes of social change which included policies (such as furthering the expansion of colonial empires, taxing inheritances, and placing restrictions on the sale of alcohol) that were anything but 'liberal'. It originated as one of the first fruits of the Enlightenment, a philosophical movement based on the belief that man was a rational being, able to work out his own salvation without the aid of tradition or the Church. Thus, in addition to free-trade and the abolition of torture, the *philosophes*, as propagandists of the Enlightenment were called, promoted a rationalist and anti-clerical climate of opinion among the educated classes in Europe and its colonies. While some of these writers still saw merit in religion, it was largely because they regarded it as a useful promulgation of moral laws - and for this purpose, one religion was as good as another. That is, they ignored Christ's invitation to His followers to share in the work of redeeming the world by radically transforming it so as to restore all things in Him. In the new view, Christianity was reduced to a thoroughly-tamed, acceptable, middle-class religion, a creed which could serve as a convenient safeguard of morality by adding the fear of eternal punishment to the restraining force of social considerations like public opinion and the power of the state. For a period, in the eighteenth century and the first decades of the nineteenth, many clergymen were influenced by the writings of the *philosophes*; and encounters with this bourgeois perversion of Christianity induced many intellectuals, including the young Marx, to deride and reject religion altogether.

Early liberalism did nothing to advance people's understanding of revolutionary phenomena, and it added little of substance to the concepts that could be invoked to justify revolution. The ideas touted by the leaders of the English Revolution of 1688-9, and indeed most of the principles proclaimed by the early leaders of the American and French Revolutions, were borrowed from the late medieval and/or monarchomac notions that sovereignty belongs to the people, that there is some kind of binding contract between rulers and their people, that kings may be overthrown if they exceed the limits of the power entrusted to them, or if they have been guilty of injustice or neglectful of their obligations towards their subjects, and that radical constitutional change - including abolition of the institution of monarchy - can be legitimate. Nevertheless, liberalism became popularly associated with revolution because the liberals presented the old ideas clothed in a noisily-propagated new rhetoric about the 'rights of man'.

The metamorphosis of natural law theories[1] into a doctrine of 'natural rights' was a reflection of the liberals' emphasis on the individual. Pre-modern writers of the natural law school had all seen the state's purpose as serving the common good. Nowhere in the writings of St Thomas Aquinas, for example, is there any mention of human rights. All his emphasis was on duties and obligations. Rulers had many obligations to their subjects, and deserved to be deposed if they failed to perform their duty. Subjects were similarly obliged to obey the lawful commands of their rulers. Inter-personal relations were handled in the same spirit. Instead of pondering what rights the individual was entitled to, pre-modern theorists stressed that each person is obliged to be active in promoting the well-being of others. They believed that the integration of the individual into the community did not confine but, on the contrary, enlarged and enriched that individual's personality. This was a corollary of the ancient notion that the full realization of a person's physical, intellectual and moral needs depends upon living with others. As Aristotle had put it, anyone divorced from the rest of the human race must be 'either sub-human' (that is, incapable of leading a rational existence) 'or super-human' (in other words, a god or a saint).[2] Accordingly, until the seventeenth century, natural law theorists insisted that the person who promotes the common good promotes his or her own good as well, because one's own good cannot be truly attained unless the common good is attained. Now it is obvious to us that if everyone has obligations and duties towards everyone else, this creates a situation in which individuals can demand a right to be treated in a certain way. However, that deduction was not drawn until modern times. The concept that each individual has certain rights (for example, a right to personal possessions such as one's own books or clothing, and 'the right to preserve one's life'), was first developed by a number of theologians, notably Jean Gerson and Francisco Suarez. Nevertheless, promoting the common good had remained their chief concern.[3] The early liberals retained the notion that there were laws of nature, but they laid emphasis on the individual rather than on society. As a corollary, they placed great emphasis on what they called the 'natural rights of man'; and because of their preoccupation with freedom and self-

1. See above, pp. 40-1.
2. The Politics, trans. Sinclair, p. 28.
3. Skinner, Foundations, vol. 2, pp. 117, 121-2, 176-8.

interest, these rights were viewed as ends in themselves rather than as means of enabling men to live the good life.

In view of the current interest in women's history, it is worth noticing that the exclusive masculinity of the seventeenth and eighteenth century liberals' rhetoric was not wholly accidental or unconscious. One of the unfortunate legacies of the Renaissance-Reformation era was the resurgence of the pre-Christian conceit that women are inferior and subject to men. It was not ever thus. In medieval England, for example, women had sat in Parliament, enjoyed manorial and other property rights, served on juries and voted for shire knights. They had been heads of monasteries and schools, and in social, religious and trading guilds were equal with men. They had held public office as sheriffs, marshals, overseers of the poor, governors of royal castles, high and petty constables, high stewards, and justices of the peace. The causes of their subsequent exclusion from public life, and the reasons why there was so little fuss about the change, are matters which someone ought to investigate. In Britain, the statute of 1539 banishing the abbesses from the House of Lords[4] and the publication of the religious reformer John Knox's First Blast of the Trumpet against the Monstrous Regiment of Women (1558) were symptoms of the new attitude. As far as England was concerned, the process was completed by a series of judicial decisions handed down in the years 1606-15, most being the handiwork of that very unhappily married Lord Chief Justice, Sir Edward Coke. It was women's further misfortune that the new orthodoxy on their position was accepted without question by the father of liberalism, the English philosopher, John Locke (1632-1704). In the 1640s, the thrice-married John Milton was able to write unselfconsciously about the rights of 'the People'. Forty years later, when the bachelor, Locke, proclaimed the rights of 'man', he took it for granted that 'a female ... is by nature and convention inferior to the male'.[5]

At the present day, talk about rights often means what it is humane or socially useful to concede to private persons. Whenever there is substantial civil disobedience in a Western nation, the correspondence columns of its newspapers are replete with claims that people have only the rights that the state grants them. Yet, however generous they may be, grants or concessions are not rights, because whatever the state gives the state can take away. The British Parliament's frequent suspension of the operation of its Habeas Corpus Act of 1679 (entitling prisoners to know the reason for their detention), is an obvious example. Concessions of that type, like modern constitutional guarantees, are not rights at all, but only more or less hopeful expressions of the legislators' or the community's kind intentions. Rights are what each person is entitled to because he or she is human, not what society is willing to let him or her have, and

4. 31 Hen. VIII, c. 13.

5. M. Seliger, The Liberal Politics of John Locke (Allen & Unwin, London, 1968), p. 212.

they are valid even against society. As subscribers to the natural-law tradition, Locke and his disciples held that man's rights are rooted in his nature. Man is a particular kind of being, and must be treated accordingly. His rights are prior to the establishment of civil society. No community is entitled to trample on them; if it does so, its laws are bad and should not be obeyed. This was nothing more than an individualistic version of the older doctrine that if a ruler persists in violating the natural law his ordinances are void and his subjects may rebel.

Locke expounded his version of natural law in his Two Treatises of Government (1690). In the second of these, subtitled An Essay concerning the True Original, Extent, and End of Civil Government, he claimed that man has certain fundamental natural rights which are antecedent to political society and which he can never surrender, namely the rights to life, liberty and estates.[6] The sole function of government is the maintenance and protection of these rights. The heart of his thesis was that the power of the state must be contained. Thus, like Aquinas and the monarchomacs, he considered that no one, petty official or king, is entitled to disregard the limits of his authority, and that separation of legislative and executive power was desirable. He defended the latter on the ground that

> it may be too great a temptation to human frailty apt to grasp at Power, for the same Persons who have the Power of making Laws, to have also in their hands the power to execute them, whereby they may exempt themselves from Obedience to the Laws they make, and suit the Law, both in its making and execution, to their own private advantage.[7]

He reaffirmed the maxim, often proclaimed in England since the rebellion which had led to Magna Carta, that the levying of taxes should be conditional upon the executive securing the consent of a majority of the people's representatives. He also adopted the monarchomac doctrines that the legislature should be superior to the executive and that the people always retain 'a Supream Power' to remove or alter the legislature when they find it acting contrary to the trust reposed in it. Rebellion and civil war are justified when those who were entrusted with protecting law and peace prove instead 'Robbers and Oppressors'.[8]

Locke's persuasive presentation of these ideas won them a wide audience, for they appealed to the self-interest of middle-class males who resented taxation and government interference with the free operation of their business, professional and trading concerns. Thus they supplied most of the theoretical basis for the American colonists'

6. J. Locke, Two Treatises of Government, ed. P. Laslett, rev. edn (Mentor, New York, 1965), pp. 309-11, 325, 329-32, 336, 395-9 and 402-3.

7. Ibid., pp. 410, 446 and 473.

8. Ibid., pp. 401, 408, 413-6, 465, 473-4 and 476-7.

revolt against British rule. They were clearly reflected in the Declaration of Independence, the United States' Constitution adopted in 1787, and especially in the Federalist essays written by Alexander Hamilton, James Madison and John Jay in 1787-8, urging the new states to ratify the Constitution.[9] The same ideas were an equally significant source of the rhetoric used to justify the first French Revolution, and so they reappeared in the Declaration of the Rights of Man and of the Citizen, issued by the National Assembly in August 1789, and yet again in the Constitution of 1791.

It has sometimes been claimed that few political thinkers have been more influential than Locke.[10] However, as far as Locke's writing on revolution is concerned, there is much more relevance in Professor Parkinson's argument that few, if any, politicians have been

> greatly influenced by a book of political theory although many have been influenced by a book of religion. The politician who reads at all will have read not only the text which the historian thinks significant but forty-nine other forgotten works of which the historian has never even heard. And if one book appears to have been his favourite, it will be because the author recommends what he, the ruler, has already decided to do; or what indeed he has already done.[11]

Locke's significance in the history of revolution is not that he guided the men of 1776 or 1789, but that his Second Treatise was relevant to the mood of their age. That is, he provided them with a more or less plausible explanation of what they (in their desire to remedy particular grievances which hurt their vanity and their pockets) had already decided to do.

Again, many writers have declared that in his Second Treatise Locke sought to justify retrospectively the so-called 'Glorious' English Revolution of 1688[12] - in which the Catholic King, James II, had been forced to flee into exile and the Protestant Dutchman, William of Orange, and his wife Mary were invited to ascend the throne. To an increasing number of critics, 1688 was 'only a coup successfully carried out by a few traitors with foreign help' - a coup, moreover, which

---

9. F.S. Oliver, Alexander Hamilton, rev. edn (Constable, London, 1907), pp. 165-75.

10. E.g., E.M. Burns & P.L. Ralph, World Civilizations, 4th edn (2 vols., Norton, New York, 1969), vol. 2, p. 127.

11. C.N. Parkinson, The Evolution of Political Thought (Longman, London, 1958), p. 9.

12. This hoary absurdity should have been finally laid to rest by the researches of P. Laslett - see the 'Introduction' to his edition of the Two Treatises, pp. 58-79 - but it still lives. E.g., P. Calvert, Revolution (Macmillan, London, 1970), p. 69, and the entry on Locke in the Dictionary of World History, ed. G.D.M. Howat & A.J.P. Taylor (Nelson, London, 1973), p. 887.

inaugurated 'an era of corruption such as few other nations have ever experienced'.[13] It perpetuated the privileged status of the propertied classes. It gave nothing to the mass of the people save religious liberty, and even that was confined to those Christians who were not Catholics. The Revolution also increased the misery of most of the Irish. It is no wonder that both of William III's nicknames ('Sweet William' and 'Stinking Billy') are still in use throughout the English-speaking world. Nevertheless, 1688 did bring significant change. It completed tasks that had been attempted in the aborted English Revolution of the 1640s and 1650s. It dealt the death blow to absolute monarchy in England, established the supremacy of Parliament, and limited the power of government by enacting the Bill of Rights of 1689. Thus it marked the victory of representative constitutional government, and it cemented a partnership between the great landowners, businessmen and government.

Locke started a hare by expressing the hope, in the Preface to his Two Treatises, that what he had written would be 'sufficient to establish the Throne of our Great Restorer, Our present King William' and 'make good his Title, in the Consent of the People'.[14] However, if government is justified by the positive consent of the governed, as Locke thought, it would be extremely difficult to defend the Revolution of 1688 and William's title to rule, for the overwhelming majority of the people were simply not asked for their opinions. The usurper was installed by force: he brought his own army across the Channel, and King James was unable to lead the British troops into battle because he was incapacitated by a nosebleed which persisted for some days. At first, only a few hundred Englishmen knew what was going on. The shibboleths and tactics employed by the small group of magnates who invited William to England and orchestrated the subsequent events were very different from Locke's. Both before the coup and in the Convention Parliament which declared the throne vacant, the revolutionary politicians invoked ideas propagated by the monarchomacs and the English judiciary. They accused James II of breaking the 'contract between King and people' and of having 'violated the fundamental laws'.[15] Now Locke was one of those theorists who regarded political society as the result of a free contract. However he adopted the ideas of one of the defenders of absolutism, Thomas Hobbes (1588-1679), that people were not by their very nature social and political beings, that there had been a state of nature, an original condition of mankind opposed to the political state, and that people had been free to choose whether or not they would live in political society.[16] So Locke, like

13. M. Salvadori, Locke and Liberty (Pall Mall Pr., London, 1960), p. xv.

14. Two Treatises, ed. Laslett, p. 171.

15. M. Ashley, The Glorious Revolution of 1688 (Hodder & Stoughton, London, 1966), p. 182.

16. T.Hobbes, Leviathan, ed. M.Oakeshott, pp. 80-92 and 109-116.

Hobbes and, later, Rousseau,[17] claimed that civil society was the result of a free contract entered into as a matter of convenience. Locke's contract was a 'social contract' between the individuals who combine to form society, not the monarchomac 'contract of government between ruler and people' concept that had become the commonplace of England's Whig politicians. Locke considered that the establishment of government had been subsequent to the formation of society, and that this had never taken the form of a contract. Instead, he held that the people gave power in trust to the government they established. So a government could be removed if it acted contrary to the trust reposed in it - rather than for the breach of some alleged contract of government.[18] If the trustee fails in its duty to protect man's right to life, liberty and property, the creators of the trust are freed from their obedience. Power returns to them, and they resume their original liberty. In short, Locke was much more interested in protecting individual liberty than in promoting political stability. For him, anarchy was preferable to any restriction on one's fundamental rights.[19] If he really meant to defend the conduct of the promoters of the Revolution of 1688, it can only be concluded that he made a poor fist of it. But it now seems clear that the reference to the Revolution in the Treatises' Preface was simply a prudent gesture: at the time of publication Locke still needed the support of his Whig patrons.

In the eighteenth century, liberalism was challenged by the rise of two further ideals, democracy and a belief in progress. These were to have a still greater impact on modern revolutions. Yet liberalism had enough vitality to be able, ultimately, to absorb them, and in the process of doing so transformed its original character.

The first modern European prophet of democracy was the Genevan, Jean Jacques Rousseau (1712-1778). When compared with liberal thinkers like Locke and Voltaire, Rousseau had no interest in defending individual rights but was primarily concerned to promote popular rule. He was also the father of romanticism. Rebelling against the rationalism then prevalent in European society, he exalted instincts, feelings and impulses, and contrasted what he believed to be the natural goodness of man with the wickedness of existing institutions. These sentiments fostered his faith in the natural equality of all men and in the wisdom of the masses. In his conception of a social contract, each individual surrenders all his rights to the general will of the community. The sovereign power of the general will is subject to no limitation. Whatever the majority decides is binding on everyone. From it there is no appeal, and the only hope for those who find themselves in a minority is that they may one day become the majority. Meanwhile, declared Rousseau, 'whoever refuses to obey the general will shall be constrained to do so by the whole body, which means nothing other than that he shall be forced to be free'. The

---

17. J.J. Rousseau, The Social Contract, trans. M. Cranston (Penguin, London, 1968), pp. 59-62 and 64-5.

18. Two Treatises, pp. 309-11, 395, 397, 413 and 425-9.

19. Ibid., 325, 369 and 454-77.

entire body of citizens is alone responsible for the making of laws. The people entrust executive power to the government, but its sole function is to carry out the general will, and the people may change or dismiss it whenever they wish.[20]

Participatory democracy of that kind could only be implemented in a city-state or a small agricultural community like a Swiss canton. Nevertheless, Rousseau's doctrines of equality and the sovereignty of the majority inspired many of the more radical leaders of the French Revolution: Robespierre was his most ardent disciple. Liberals were initially appalled by Rousseau's notion of forcing men to be free. They feared that his new absolutism, the tyranny of the majority, might be worse than royal absolutism. But in time liberals became more democratic, and were able to join forces with democrats in pursuit of common objectives for at least part of each of the great revolutions of the late eighteenth and the nineteenth centuries.

Like liberalism, the theory of progress was a child of the Enlightenment. In attacking injustice, ignorance and prejudice, and in lauding the contemporary discoveries of Newton and other scientists, the *philosophes* implicitly assumed that the growth and diffusion of knowledge must result in the upward progress of the human race. This assumption became explicit in the second half of the eighteenth century in the writings of the Germans J.G. Herder and G.E. Lessing, and the Frenchmen A.R.J. Turgot and the Marquis de Condorcet. Whereas the mainstream of orthodox Christianity had always taught that every person was called to strive, with God's help, for his or her own perfection, so as to achieve eternal life, the *philosophes* developed a quasi-religion of the perfectibility, not just of individuals, but of all societies and their institutions.[21] As Condorcet put it:

> Our hopes, as to the future condition of the human species, may be reduced to three points: the destruction of inequality between different nations; the progress of equality in one and the same nation; and lastly, the real improvement of man.
>
> Will not every nation one day arrive at the state of civilisation attained by those people who are most enlightened, most free, most exempt from prejudices...? Will not the slavery of countries subjected to kings, the barbarity of African tribes, and the ignorance of savages gradually vanish?[22]

---

20. *The Social Contract*, pp. 62-78, 146 and 151-4.

21. C.L. Becker, *The Heavenly City of the Eighteenth-Century Philosophers* (Yale U.P., New Haven, 1932), pp,. 139-40; L. Gottschalk, 'Becker and the *Philosophes*' Dilemma', in *Carl Becker's Heavenly City Revisited* (Archon, Hamden, Conn., 1968), p. 95.

22. M.J.A.N. Caritat, Marquis de Condorcet, *Outlines of an Historical View of the Progress of the Human Mind*, trans. anon. (Johnson, London, 1795), pp. 316-7. For a more accessible but less elegant rendering see J. Barraclough's translation (Weidenfield & Nicolson, London, 1955), pp. 173-4.

Turgot and Condorcet were two theorists who seized opportunities to implement their ideas. When Turgot was appointed Louis XVI's Comptroller-General of Finance in 1774, he embarked on sweeping reforms of the French bureaucratic machine, removed fiscal and other barriers which had hampered trade between the provinces and, in particular, attempted to break down the aristocracy's immunity from taxation. His campaign for a more economical, efficient and equitable administration prompted the privileged classes to combine to overthrow him, and they accomplished that object in May 1776. However, his plans for radical social and economic change led others to speculate about the benefits of winning power, and the King's failure to back him greatly diminished France's chances of being reformed by peaceful means.

Condorcet's turn came at the end of his life, in 1792-3, when he won leadership of the moderates in the French National Convention. Besides securing the abolition of slavery in the French colonies and other 'progressive' measures, he insisted that the elimination of poverty should be one of the first objects of government. As a result of his efforts and those of Robespierre (of whom more later), the Constitution of 1793 declared that society owes a living to the poor, either by finding work for them or giving them the means of subsistence, and that the state was obliged to make provision for educating the masses. He also advocated pensions for the aged, co-operative banks to provide cheap credit, and establishing a perfect equality of civil and political rights between the individuals of both sexes. While his views on the last-mentioned questions were rejected, and though the Constitution of 1793 was never implemented, he was successful in convincing the right-wing of the Convention, the Girondists, that the Revolution should proceed beyond political and constitutional change.[23] Thenceforth, promoting social and economic change was increasingly prominent as an activity of all revolutionaries, for even the more sceptical liberals accepted its desirability once they had succumbed to the cult of the idol of progress.

Across the Atlantic, in the majority of Britain's North American colonies, the evolution of liberalism was not the work of a few outstanding thinkers but rather a mass movement. Much recent research on the American Revolution confirms that it was not just a crisis of empire, and that there was truth in contemporary claims that the War for Independence was but one act of a long-term revolution in the 'minds and hearts of the people'.[24] The war was primarily a struggle in defence of values the colonists had developed over a period

23. J.S. Schapiro, Condorcet and the Rise of Liberalism (Octagon, New York, 1963), pp. 142-55.

24. P.F. Bourke, 'Interpreting the American Revolution', Tradition, no. 16 (June 1977), p. 9, quoting Benjamin Rush (1745-1813) and John Adams (1735-1826).

of 150 years. Compared with other empires, the British administration of the North American plantations had been extraordinarily lax. 'The apparatus of the imperial state, which independence eliminated, had been a superficial overlay on American society': in many matters the colonists had long been self-governing.[25] Meanwhile, the colonies exhibited an equally remarkable diffusion of wealth. This incubated a colonial stream of democratic thought, initiated by people like Roger Williams of Rhode Island and John Wise of Massachusetts before Rousseau began propagating similar ideas in Europe.[26] It also meant that though the property qualifications for voting for the colonial legislatures were broadly comparable with the qualifications for voting in House of Commons elections, well over half the adult white male colonists could vote while less than twelve per cent of Englishmen were enfranchised.[27] A further consequence of the uniquely widespread opportunities for the enjoyment of property was that while in England liberal ideas remained confined to the coffee houses and the radical fringe of the Whigs, in America they became the dominant political ideology. Thus, from the beginning of the eighteenth century, colonial politicians were preoccupied with the corruptions of power. 'Liberty needed constant vigilance and was ever in danger from conspirators' - governors, customs officers, and other agents of the British government.[28] Prior to 1763 that was paranoid nonsense. But from that date onwards, when Britain tried to induce the colonists to share part of the cost of their own defence, the imperial authorities' efforts were greeted with a vast flood of denunciatory pamphlets, tracts, sermons and books,[29] and ultimately, armed rebellion. Thomas Paine's pamphlet, Common Sense, published on 10 January 1776, urging an immediate declaration of independence as the fulfilment of America's moral obligation to the world, quickly sold 150,000 copies.[30]

By twentieth-century standards the American Revolution has seemed a relatively tame affair. Yet while economic interpretations

25. B. Bailyn, 'Lines of force in recent writings on the American Revolution'. A paper presented to the International Congress of Historical Sciences, San Francisco, 1975, p. 29.

26. J.M. Jacobson, The Development of American Political Thought: a Documentary History (Century, New York, 1932), pp. 71-6; A.C. McLaughlin, Foundations of American Constitutionalism, new edn (Fawcett, New York, 1961), pp. 34, 73-5 and 112.

27. J.P. Greene, All Men are Created Equal (Clarendon Pr., Oxford, 1976), pp. 12-16. In some colonies the proportion of voters exceeded 80%. Bailyn, 'Lines of force', p. 30.

28. Bourke, 'Interpreting the Revolution', p. 11.

29. See the collection, Pamphlets of the American Revolution, ed. B. Bailyn (Harvard U.P., Cambridge, Mass., 1964), and Bailyn's general study, The Ideological Origins of the American Revolution (Harvard U.P., 1967).

30. E. Foner, Tom Paine and Revolutionary America (O.U.P., New York, 1976), p. 79.

have been discredited, Bernard Bailyn's studies of the colonists' ideology has reminded us that from the viewpoint of an eighteenth-century European, a revolution did indeed take place. It was a revolution against the characteristic institutions of Europe: monarchy, aristocratic privilege and patronage, imperialistic wars, colonialism, vestiges of feudalism (like primogeniture, discriminatory game laws and manorial rights), mercantilism, and established churches. The preoccupation with constitutionalism, scorned by some who overlook the same phenomenon in the French and Chinese Revolutions,[31] was itself an attempt to realize in new forms of government the radically different character of American society. That is, the British authorities' attempts at intervention had triggered an explosion of thought which eventually moved away from a narrow focus on independence.[32] The radical character of the Revolution found expression in: institutionalising the sovereignty of the general citizenry (especially through the rebels' invention of the constitutional convention), separating the main branches or organs of government, further dividing power between the new central government and the states, insisting that officials be elected representatives of the people, and ordaining that all public authority must be exercised within the bounds of constitutional prescriptions and the declared rights of the citizens. The state and federal constitution-makers established a society dedicated to the provision of opportunity for all - at least all who accepted the republican ideal. Radicalism found further expression in the violence directed against those who either supported the British connexion or opposed other aspects of the Revolution: 80,000 former colonists fled into exile. On a population basis, there were more than five times as many emigres from the American Revolution as there were from the French Revolution, and their property was confiscated at a comparable rate.[33]

There was more radicalism in the rebels' confrontation of social anomalies. Established churches were attacked; the franchise was broadened; non-Christians were granted political rights; freedom of the press was secured; measures to relieve the plight of debtors were enacted in several states; and slavery began to be abolished. It took time before these social reforms were implemented throughout the country. Yet it was only a matter of time, for they seemed a logical and necessary consequence of the spirit of 1776. So did many reforms - such as the emancipation of women - first thought of by later generations, for the Declaration of Independence had provided Americans with a programme for their future guidance. It dedicated them to the establishment of a truly competitive society in which individual creativity would be given free play.

---

31. E.g., H. Arendt, On Revolution (Penguin, London, 1973), pp. 141-54 and 166-9.

32. Bourke, 'Interpreting the Revolution', p. 11.

33. R.R. Palmer, The Age of the Democratic Revolution (2 vols., Princeton U.Pr., Princeton, 1959), vol. 1, p. 188.

Moreover, the American Revolution produced some new versions of Milton and Locke's notion that revolutions are usually good things. In 1787, Thomas Jefferson, chief author of the Declaration of Independence, and subsequently the third President of the United States, declared in a much quoted passage:

> what country can preserve its liberties if their rulers are not warned from time to time that their people preserve the spirit of resistance? ... What signify a few lives lost in a century or two? The tree of liberty must be refreshed from time to time with the blood of patriots and tyrants. It is its natural manure.[34]

Similar statements have been made, not only by later Americans such as Abraham Lincoln, but by overseas admirers of the example America had set. Thus in 1792, Bertrand Barère, arguing in the French National Convention for the execution of Louis XVI, said: 'The tree of liberty grows when it is watered with the blood of tyrants.'[35] As Jefferson observed, the American Revolution addressed itself 'to the world', urging oppressed peoples everywhere 'to assume the blessings and security of self-government', and to assert their 'right to the unbounded exercise of reason and freedom of opinion'.[36] By 1824 the republic's foreign policy and the conduct of its representatives abroad led the conservative Austrian Chancellor, Metternich, to complain of the United States that by 'fostering revolutions wherever they show themselves, in regretting those which have failed, in extending a helping hand to those which seem to prosper, they lend new strength to the apostles of sedition, and reanimate the courage of every conspirator'.[37] Few people of that era had any doubts about the radical nature of the challenge the Americans had presented to mankind.

The liberal ideas trumpeted by the founders of the United States were proclaimed again by those who led the first stage of the revolt against absolute monarchy in France. The immediate prophet of the French Revolution was the Abbé Emmanuel Sieyès. In January 1789, after Louis XVI had consented to summon the Estates-General for the first time in 175 years to deal with the crisis resulting from the government's bankruptcy, Sieyès published a popular pamphlet entitled What is the Third Estate? Summarizing the grievances of the ninety-eight per cent of Frenchmen whose representatives were to have only a

---

34. D. Malone, Jefferson and his Time (6 vols., Little, Brown, Boston, 1948-81), vol. 2, pp. 165-6.

35. F.P.G. Guizot & Mme Guizot de Witt, France, trans. R. Black (8 vols., Collier, New York, 1898), vol. 6, p. 133.

36. Writings of Thomas Jefferson, ed. P.L. Ford (10 vols., Putnam, New York, 1892-9), vol. 10, pp. 390-2. Republished in Jefferson Himself, ed. B. Mayo (Virginia U.P., Charlottesville, 1970), pp. 344-5.

37. Quoted in W. Ebenstein, Great Political Thinkers, 4th edn (Holt, Rinehart & Winston, New York, 1969), p. 474.

third of the voting power in the Estates-General, he declared that the Third Estate was the nation, and that the nobility and clergy could easily be ignored. The people's representatives should either have the courage to assemble and legislate alone, or else appeal to the nation and let it decide once and for all where sovereignty lay.[38] As a priest, Sieyès was a member of the privileged orders he denounced so caustically. He had become a canon of Chartres, and vicar-general and chancellor of that diocese, once ruled by the begetter of the doctrine of tyrannicide, John of Salisbury.[39] Yet because he had been born a commoner in the eighteenth century rather than the twelfth, he, unlike John, could never rise to a French bishopric, as all senior appointments in both Church and state had become the exclusive property of the aristocracy. Sieyes was sent to the Estates-General by the electors of Paris. At his urging the Third Estate proclaimed itself the National Assembly, in June, and he remained one of the most radical members in the debates on the Declaration of the Rights of Man and of the Citizen, and on the Constitution of 1791. He was being quite consistent with his earlier pronouncements when, as a member of the Convention, he voted for the death of the King - a sentence carried by a majority of one. However he quailed at the excesses of Jacobinism, and, fearful of democracy, assisted Bonaparte's coup in 1799, 'so that by a strange destiny he became gravedigger to the political liberty for which he had been godfather'.[40]

The fast pace of events in the first stage of the French Revolution, like the collapse of the old regime, resulted from the economic crisis. Over a fifty-year period, prices had increased three times faster than wages. Commercial treaties and bad seasons had produced high unemployment in the cities, and severe food shortages amounting to famine in some regions. Gangs of desperate beggars terrorized city and country-dwellers, and some towns in the Beauvais lost a quarter of their population through malnutrition and epidemics.[41] Thus the liberals in the National Assembly were able to promote sweeping changes because it was not hard to convince their colleagues that the frequent outbreaks of popular violence would become ever more serious if reform was delayed. On one night, 4 August 1789, the Assembly abolished serfdom, the nobles' hunting privileges and their exemption from taxation, ecclesiastical titles, and the peasants' obligation to give a day's unpaid labour on the roads. Other noble and clerical privileges soon went the same way. In

38. J.H. Stewart, A Documentary Survey of the French Revolution (Macmillan, London, 1951), pp. 42-52.

39. See above, pp. 42-3.

40. G. Lefebvre, The Coming of the French Revolution, trans. R.R. Palmer (Princeton U.P., Princeton, 1947), pp. 69-70, 81-4, 171-2 and 174-80.

41. O. Hufton, 'Towards an understanding of the poor of eighteenth century France', in French Government and Society, ed. J.F. Bosher (Athlone Pr., London, 1973), pp. 145-63.

December, the Church's lands were confiscated and used as collateral for the issue of paper money. The Declaration of Rights, adopted on 26 August, had enshrined the catchwords of the revolution, liberty, equality and fraternity, in constitutional terms. It stated that men are born and always remain free and equal in respect of their rights, and that the purpose of all political associations is the preservation of man's natural and imprescriptible rights to liberty, property, security and resistance to oppression. The nation was declared to be the source of all sovereignty, and it therefore had the right to change its constitution and to demand of all office holders an account of their conduct. Political liberty was defined as the power of doing whatever does not injure another. Within that constraint, to be defined by law, freedom of speech, religious toleration and the liberty of the press were established. Law was to be made by all citizens or their representatives, so that it would be an expression of the general will of the community. All citizens were made equally eligible for all honours, places and employments according to their abilities, without any distinction other than that created by their virtues and talents. Furthermore, the Declaration launched a juridical revolution by announcing that no man was to be arrested or imprisoned except by due process of law, that no one was to suffer because of retrospective legislation or be deprived of his property without fair compensation, and that every man was to be presumed innocent until he was convicted.

The authors of the Declaration could find support for their proposals in the writings of the liberal political theorists, Rousseau's dreams of democracy, the American Declaration of Independence, the Bills of Rights that had been appended to the constitutions of most American states, and the brand-new 'principle of utility' promulgated by the English philosopher, Jeremy Bentham (1748-1832), according to which action is right if it achieves the greatest good of the greatest number.[42] Yet, as Robert Palmer pointed out, in comparison with earlier documents and ideas, the French Declaration 'gave a sharper definition to the conception of citizenship, individual liberty, and rightful public authority'. It 'derived both liberty and authority from the same principles, while relating both to legal equality' and recognising the importance of requiring each individual to respect the rights of others. In contrast to the Declaration of the Rights of Man published by the United Nations in 1948, it affirms that citizens possess power as well as rights. Moreover, 'by laying down the principles of the modern democratic state', it 'remains the chief single document of the Revolution of the Western World'.[43] The fact that the bourgeois majority in the Assembly then proceeded to confiscate Church property

42. J. Bentham, A Fragment on Government and An Introduction to the Principles of Morals and Legislation, ed. W. Harrison (Blackwell, Oxford, 1948), pp. v and 125-8.

43. R.R. Palmer, Age of the Democratic Revolution, vol. 1, pp. 487-8.

and to draft a Constitution in which the franchise was restricted to taxpayers in no way detracted from the domestic and foreign impact of the Declaration itself.

In defining the principles of modern democracy the revolutionaries looked to the future. Their most decisive blow against the past was their judgment condemning the King. The liberals who dominated the National Assembly had been content to establish a constitutional monarchy. Louis XVI had formally accepted the Constitution of 1791, but his attempt to flee the country in June of that year, and his endeavours to encourage foreign rulers to threaten to invade France and crush the Revolution, made it obvious that he had not accepted his new role in good faith. Even the moderates in the Convention insisted that the people's right to judge their rulers could never be validly renounced, and that as kings were citizens they, like any other citizens, could be tried for treason.[44] Again, as long as Louis lived, he was an inspiration to internal and external counter-revolutionary forces. Kings were still magical figures to many of their subjects. To break the royal spell, the monarchy had to be destroyed. When Louis was put on trial, so was the modern theory of the divine right of kings. When he was executed, in January 1793, that doctrine was buried forever. Those delegates who used the language of the monarchomac justifications of tyrannicide[45] agreed with their less-religious colleagues that it was no longer a matter of getting rid of a single tyrant. The Crown had been intimately connected with the discredited complex of intolerable abuses and antiquated privileges. Louis's conduct had demonstrated that the monarchy was still corrupt. It had to go.[46] he blow thus delivered at absolute monarchy was the more dramatic because no monarchy in Western Europe had been as absolute as the French. Thereafter, few kings ventured to claim unlimited power; and when a Bourbon was restored to the French throne in 1814, he had no pretensions to a divine commission to rule as he wished.

In 1793, serious internal disorder - provoked by continuing high prices and unemployment, and still more by the reverses the French armies were suffering in battle following the National Convention's declaration of war against Prussia and the Holy Roman Empire - enabled Jacobin extremists like Danton, Hébert, Saint-Just and Robespierre to become ever more prominent and gain a share of executive power. The outstanding extremist leader of this radical phase of the Revolution was Maximilien Robespierre (1758-1794).

Robespierre's political creed sprang from Rousseauist assumptions that government should be based on moral principles, that the people (as a whole) are naturally good, and that the people's will must therefore be sovereign. From 1789 he had campaigned for

---

44. Regicide and Revolution, ed. M. Walzer (C.U.P., Cambridge, 1974), pp. 54-8.

45. See above, pp. 51-6.

46. Regicide and Revolution, Chs 4-5.

manhood suffrage, frequent elections, and the use of the recall. He also called for political rights to be extended to the coloured population of the French West Indies.[47] But besides being a democrat, in the early years of the Revolution he had been 'one of the first and most uncompromising of liberals', warning against 'over-government', and demanding an absolute separation of executive from legislative power as the best safeguard of liberty.[48] However, in 1793, when he joined the Committee of Public Safety (the twelve-man body entrusted with executive power) he became an advocate of state power. In December of that year, after the Jacobins had purged the National Convention, Robespierre proclaimed the doctrine that the principles of revolutionary government were to be sought, not in the ideas of political theorists, 'but in the laws of necessity and of the welfare of the people'. Sovereignty, unfettered by any constitutional limitations, belonged to the rump of the Convention (the Jacobins and their supporters) who represented the 'real' will of the people of France, whether the latter recognized it or not.[49]

One consequence was the Reign of Terror of 1793-4, when freedom of opinion was controlled by 'revolutionary justice', institutionalised in 'people's courts'. Another was an attack on freedom of trade. In response to the Paris mob's cries against monopolies, Robespierre became a prophet of the right to subsistence. To promote equality, he advocated progressive taxation and the limitation of property rights. Laws were passed against speculation and hoarding, and to control the price of basic commodities. Supplies for the army and the cities were requisitioned. The property of the 20,000 enemies of the Revolution guillotined during the Terror was confiscated for the benefit of the government and the lower classes. Again, until the early months of 1793, when Britain declared war on France, Robespierre had been a pacifist, scorning those who called for a crusade to take the good news of revolution to the rest of Europe. No one loves armed missionaries, he said: 'those who try to dictate laws with arms in their hands will never be regarded as anything but foreigners and conquerors'.[50] Here too he did an about-face when he had to share the responsibilities of power. He supported the introduction of conscription for military service. To stir the people's will to defeat the invaders, he used every available instrument of propaganda - the press, the theatres, art, education, and his own state-sponsored deistic religious cult of the Supreme Being - to foment hatred of the Germans and especially the British, as well as to present the struggle as a people's war for justice and liberty. Thus he inaugurated modern ideo-

---

47. A. Cobban, ' he fundamental ideas of Robespierre', reprinted in his Aspects of the French Revolution (Jonathan Cape, London, 1968), pp. 137-52.

48. A. Cobban, 'The political ideas of Maximilien Robespierre during the period of the Convention', reprinted in Aspects, pp. 159-60.

49. Ibid., pp. 161-2.

50. Ibid., pp. 180-2.

logical warfare and the era of bellicose nationalism.[51] So many of Robespierre's policies alienated the middle classes that in the summer of 1794 they exerted themselves sufficiently to regain power and redirect the Revolution on a more moderate course, which persisted until Bonaparte's coup. Robespierre was executed on 28 July 1794; but later generations remembered him as the model of a liberal-democratic revolutionary who, when confronted with the realities of office, became converted to political pragmatism and threw both liberalism and democracy to the winds while ruthlessly pursuing his goals.

The French Revolution has had many critics, the most influential being the Irishman, Edmund Burke, whose ideas are analysed in the next chapter. But naturally it has had its apologists. Tom Paine's book, The Rights of Man (1791-2), written in answer to Burke's Reflections on the Revolution in France, outsold the latter by ten copies to one, and many others have defended what the revolutionaries did.[52]

The reaction of the great nineteenth-century French liberal theorist, Alexis, Comte de Tocqueville (1805-59), was cautious, and it reflected his own experiences in public life. He recognised political and social equality as just,[53] but liberty remained his first passion. At the time of the July Revolution of 1830, when the Bourbons were finally overthrown and replaced by the 'bourgeois' constitutional monarchy of Louis Philippe, Tocqueville was a judge of the district court at Versailles. Expecting little from the new government, and believing it was necessary to accept the coming age of democracy, he found an excuse for making an official visit to the United States so he could study democracy where it was most firmly established. His Democracy in America (1835-40) presented a penetrating analysis of the American experience.

In one of the many perceptive and prophetic passages in that work, Tocqueville argued that democracy was creating a potential for social revolution, because of the nature and behaviour of a new 'class of masters' it was giving rise to: an aristocracy of manufacturers. He saw that democracy favours the growth of industry because it fosters an emphasis on material welfare for everyone, so that demand for manufactured goods increases. Manufacturing also prospers because the equality of opportunity that democracies promote encourages the talented to pursue wealth in commerce and industry, where there are no birth, class or caste barriers to success.[54] He also saw that the growth of manufacturing was producing a new type of worker, highly

---

51. Ibid., pp. 182-90.

52. For a general survey, see G. Rudé, Interpretations of the French Revolution (Historical Association, London, 1961).

53. M. Zetterbaum, 'Tocqueville: neutrality and the use of history', American Political Science Review, vol. 58, no. 3 (September 1964), pp. 611-21.

54. Democracy in America, trans. H. Reeve et al. (2 vols., Vintage, New York, 1947), vol. 2, pp. 163-6.

specialised through the division of labour and mass production. However, while the new mode of production was economically efficient, it was having serious social effects. As Tocqueville put it, while the employer dealt with a widening range of interests and became 'the administrator of a vast empire', the employee had his vision narrowed and became more and more 'a brute'. There was no real partnership between an employer and his workers, and social relationships were becoming more rigid. Workers would become ever more dependent on their master and would seem 'as much born to obey as that other is to command'. In the old landed aristocracy there had been mutual ties of habit, duty and custom between master and servant. Moreover, masters and servants had shared labour, experiences and objectives. In democratic society, the employer asks nothing of his workers but their labour, and the workers expect nothing but their wages. Besides, the manufacturing aristocracy has no sense of public responsibility. Its aim is 'not to govern' the people 'but to use' them. It would first debase and impoverish those who serve it, and then abandon them to public charity.[55]

Tocqueville also predicted that a democratic people would not indefinitely tolerate the discrepancy between political equality and economic inequality. He saw that the first phase of a democratic revolution, the political phase, would lead inevitably to a second, social and economic phase. He believed the July Revolution of 1830 was the last purely political revolution France would experience. The next revolution would spring from economic grievances, and it would attempt to change, not just the form of government, but society itself. In all this he anticipated much that was later taken up by Karl Marx; and as a member of the French Chamber of Deputies, he predicted the February Revolution of 1848 in which the July Monarchy was swept from power by people seeking to establish a social democratic republic.[56] He accepted the Revolution, and as a deputy in the Constituent Assembly voted with the majority for a new Constitution. Meanwhile he vigorously opposed Louis Napoleon Bonaparte, who nevertheless was elected President of the Second Republic. Tocqueville was elected to the National Assembly and became Minister of Foreign Affairs, but because he would not compromise on matters of principle was dismissed in October 1849. He contracted tuberculosis and watched helplessly as Louis Napoleon undermined democratic institutions and established a dictatorship, converted a year later into the Second Empire.

Tocqueville's only weapon was his pen. He embarked on a study of French history to discover and explain why the first French Revolution had produced a society that was dedicated to equality but

---

55. Ibid., pp. 168-71.

56. See the manifesto Tocqueville drafted in October 1847, and his speech of 27 January 1848, both reproduced in his Recollections, trans. G. Lawrence, ed. J.P. Mayer & A.P. Kerr (Macdonald, London, 1970), pp. 12-15.

not liberty, a society which had permitted the establishment of Napoleon I's dictatorship. He found a striking continuity of ideas and institutions linking the Revolution and the first Empire with the Old Regime. In particular, the centralised administration of the later years of the Revolution and the Empire was but a logical sequel to developments begun by Louis XIV and stepped up by Louis XVI. The latter had effected an 'administrative revolution' by increasing the power of the King's Council, authorising the all-pervading activities of the royal officials in each district and keeping them under close scrutiny, undermining the powers of the old local-government institutions, and replacing local courts with royal courts. Thus there was a link between the Monarchy and the Revolution. The driving principle of the Revolution was equality, and it was equality before the law which the old regime had been striving to establish in its long struggle with feudalism.[57]

No one had expected Tocqueville, as a scion of the oldest Norman nobility, to eulogize the Revolution. However, for a few months in 1789 its leaders had been fired by the twin ideals of equality and liberty, and Tocqueville described that period as a 'rapturous' time of 'bright enthusiasm, heroic courage, lofty ideals ... a historic date of glorious memory' which later generations would always admire and respect. The trouble was that liberty had soon been sacrificed to equality. While the hatred of inequality was of long standing and inextinguishable, the love of liberty was more recent and less profound. In the anarchy arising from the economic crisis, made worse by wars, the ideal of freedom 'lost much of its appeal and the nation, at a loss where to turn, began to cast around for a master - under these conditions the stage was set for a return to one-man government'. By favouring and flattering the people's desire for equality, but failing to secure liberty, the Revolution had left its work half-done.[58]

Tocqueville also discovered that the drive for equality had accelerated towards the end of the old regime because the monarchy's undermining of feudal and provincial institutions had been accompanied by a phenomenal increase in trade and national prosperity. The resultant rise in the middle classes' wealth and economic power led them to regard the nobles' privileges as more and more anachronistic. Likewise, the peasants' lot was not nearly so squalid and miserable as town-dwellers had imagined, and on the eve of the Revolution they were already the owners of half the land in France. Despite the occasional famine, they were far better off and much less oppressed than the peasants of Russia, Prussia and the Holy Roman Empire. Thus they found the vestiges of feudalism intolerable. Some Marxist writers have tended to be sceptical about Tocqueville's deduction that revolutions are more likely to occur in a period of increasing prosperity. However, the development of a 'youth revolution'

57. Tocqueville, The Ancien Regime and the French Revolution trans. S. Gilbert (Fontana, London, 1966), pp. 61-106.

58. Ibid., pp. 225-7.

throughout the Western world in the unprecedentedly prosperous 1960s won more supporters for his view. Meanwhile, Tocqueville had also observed that in the last decades of the old regime, the royal officials, who should have been defending the status quo, had been among the first to fall under the influence of the philosophes' demands for reform. Tocqueville found that 'it was precisely in those parts of France where there had been most improvement that popular discontent ran highest'. His historical research led him to develop the highly original and important thesis that

> it is not always when things are going from bad to worse that revolutions break out. On the contrary, it oftener happens that when a people which has put up with an oppressive rule over a long period without protest suddenly finds the government relaxing its pressure, it takes up arms against it. Thus the social order overthrown by a revolution is almost always better than the one immediately preceding it, and experience teaches us that, generally speaking, the most perilous moment for a bad government is one when it seeks to mend its ways.[59]

Revolutionaries, despots and political sociologists have taken note of the lesson drawn in this famous passage.

A contemporary of Tocqueville's, the Italian patriot, Giuseppe (Joseph) Mazzini (1805-72), was a liberal who deplored the French Revolution while simultaneously insisting on a Robespierre-like cult of the nation. He felt the French Revolution was 'crushing' his own generation - 'It weighs like an incubus upon our heart'[60] - because it had placed too much emphasis on individualism and on rights, the gaining of which had done nothing to improve the condition of the mass of the people. Only the capitalists had benefited. Instead, like the pre-modern political theorists, he emphasised men's duties. Professor Beales has neatly summarised Mazzini's argument: 'If all would do their duty, then they would become different people, and society as a whole would be transformed. Then rights would be worth having, and spiritual as well as material progress would be open to everyone.'[61] Mazzini held that everyone's first duty is to humanity. However, he also contended that humanity manifests itself in nationalities. For the people of Italy - still divided into a number of separate states, with

---

59. Ibid., pp. 52-60, 193-5 and, for the quotations, 196. For critical appraisals see R. Herr, Tocqueville and the Old Regime, rev. edn (Princeton U.Pr., Princeton, 1966), and H. Brogan, Tocqueville (Fontana, London, 1973), pp. 82-93.

60. Faith and the Future (1835), in Mazzini, The Duties of Man and other essays, ed. T. Jones, rev. edn (Everyman, London, 1955), p. 170.

61. D.E.D. Beales, 'Mazzini and revolutionary nationalism', in Political Ideas, ed. D. Thomson (Penguin, London, 1969), p. 145. See also The Duties of Man etc., pp. 8-20 and 256-8.

large areas still under foreign rule - their most urgent duty was to win freedom and unity for their country. Only when that was accomplished could they do their duty to humanity and make social progress.[62] In accordance with these principles, in 1831 he founded Young Italy, an organisation dedicated to expelling foreign despots from the Italian peninsula and establishing a united republic. In 1834 he established additional revolutionary societies, Young Switzerland and Young Europe, to form national committees for patriotic agitation in Switzerland, Germany, and Poland.[63] He long remained the most active political agitator in Europe, but his ability as an administrator was inferior to his skill as a propagandist. The Swiss, by and large, resented his intrusion; the Poles remained divided and enslaved. Italy and Germany were united, as monarchies, by the realpolitik of Cavour and Bismarck respectively, not by high-minded idealists leading popular revolutions. Nevertheless, Mazzini was important as the prophet of national revolutions, and his activities and voluminous writings directly inspired Young Ireland, the Young Turks, and, especially, the Indian nationalist leader, Gandhi, who revered him as a saint.[64]

In some respects the type of nationalism Mazzini fostered remained liberal, for he was a liberal in his faith in education and self-help, and in his anticlericalism and republicanism. Initially he advocated a humanitarian form of nationalism, which is better called patriotism - a selfless love of one's country and its people. Many of his admirers shared his belief in progress, and in the long run they came to agree with his feminism: from the 1830s, he had claimed that women should be granted full civil, political and social equality with men.[65] However there was also a selfish element in his schemes which foreshadowed the agressive, totalitarian nationalism of the twentieth century: 'he ranked national unity and equality above liberty, and he thought a nation needed a unifying religion and a unifying system of education'. He even anticipated the recent fashion for making dubious territorial claims under the cloak of nationalism, in his agitation for the annexation to Italy of Nice (with its French population), Istria (predominantly Slav), and the Tyrol (peopled by German-speakers with an Austrian culture).[66] The same phenomenon has been evident in India's invasion of Goa, Indonesia's invasion of East Timor, Argentina's invasion of the Falklands, and so on.

Mazzini stood at yet another turning point in the literature of revolution. While he inspired the last batch of liberal revolutionary movements, it must be remembered that his early liberalism, like

---

62. The Duties of Man, pp. 51-66.

63. B. King, The Life of Mazzini (Everyman, London, 1912), pp. 62-4.

64. Beales, 'Mazzini', pp. 143-5, reproducing Gandhi's essay, 'Joseph Mazzini', first published in Indian Opinion (Durban), 22 July 1905.

65. See especially The Duties of Man, pp. 62 and 122.

66. Beales, 'Mazzini', p. 148.

Robespierre's, was ultimately eclipsed by the potency of the vision of national greatness he had developed. But in contrast to Robespierre, who had believed that all citizens who were alleged to be enemies of the French nation should be brought to public trial, several of Mazzini's methods - the use of secret organisations, terrorism, assassination and guerilla warfare - were intrinsically hostile to the survival of the classic liberal notion that each and every person has certain fundamental natural rights. Thus it is not surprising that, in their appeal to people's passion for self-aggrandisement, practically none of the twentieth-century national revolutions or 'wars of national liberation' which owe something to Mazzini's inspiration has left any room for individual liberty.

Chapter Five

BURKE AND THE CONSERVATIVE TRADITION

Carl Bridge

> The sycophant - who in the pay of the English oligarchy played the romantic *laudator temporis acti* against the French Revolution just as, in the pay of the North American colonies at the beginning of the North American troubles, he had played the liberal against the English oligarchy was an out-and-out vulgar bourgeois.[1]

Thus did Marx attempt to discredit Edmund Burke whose conservative analysis of the nature of society and revolution Marx rightly saw as rival and contradictory to his own. Nonetheless, Burke has remained the key thinker in what can be called the conservative tradition in thought about revolution.[2] A convenient way of explaining Burke's position is to take up Marx's challenge and resolve the implied inconsistency between Burke's reactions to the American and French revolutions. We can then review the main lines of criticism of his thought, discuss some of the commentators on it, and assess his influence on later conservative thinking about revolutions. First, however, there are some basic points to make about his background and his views on the nature of society and politics.

Burke's Background

Born in Dublin in 1729, Burke was the son of a lawyer who had turned Protestant in order to be able to practise his profession. His mother remained a Roman Catholic. Burke graduated from Trinity College, Dublin, and began reading for the Bar in London but was diverted by literary pursuits. His first works, *A Vindication of Natural Society*

---

1. K. Marx, *Capital*, I (Moscow, 1954), p. 760, fn. 2, cited in C.C.O'Brien's introduction to Edmund Burke, *Reflections on the Revolution in France* (Penguin, Harmondsworth, 1969), p. 9. All references are to this edition. The Latin in the quotation means 'praiser of times past' (Horace, *Ars Poetica*).

2. See R. Kirk, *The Conservative Mind from Burke to Eliot* 6th edn (Gateway, South Bend, Indiana, 1978).

(1756) and On the Sublime and the Beautiful (1757), were commonsense attacks on the then fashionable mechanistic rationalism in religion and art criticism respectively. In 1766 he was elected to parliament in the Whig interest and he remained an MP till 1794, three years before his death in 1797. His parliamentary career was spent mostly on the opposition backbenches where he fought several great crusades: in favour of the rights of the American colonies; for the better government of Ireland and India, and hence the impeachment of Warren Hastings; and against the extension of royal power and patronage. Outside the House he was known as a controversialist, orator and publicist. Samuel Johnson held him in great respect for his wit and sense. Burke's last great mission, against the French revolution and the export of its Enlightenment principles, occupied the last seven years of his life and is what he is best remembered for. Though constantly in debt and always regarded as a parvenu in English governing circles, his powerful pen made him their greatest spokesman and apologist after 1789 and still.[3]

Burke on Society and Politics

The fundamental point to grasp about Burke's view of society is that he held that habit, time, and what he called 'prejudice', by which he meant the distilled pre-judgements which make up the received wisdom in a society, are the main determinants of social organisation and behaviour.[4] Contrary to Locke and Rousseau, he argued that there could be no such thing as an ideal, logically arrived at, set of social arrangements based upon self-evident, natural rights. For Burke, society is not made up of a set of social contracts, but rather is a complex and mysterious organism in which chance, prejudice and habit have as much of a role to play as enlightened self-interest and abstract reason. Real human reason is specific and historical, based on the distilled wisdom of generations, not the abstractions of theorists.

In Burke's historically-determined state, political power had to rest in the hands of the landed gentry and aristocracy simply because they had had it for many generations and understood its use. The social hierarchy as it had evolved over millenia was, in his words, a 'natural order', ordained by Nature. Where Aristotle and the Medieval schoolmen had seen God as creator and head of a great chain of being, with each unit related by duty and obligation to those above and below it, Burke saw the infinite variety of checks and balances in Nature as constituting an ordered, though constantly evolving, universe. Man always hovered on the brink of chaos, his only protection being his faith, for God's laws could not be fully understood; and God had ordained through Nature that religion, deference and private property were the cement of the social and political system.

---

3. The best biography is C. B. Cone, Burke and the Nature of Politics (University of Kentucky Press, 2 vols, 1957 and 1964).

4. E.g., see Reflections, pp. 182-3.

This is not to say that all things should stay as they are, which is what the schoolmen thought. Burke was the author of the great aphorism: 'A state without the means of some change is without the means of its conservation.'[5] With Burke, circumstances always altered cases; reason ought always to be tempered by experience. Thus constitutions and rights are prescriptive and vary with local conditions:

> circumstances (which with some gentlemen pass for nothing) give in reality to every political principle its distinguishing colour and discriminating effect. The circumstances are what render every civil and political scheme beneficial or noxious to mankind.[6]

He was certainly an empiricist; but for him observation justified the natural order. The experiences of the past are an integral part of the present held in trust for the future: 'Society is . . . a partnership not only between those who are living, but between those who are living, those who are dead, and those who are to be born.'[7]

It is important to be clear about what Burke meant by the natural order. He did not mean merely an order determined in a law of the jungle sense; rather he said that there were certain constant elements in any stable society, which, by reason of experience, could be identified as religion, deference and private property.

Burke on the American Revolution

Burke's attitude to the American revolution was that the British monarch, George III, had overstepped his customary rights by taxing and otherwise regimenting his American subjects without their consent. In this case the Crown, though the natural ruler of the colonies, was not justified by previous practice to interfere with the longstanding convention that Britain would not tax the colonies. As with the Glorious revolution of 1688, when James II similarly overstepped the mark by keeping a standing army and trying to re-introduce Roman Catholicism, it was the monarch who was the revolutionary. The American colonists (or in 1688, the Whig politicians) who opposed the revolutionary monarch were fighting to protect the social and political order as they knew it. Burke believed that the American revolution, like the Glorious revolution, was a conservative revolution.[8]

Burke's commentary on the American revolution also reveals another strain in his thought. Thirty years a practising politician in the House of Commons, Burke was pre-eminently a pragmatist. He did not base his argument on legal refutation of the King's theoretical right to tax the colonies, a right which legally speaking he accepted, rather he

---

5. Ibid., p. 106.
6. Ibid., p. 90.
7. Ibid., pp. 194-5.
8. This is the principal argument of A Letter to the Sheriffs of Bristol, 1777.

stressed that it was impractical as well as imprudent to attempt to coerce two million colonists three thousand miles away. Circumstance, as always, coloured the case.[9]

Burke on the French Revolution

The French revolution, he perceived as an opposite case. His response to it, Reflections on the Revolution in France and on the Proceedings of Certain Societies in London Relative to that Event (1790), is the volume in which, more than anywhere else, he elaborated his political philosophy and his thoughts on revolution.

In the Reflections Burke imagines himself writing to a young French gentleman about the events of 1789. It must always be remembered that Burke was writing in the early, moderate, constitutional-monarchy phase of the revolution before the execution of Louis XVI and the advent of the Jacobin dictatorship. Burke spends as much time justifying political practice in England as he does condemning it in France. This was quite intentional, as his purpose in writing the book was as much to combat the spread of revolutionary ideas across the channel (hence the second part of the title) as it was to influence events in France.

What did Burke think was so wrong with the setting up of the Constituent Assembly in France, the Declaration of the Rights of Man and the Citizen, and the Civil Constitution of the Clergy? For one thing, it was all done too precipitately:

> it is with infinite caution that any man ought to venture upon pulling down an edifice which has answered in any tolerable degree for ages the common purpose of society, or on building it up again, without having models and patterns of approved utility, before his eyes.[10]

But more annoying for Burke was the attempt of the Constituent Assembly to define in the abstract the rights of man (i.e. to life, liberty and property).

> These metaphysic rights entering into common life, like rays of light which pierce into a dense medium, are, by the laws of nature, refracted from their straight line. Indeed in the gross and complicated mass of human passions and concerns, the primitive rights of men undergo such a variety of refractions and reflections, that it becomes absurd to talk of them as if they continued in the simplicity of their original direction. The nature of man is intricate; the objects of society are of the greatest possible complexity; and therefore no simple disposition or direction of power can be suitable either to man's nature, or to

---

9. See T.E. Utley, Edmund Burke (Longman, London, 1957), pp. 18-25.

10. Reflections, p. 152.

> the quality of his affairs. The pretended rights of these theorists are all extremes; and in proportion as they are metaphysically true, they are morally and politically false. The rights of men are in a sort of middle, incapable of definition, but not impossible to be discerned.[11]

Rights were defined by specific context. Thus the 'speculative' grievances of academics and lawyers who spoke of such matters as social and economic inequality were 'false' whereas the 'practical' grievances of the poor about the price of bread or a brutal master were 'real'. Running problems could be rectified; but the overall social, political and economic system was natural and impossible to change simply by decree.[12]

Burke lampooned the newly elected members of the governing Constituent Assembly as politically unnatural. It was government by 'hairdresser' and 'tallow chandler':

> Such descriptions of men ought not to suffer oppression from the state; but the state suffers oppression, if such as they, either individually or collectively, are permitted to rule. In this you think you are combating prejudice, but you are at war with nature.[13]

Only the gentry and aristocracy had the time, education and inheritance to know the science of government.

France and Britain were within what Burke called 'the vicinage of Europe' where certain rules of government had naturally evolved based on religion, inheritance, private property and deference. Not the least of Burke's concerns in attacking government based on wrong-headed abstract principle was to defeat what he saw to be behind it, a conspiracy of men of talent without property. (He should have known because he began as one.) The causes of the revolution for him were a combination of specific grievances (bad harvests, an unreformed taxation system), a governing class toying foolishly with abstract ideas, and a conspiracy of gifted propertyless desperadoes: 'I never yet knew of any general temper in a nation that might not have been tolerably well traced to some particular persons.'[14] The revolution in France, to Burke, boiled down ultimately to a conspiracy by a group of frustrated lawyer philosophers to seize power and rearrange things to their material advantage. To those gentry in England who approved the

---

11. Ibid., pp. 152-3.

12. See M. Freeman, 'Edmund Burke and the Theory of Revolution', Political Theory vol. 6, no. 3 (August 1978), p. 283.

13. Reflections, p. 138.

14. Burke's correspondence cited in R.A. Smith, Introduction, Burke on Revolution (Harper, New York, 1968), p. xviii. The phrase 'the vicinage of Europe' from On a Regicide Peace, 1796, is also cited by Smith, p. X. 'Vicinage' means neighbourhood or community.

early revolutionaries' removal of aristocratic abuses and confiscation of church property, he warned that this would lead the revolutionaries 'to subvert all property of all descriptions'.[15] It was the thin end of the wedge. Of course Burke was alarmist and wrong: in the end bourgeois property holding was strengthened by the revolution, but this was not obvious in 1790.

Some Criticisms of Burke

Burke's thought is open to several lines of criticism which I shall do little more than list here.

Perhaps the most serious weakness in his thinking is that he regards the status quo as he knew it so highly, and man's capacity for reasoned fundamental change so poorly, that he offers no adequate mechanism for rectifying the ills of society. Since it so happened that a small percentage of the population controlled the overwhelming proportion of the nation's wealth, and had done so for a long time, this was held to be the only possible system, and therefore had, in the main, to be tolerated for fear that large-scale change would lead to chaos. What exists is defined as the natural order rather than what ought to exist. At bottom Burke's prescriptive definition of rights tends to be amoral and self-fulfilling.[16]

Consequently Burke does not recognise any deep social and economic structural causes in his analysis, nor does he pay any serious attention to the plight of the poor. All attempts at substantial modification of the existing order are assigned to the plotting of a foolish minority rather than a reaction to widespread social ills.

It can be argued that Burke's antagonism to the French revolution is so complete that it is itself a dogmatic abstraction, and therefore, in his own terms, suspect. Burke's argument, despite its constant pleas about the importance of circumstances, experience, and empirical proof, is mostly devoid of evidence and overburdened with vituperative rhetoric: e.g. there were very few tradesmen in the Constituent Assembly.[17] As George Rude comments, Burke 'dipped his pen in vitriol when he wrote his Reflections'.[18]

Burke's wholesale rejection of the revolutionaries' achievement produced some peculiar side-effects. He evoked the spectre of communistic Jacobinism as the only alternative to the old order, when in fact the middle ground of a state based on bourgeois private

---

15. Reflections, p. 261.

16. Cf. H. Laski's 'The case aginst Burke's aristocracy has a moral aspect with which he did not deal. He did not inquire by what right a handful of men were to be hereditary governors of a whole people', cited by P.W.Buck, in his introduction to How Conservatives Think (Penguin, Harmondsworth, 1975), pp. 13-14.

17. A partial exception is his analysis of the political economy of France in the last third of the work.

18. G. Rude, Interpretations of the French Revolution (Historical Association, London, 1961), p. 3.

property was what emerged. His failure to predict liberal democracy must not be forgotten (though, paradoxically, in Britain Burke's thought smoothed the way for the gradual admission of new classes into politics). It is often said that he foresaw the Reign of Terror and Napoleonic dictatorship; but it is better history to argue that the invasion of France which Burke's writings encouraged created the situation for the collapse of the moderate Girondins and their replacement by the radical Jacobins and Napoleon. Burke himself helped cause the radicalisation of the revolution. Further, his identification of the French Ancien Regime with the eighteenth century British settlement is extraordinarily questionable. Nobody but Burke could try to ignore the gross inequalities of unreformed France. One cannot help wondering that had Burke been permitted a look into a crystal ball at France in the 1980s, where private property is still an enshrined right, his worst fears might have been allayed.

Some Commentators

Many writers have called Burke a liberal who became a tory in old age; though only Marx was uncharitable enough to say that the change was induced because he was paid to play a different tune.[19] Isaac Kramnick, in The Rage of Edmund Burke, sees Burke as a split personality - both liberal and tory at the same time - tearing himself apart trying to resolve a dilemma which had him side with the American revolutionaries of the 1770's and the French Crown in 1790.[20] Conor Cruise O'Brien thinks it enough to explain this perversity by saying that he was an Irishman.[21] However, as we have seen, there is no irreconcilable inconsistency in his views, which were always characterised by a pragmatic conservatism, while influenced by the emphases of the moment and rhetorical exaggerations.

The most stimulating recent analysis comes from C.B. Macpherson.[22] He argues that Burke's striking and original contribution to political thought was to take the Natural Law theory of the medievals and to graft it onto the new capitalist order. Thus, according to Macpherson, the feudal justification for property-ownership - that it was a time honoured God-given responsibility - was stretched by Burke to justify also the new capitalist property-owners whose property was won via the market-place. Commercial profit became as natural as landed property. Macpherson is right to conclude that this was the ultimate effect of Burke's writings in Britain; but he is probably wrong to see it as a conscious slide in his logic. In Burke's time in Britain commercial wealth was readily absorbed into the landed ruling classes and hence in his eyes purified

---

19. John Morley and H.T. Buckle both thought the liberal Burke was mentally disturbed in his later tory years, see Macpherson, Burke (Oxford Univ.Pr., London, 1980), pp. 3-4.

20. Basic Books, New York, 1977.

21. In his introduction to Reflections.

22. Burke

and legitimised. In France, however, this did not happen: traditional landed wealth remained separate from new capitalist wealth; hence Burke condemned the bourgeoisie as misguided revolutionaries. Neverthless there are sufficient ambiguities in Burke's writings to allow Macpherson to argue seriously that 'Burke's achievement was to see, and make others see, the market society as traditional society'.[23] Later writers certainly have done so.

The Conservative Tradition

One of Burke's early critics acutely described Reflections as 'the manifesto of a counter-revolution.'[24] Burke identified and tried to counter the major challenge to the economic, social and political order of his time: the liberal secular ideas of the Age of Reason. His remains the classical statement of the conservative view, the paradigmatic response of the conservative frame of mind to revolution. It can be summarised in six points.

1. He argued that the social, political and economic order cannot be restructured in terms of abstract theories of rights and contracts. Rather, society has a complex natural order, which men of true reason can appreciate but not fully understand. Men should recognise that they are fallible, often illogical, creatures of habit.
2. Thus abstract democracy and the wholesale redistribution of property are chimerical and a threat to real freedom, which comes from a faith in prescriptive rights.
3. Consequently existing institutions - primarily the church and private property - must be preserved as the only alternative to chaos.
4. By and large those with power are those best trained to exercise it. The only justifiable revolutions are those in defence of the natural order.
5. Nevertheless, a rigid defence of entrenched privilege fails. The best means of ensuring a stable and civilised society is to make piecemeal changes to rectify specific grievances. Thus, by slow degrees, real reforms are brought about.
6. Since the natural elite is best fitted to govern, it is also best equipped to deal with hardships and grievances (famines, wars, etc.). Radical revolutions occur when talented men without

---

23. Macpherson, 'Edmund Burke and the New Conservatism', Science and Society, vol. 22, no. 3 (Summer, 1958), p. 236.

24. Sir J. Mackintosh, Vindiciae Gallicae, 1791, cited in O'Brien, p. 51.

> property conspire to exploit crises in order to usurp government for their own ends. Chaos and misery can be the only results.

Burke's reasonableness and superb pen have enlisted many in the conservative cause. So canny is his ability to describe the foibles and irrationalities of political man that his writings are admired by many on the other side of the political fence.[25]

There are other strands in the conservative tradition which are alien to Burke and which have not survived so well. In France Bonald and de Maistre erected a conservatism based upon a reactionary religious mysticism; and in Austria Metternich insisted on no change at all. In our century the fanaticism of fascism emerged when traditional ruling classes allied themselves with a revolutionary mass ideology. Each of these - reactionary conservatism and fascism - is alien to Burkean thinking, though all three are opposed to communism, socialism and liberalism.[26]

A fourth strand in conservative thought is elite theory, which had its origins at the end of the nineteenth century. Pareto and Mosca in Italy, and later Ortega in Spain, stripped the traditional underpinnings from Burke's aristocracy and described politics in terms of an elite of gifted, cultured, or just plain powerful individuals who would always dominate over the masses. They maintained that such elites existed in all societies, communist and socialist too. Apart from demonstrating the Burkean truism that in all human society absolute equality is a myth, these theorists had little to say about religion, stability and morality, all of which were crucial to Burke.[27]

Elements of Burke persist in much modern political thought about revolution. His interpretation of revolution as an aberration of the political process, as a disease with a particular pathology, is evident in Crane Brinton's attempt to delineate the stages through which the classical revolutions moved, ending in dictatorship. More recently, other conservative political scientists in the United States, like S.P. Huntington and Chalmers Johnson, have seen their own modern American industrial society as the ideal society and treated revolution

---

25. E.g., 'His flashes of insight are things that go, as few men ever have gone, into the hidden deeps of political complexity', H. Laski, Political Thought in England (Oxford Univ.Pr., London, 1950 edn), p. 182; and 'His spirit informs the progressive movement as much as it informs the Conservative party', R.H.S. Crossman, 'British Political Thought in the European Tradition', in J.P. Mayer (ed.), Political Thought: the European Tradition (Dent, London, 1942 edn), p. 188.

26. N. O'Sullivan Conservatism (Dent, London, 1976), is an excellent survey.

27. For discussion see J.H. Meisel (ed.), Pareto and Mosca (Prentice Hall, Englewood Cliffs, 1965); D. Bell, The End of Ideology (Free Press, New York, 1960), ch.1; and J. Burnham, The Managerial Revolution (Penguin, Harmondsworth, 1962), 1st published 1941.

as an undesirable 'disfunction' in the process of modernisation.[28]

Following Burke, many liberals and conservatives have emphasised that freedom is an imperfect condition, guaranteed only by constant vigilance against the dictatorship of the majority and the incursions of the all powerful modern state. Liberals and conservatives have now joined forces in defence of property and their notion of freedom. Communist revolution, or full social and economic democracy (which the new so-called liberal-conservatives like Strauss, Hayek and Friedman fear in the train of political democracy), they regard, along with Burke, as the ultimate enemy of true freedom. They, like Burke, however, are still open to the fundamental criticism that for the mass of people, the Friedmanite free society is not necessarily a just one.[29]

It is hardly surprising that during the Cold War, that heyday of conspiracy theory, Burke was revived as an antidote to Marxism, and the American revolution held up as a real revolution as opposed to the Russian and Chinese counterfeits. His crying wolf over the French revolution became an early warning of the communist revolutions to come.[30] Conservative analysts of Russian and Chinese society have constantly looked for the re-emergence of social inequalities and entrenched governing elites as evidence that these are the natural condition of man.[31] Marx was extraordinarily perceptive when he signalled out Burke for special treatment; he had discovered the principal exponent of counter-revolutionary theory. Burke's eloquent and convincing description of the nature of politics, and his criticisms of the pitfalls of abstract rights and wholesale reform, survive as constant warnings to all revolutionaries and radical reformers. Nevertheless, the sort of political order he tried to justify as 'natural' will also inspire them to action.

---

28. Crane Brinton, The Anatomy of Revolution (Vintage Books, New York, 1960); S.P. Huntington, Political Order in Changing Societies (Yale Univ.Pr., New Haven, 1970); Chalmers Johnson, Revolution and the Social System (Hoover Institution, Stanford, 1964).

29. O'Sullivan, ch.5.

30. O'Brien, pp. 56 76; Macpherson, Burke, p. 4.

31. E.g., Burnham.

Chapter Six

MARX, LENIN AND MODERN REVOLUTIONS[1]

Norman Wintrop

The influence of the ideas of Karl Marx (1818-1883) and Lenin (1870-1924) on twentieth-century revolutions has been enormous. But the influence has not been entirely one way. The ideas of both Marx and Lenin have come to be interpreted in terms of the revolutions that have been made in their names and the revolutionary movements that have claimed a descent from them. A problem in understanding their ideas is that there is no way of knowing how Marx or Lenin would have responded to the revolutionary movements and actors of the past six decades who have acted in their names. Similarly, there are no ways of knowing what Marx would have thought of Lenin.

The precise relationship of Lenin's thought and practice to those of Marx and the question of whether Lenin is the great twentieth-century exponent of Marx's revolutionary theory and practice or the founder of a new approach to the waging of revolutionary struggle are controversial issues. They have been debated by Marxists and others since the post-World War One split between Lenin's supporters, who established independent Communist Parties and the new Communist International, and rival Marxists, such as the German, Karl Kautsky, and the Austrians, Otto Bauer and Rudolf Hilferding, who remained loyal to the second Socialist International. Likewise, the questions of how Lenin would have reacted to the Communist disputes and splits between Stalin, Trotsky and Bukharin, in the 1920s and 1930s, and between Stalin and Tito, Khrushchev and Mao, and Deng Xiaoping and the Gang of Four, after World War Two, though often regarded by those who do not share their faith as reminiscent of Byzantine theology, have been matters of concern for the participants and their Western and other partisans.

This chapter will not try systematically to review the rich history of the Marxist revolutionary tradition, but will concentrate on Marx

1. I am indebted to David Close and Richard DeAngelis of Flinders University and David Lovell of the Australian National University for extensive comments on an earlier draft of this chapter.

and Lenin.[2] It will begin with an analysis of Marx's thinking about revolution, it will deal with the changes made to Marx's ideas and project by Lenin, as a result of both his written work and his participation in the Russian Revolution, and it will discuss the influence exercised by Marx and Lenin on subsequent revolutionaries, revolutionary movements and revolutions.

MARX

Most accounts of the revolutionary theory of Karl Marx begin with the proposition to be found in discussions by his friend and colleague, Frederick Engels (1820-1895), and his most influential twentieth-century disciple, Lenin, that there were three principal sources and components of Marx's thought, including his general theory of revolution. These were (1) classical (late eighteenth and early nineteenth-century) German philosophy, (2) French socialism and (3) British classical economics, or political economy as it was called early in the nineteenth century. The proposition is not as helpful as is often supposed because it neglects some important sources and features of Marx's thought.[3] In this chapter, therefore, the usual threefold framework will be replaced by a sixfold classification of Marx's principal ideas. It will be maintained that these six components of Marx's revolutionary theory had been discovered by 1848, the year of European-wide revolutions, and that they were never subsequently abandoned by Marx. The discussion will begin with some frequently neglected ideas and aspirations: those taken by Marx from the liberal democratic tradition.

Liberalism and Democracy

One of the most misleading features of the view that the three components of the Marxism of Marx are German philosophy, French socialism and British classicial economics is its suggestion that Marx's first encounter with political ideas was with those of socialism. This view of Marx ignores the fact that before he discovered socialism he had participated in the German liberal-democratic movement. In 1842 and 1843 Marx was a contributor to and eventually the editor of the *Rheinische Zeitung*, a newspaper which promoted the modern liberal ideal of the maximisation of individual liberty and the modern democratic ideal of self-government by citizens by means of representative institutions. Before encountering French socialism,

---

2. For a comprehensive review and examination of the Marxist tradition, see L. Kolakowski, *Main Currents of Marxism: Its Rise, Growth and Dissolution* (3 vols., Clarendon Pr., Oxford 1978).

3. For a systematic study of the origins of Marx's thought, see A. Cornu, *The Origins of Marxian Thought* (C. Thomas, Springfield, Ill., 1957).

therefore, Marx committed himself to, familiarised himself with, and absorbed and developed liberal and democratic values, of which the one he most emphasised was freedom.[4]

For Marx, the idea of freedom expressed both the liberal ideal of the independent, end-choosing individual and the democratic demand for citizenship (self-government). In 1842 and 1843, first in the Rheinische Zeitung and then in the seclusion of his study, Marx outlined a view of freedom which anticipated the New (social) Liberalism of T.H. Green and his followers at the end of the nineteeth century. This was an amalgam of liberalism and democracy whereby an earlier liberal emphasis on legal rights as the means to protect the property and promote the liberty of individuals gave ground to seeing participation in a rational state and community as the means to promote self-development. A self-determined, co-operative and public-spirited, activity was stressed rather than the protection of private interests. For Marx, the human capacity and need for such a freedom defined human beings, and distinguished them from the other inhabitants of the natural world. In a Rheinische Zeitung article in 1842, a year before he was converted to socialism, Marx wrote that

> freedom is so much the human essence that even its opponents implement it while combating its reality; they want to appropriate for themselves as a most precious ornament what they have rejected as an ornament of human nature.[5] [Emphasis added.]

The idea that freedom is the essence of being human was never abandoned by Marx. It is an idea which explains rather than contradicts the later argument in Capital that labour is the most distinctive of human qualities. The emphasis on labour was simply the old idea in a new guise. What Marx emphasised about human labour was its distinctively free character. Unlike in animal labour, he wrote, human beings possessed the capacity to produce artefacts, institutions and culture not as a result of physical need but of choice. They refashioned nature, created new social institutions and engaged in new ways of living on the basis of new, freely chosen ideas. History was the ultimate product of such human labour. The following formulation of the idea comes from Capital.

> Primarily, labour is a process going on between man and nature, a process in which man, through his own activity, initiates, regulates and controls the material reactions between himself and nature...By thus acting on the external world and changing it, he

---

4. For an analysis of Marx's 1842-3 journalism, see N. Wintrop, 'Karl Marx's Political Philosophical Journalism of 1842-43', Australasian Political Studies Association Conference paper, 1979.

5. K. Marx and F. Engels, Collected Works, vol. 1 (Lawrence and Wishart, London, 1975), p. 155.

> at the same time changes his own nature. He develops the potentialities that slumber within him, and subjects these inner forces to his own control...We have to consider labour in a form peculiar to the human species. A spider carries on operations resembling those of a weaver; and many a human architect is put to shame by the skill with which a bee constructs her cell. But what from the very first distinguishes the most incompetent architect from the best of bees, is that the architect has built a cell in his head before he constructs it in wax. The labour process ends in the creation of something which, when the process began, already existed in the worker's imagination, already existed in an ideal form...in the nature that exists apart from himself, he the worker realises his own purpose.[6]

The idea that freedom characterised human labour was the moral basis for Marx's objections to industrial capitalism and his commitment to its revolutionary destruction. Whereas economic activity, according to Marx, should be the co-operative undertaking of free subjects, under modern capitalism labour had become an object. It had become a commodity which was bought and sold, the result of the processes of production being controlled not by the producers but by external forces. These criticisms of modern capitalism were linked to Marx's concepts of alienation and commodity fetishism. Human beings were alienated because they were separated from a life of free, creative labour. Commodity fetishism occurred in modern life when economists and others had a distorted view of economic life: instead of seeing production for the satisfying of human need as the essence of economic activity, they saw the exchange of commodities and the price mechanism. It was, therefore, the liberal and democratic emphasis on freedom and the human capacity for self-government, which Marx extended into economic analysis and criticism, that led Marx to a revolutionary opposition to modern capitalism.

But not only did liberal and democratic ideas enter into Marx's economic evaluations, they also entered into his revolutionary project for the construction of a classless and stateless society. Between 1842 and 1843 Marx developed a conception of and advocated a state which combined the liberal principles of freedom of speech, publication, assembly and association with the modern democratic objective of self-government by freely-elected representatives. This was his original revolutionary alternative to the bureaucratic and authoritarian governments of Prussia and other German states. Later, as a communist, Marx proposed not a liberal democratic state but a new kind of post-state, post-liberal-democratic politics. His political principles, however, had not changed. The classless and stateless communist society of the future, and the transitional societies which would establish it, still consisted of the original liberal and democratic

---

6. K. Marx, Capital, 2-vol. edn of vol. 1 (Dent, London, 1930), pp. 169-70.

ideal: individuals and groups co-operating to resolve differences, govern themselves and initiate new undertakings. The commitment to communism did not mean abandoning liberal democratic ideals, but adding to them the project of freeing humanity from economic as well as political coercion. Marx's communism was an economic as well as a political project. It proposed to liberate men and women from economic scarcity and from the private ownership of economic resources, which Marx believed led to the exploitation of one class by another. Some critics see this proposal to refashion economic life as a dangerous delusion, incompatible with liberal democratic norms. Whether or not this criticism is justified, Marx's position is more accurately described as a perfectionist application of liberal democratic principles than as the abandonment of liberal democratic politics for something else.

But - and this is crucial to the argument that liberal and democratic values were always a part of Marx's revolutionary theory - not only did a perfectionist variety of liberalism and democracy remain a part of Marx's ends but attempts were made by him to integrate liberal and democratic principles into his revolutionary means. It may be true that from 1848 to 1850, when Marx's immediate political concern was the possibility of a German revolution, he went through what is sometimes described as a _Jacobin_ phase in which he briefly supported conspiratorial revolutionary groups and the idea of a minority dictatorship.[7] It is also true that - in common with most democrats - he supported the use of force and violence in nations which lacked a democratic constitution. Nevertheless, from the end of 1850, Marx overwhelmingly relied on peaceful and democratic means to achieve socialist revolution: industrial growth, constitutional change, and an anticipated economic and political education and organisation of the industrial workers. He opposed the idea that socialist revolution required not the industrial workers, trade unions and labour parties but elites of professional revolutionaries organised in conspiratorial or vanguard parties, with a strategy of utilising social and political crises for insurrectionary purposes. For this reason he rejected the revolutionary strategies of Blanqui, Mazzini and Bakunin. For the mature Marx, a revolution intended to inaugurate an era of free, co-operative political and social activity could not be inaugurated by a manipulative minority. It required the conscious activity of the overwhelming majority of the members of a society.

As early as 1845, in his 'Theses on Feuerbach', Marx had

---

7. For Marx's encouragement of a permanent-revolutionary strategy and a Jacobin-type dictatorship, see the 'Address of the Central Committee to the Communist League', K. Marx and F. Engels, _Selected Works in Two Volumes_, vol. 1 (Lawrence and Wishart, London, 1950). But see also Marx's other 1848-51 writings on Germany, K. Marx, _The Revolutions of 1848_, ed., D. Fernbach (Penguin, Harmondsworth, 1973); and Marx-Engels, _Collected Works_, vols. 7-10 (1977-8).

formulated a revolutionary practice which emphasised the self-education of the masses and which pilloried the pretensions of socialist intellectuals and revolutionary leaders. In the third thesis, Marx noted the authoritarian, illiberal and anti-democratic dangers in socialist theories which divided society into two parts, the educators and those being educated, and he rejected those theories for a conception of revolution as self education.

> The materialist doctrine concerning the changing of circumstances and upbringing forgets that circumstances are changed by men and that the educator must himself be educated. This doctrine must, therefore, divide society into two parts, one of which is superior to society. The coincidence of the changing of circumstances and of human activity or self-change can be conceived and rationally understood only as _revolutionary practice_.[8]

This conception of revolution was liberal as well as democratic, because, without the pluralism, criticism and debate of liberalism, this proposed self-change of large numbers of people is not possible, only their manipulation and indoctrination.

For the mature Marx, socialist revolution was the rational and inevitable response to modern capitalism on the part of the industrial workers, a response which was not dependent upon the propaganda or organisational work of revolutionary elites. Socialism meant that, for the first time, there would be a ruling class which comprised a majority of the population and who were conscious of their objectives. 'All previous historical movements were movements of minorities. The proletarian movement is the self-conscious, independent movement of the immense majority, in the interest of the immense majority.'[9] The new society, possessing the support of an overwhelming majority of the population, would thus be able to grant full political rights to the defeated classes and their parties: 'the struggle for the emancipation of the working classes means not a struggle for class privileges and monopolies, but for equal rights and duties, and the abolition of all class rule.'[10]

Arguably, Marx's socialist revolutionary project for the abolition of private property and the state, and the organising of society on the principle of free co-operation, was so absurd, fantastic or threatening, and so likely to provoke the hatred and resentment of opponents, that movements which took it seriously would be compelled to abandon liberal democratic principles for force and compulsion. Similarly, particularly if working class self-change was slow, the tendency would

---

8. Marx-Engels, _Collected Works_, vol. 5 (1976), p. 4.

9. Marx-Engels (_Communist Manifesto_), _Selected Works_, vol. 1, p. 42.

10. _General Rules of the International Working Men's Association_, ibid., p. 350.

be for groups of communists, initially engaged in contributing to the education of workers, increasingly to substitute their propaganda, leadership and organisational skills for the independent activity of the working class. But, if so, these developments were not the result of Marx's intentions. They arose more from the fact that Marx took the ideas of freedom and democracy to extremes.[11] This uncompromising commitment to certain ideals - at the expense of others, for example toleration and minority rights - was linked to another component of Marx's revolutionary theory: utopianism.

Utopianism

By utopianism is meant a demand for perfection and harmony in human affairs, based on an unrealistic and excessively optimistic view of individual and social potential. The term, therefore, is being used both descriptively and critically.

One utopian feature of Marx's thought was the belief that economic scarcity could be overcome. He believed that people would learn to moderate their cravings for possessions and material pleasures, and would use modern industry and technology to produce more goods and services then the demand for them. A second utopian feature was the belief that people would work and co-operate without any material incentive. Economic activity would require no other motive than moral commitment. A third utopian feature was the belief that not only would economic abundance bring to an end conflicts over the distribution of economic resources, but it would end all other permanent conflicts. The proposal to transcend or go beyond the state, partly in the sense of abolishing armies, police forces and permanent bureaucracies, assumes that, in a socialist society, a combination of individual restraint, social restraint and industrial growth will enable the problems of psychological differences, personal rivalries, power struggles, territorial disputes, religious controversies and disputes about social ends and means to be solved by discussion and agreement. This is the anarchist part of Marx's thought: the belief that socialism will eventually end all permanently divisive social conflicts and dispense with a need for laws backed by force.

Needless to say, Marx denied that he was a utopian; he regarded his revolutionary project as realistic, and he denounced the utopianism he attributed to others. It should be noted, however, that though Marx

---

11. Studies of Marx which emphasise and document the liberal and democratic features of his thought include S. Avineri, The Social and Political Thought of Karl Marx (Cambridge Univ. Pr., Cambridge, 1968); W. Blumenberg, Karl Marx (New Left Books, London, 1972); R.N. Hunt, The Political Ideas of Marx and Engels (Univ. of Pittsburgh Pr., Pittsburgh, 1974); and J. Lewis, The Life and Teaching of Karl Marx (Lawrence and Wishart, London, 1965) and The Marxism of Marx (Lawrence and Wishart, London, 1972). For a counter-attack, see A. Gilbert, Marx's Politics (Rutgers Univ. Pr., New Brunswick, N.J., 1981).

and Engels polemicised against the utopianism of Robert Owen, Fourier and Saint-Simon, and though they - particularly Engels - claimed to have replaced utopian with scientific socialism, it was the means and not the ends of the utopian socialists that were the targets of their criticism. In common with the utopians and the anarchists, Marx believed that society could be reconstituted on the assumption that, once private property and the state were abolished, people would act fraternally and morally. His objection to the utopians and the anarchists was not that their assumptions were unsound but that their means were unrealistic. They were accused of neglecting the objective historical trends and forces which promoted their ends for a reliance on social blueprints that rested on nothing but their subjective wishes and powers of persuasion. Marx claimed that, in contrast to the utopians who set themselves against history, the social ends he favoured were built into history and expressed themselves in objective trends and forces.[12]

Before discussing Marx's view of history, it is pertinent to note some further utopian features of his revolutionary theory, features sometimes described as Promethean and Romantic. Prometheus was the Greek god, frequently referred to by Marx in glowing terms, who stole fire from heaven to give to mankind and who championed men against Zeus. The Promethean theme in Marx's revolutionary thought is the desire to replace the Judaic and Christian acceptance of the sovereignty of a revealed God with the secular political undertaking of building a heaven on earth in accordance with human wishes. The Romantic themes are the beliefs that (1) societies can be created which will be inhabited by noble, autonomous and unique individuals and that (2) these societies will also be natural and organic communities. These utopian and quasi-religious features of Marx's revolutionary theory help to explain its enduring attraction.[13] But what is more exciting, certainly for devotees, is Marx's insistence that by means of a proper understanding of history, science, the proletariat and economics he had turned apparently utopian hopes into realistic aspirations.

---

12. Utopian socialism is discussed and criticised by Marx in the Communist Manifesto. See also, F. Engels, Socialism: Utopian and Scientific, Marx-Engels, Selected Works, vol. 2.

13. For secondary discussions of the Romantic, Promethean and other utopian themes in Marx's work, see Kolakowski, vol. 1; R.C. Tucker, Philosophy and Myth in Karl Marx (Cambridge Univ. Pr., Cambridge, 1964 - the argument is toned down in the second edition, Cambridge Univ. Pr., Cambridge, 1972) - and E. Voegelin, 'The Formation of the Marxian Revolutionary Idea', Review of Politics, vol. 12 (1950), pp. 275-302. See also J.L. Talmon's critical work on late-eighteenth century and early-nineteenth century radical thought, The Origins of Totalitarian Democracy (Praeger, New York, 1960) and Political Messianism: The Romantic Phase (Praeger, New York, 1960).

Historical Progress and Scientific Method

According to Marx, who was influenced by Hegel's philosophy of history but who had independently reflected on the political revolutions, economic changes and industrial growth of the preceding three hundred years, progress occurred in history. Sometimes he wrote as if progress were predestined and inevitable, and apparent departures from it were no more than a temporary thwarting of history, as in Capital with its epic tale of the rise of industrial capitalism and its conquest by socialism. At other times, as in his remark in the Communist Manifesto that class struggles sometimes ended with the mutual destruction of the contending classes, progress became only a possibility. A belief in progress was widespread during Marx's lifetime. But progress was defined differently and given different contents by different writers. For Marx, social formations (for example feudalism or capitalism), classes, political movements and the activities of individuals were progressive to the extent that they brought nearer a society of economic plenty, individual freedom and social co-operation. Historical progress, for Marx, meant progress toward a new kind of human condition.

Though Marx used the term revolution in as many ways as most political thinkers, it was always related to this understanding of history and progress. By revolution, he sometimes meant a centuries-long process of social evolution in which one ruling class replaced another and one social formation was transformed into another. The term is used in this way when, for example in the Communist Manifesto, Marx discussed the origins of modern capitalism. At other times, however, the term was given the more cataclysmic meaning of a continental-wide if not world-wide social transformation within a few decades or years. In this use of the term, Marx was influenced by the European-wide character and rapid effects of the French revolutionary wars and, later, the 1848 revolutions. Also, by revolution, Marx sometimes meant political violence intended to overthrow a government,in other words an insurrection or coup. But in all these uses of the term, revolution and progress were closely linked. Revolution was the agency of progress, and it was their contributions to historical progress that distinguished revolutionary challenges and changes from others. In contrast to many subsequent historians, sociologists and other analysts of revolution, who have tried to use the term revolution in value-neutral ways, to describe all radical, violent or swift social or political changes, Marx distinguished revolution from counter-revolution and from self-defeating struggles and changes. Revolutions occurred, for Marx, only when historical progress was advanced. By definition, revolution was constructive and creative.

In some ways Marx's approach to the understanding and forwarding of revolution resembled Greek political thought, which similarly had tried to be both empirical and evaluative. But, whereas the Greeks held a cyclical philosophy of history in which social and political change could not go beyond the boundaries set by human nature, Marx saw revolutions as potential challenges to all such boundaries, and he saw history as progressing toward an end - the overcoming of economic scarcity and the organising of society on the principles of freedom and co-operation. It followed from this eschatological view of history that the eras of history that had facilitated the emergence of industrial capitalism, the proletariat and, consequently, the conditions for the achievement of a new kind of history represented stages of development. Thus slave societies were superior to what Marx believe were the primitive communal and Asiatic-type societies preceding or co-existing with them, feudalism to slavery, modern capitalism to feudalism, and socialism to capitalism. Each was superior to its predecessor because it increased economic production and because it increased the areas and possibilities of freedom, thus making possible richer cultures. And each was progressive because it brought nearer the possibility of communism.

But it is misleading to see Marx as simply making a moral evaluation of history and having a visionary conception of its possibilities. Marx claimed a scientific status for at least some of his work, and Marxists, beginning with Engels, have claimed a scientific status for both his understanding of history and the linked revolutionary project. It is because so many present day sociologists share the view that Marx tried to construct a science of society that they regard him as one of the founders of their discipline - despite his disdain for his contemporary Auguste Comte who pioneered the term and concept of sociology. But precisely what Marx meant by his claim to have forsaken the methods of philosophy for those of science is a controversial issue among Marxists and writers on Marx, and an issue that has been aggravated in recent years by the disputes over what constitutes a science. Contrary to what was once widely believed, Marx does not appear to have shared Engels' view that changes from one historical stage to another are produced almost entirely by economic laws, and that the purpose of a social and socialist science is to discover and forward these laws. Marx, in his detailed explanations of the transition from one stage to another, finds a place for economic and other factors which do not possess the regularity of laws. These factors include the growth and decline of populations, geographic and climatic changes, migrations, conquests, gold, silver and similar discoveries, new technologies and the activities of outstanding individuals.[14] It is only with regard to modern industrial capitalism, where not only economic life but all other areas of society are subordinated to the extraction of a social surplus by the economically dominant class, that Marx appears to think it possible for social laws of an economic kind to be discovered and predictions of large-scale change made. But the analysis of the laws of capitalist development, in Capital, do no more than predict economic crises and the centralisation of property and production. The additional claim that capitalism

---

14. For Marx's detailed examinations of historical change, see The German Ideology, section on 'Feuerbach', Marx-Engels, Collected Works, vol. 5 (1976), pp. 27-93; and K. Marx, Pre-Capitalist Economic Formations, ed. E.J. Hobsbawm (Lawrence and Wishart, London, 1964).

will be succeeded by socialism rests not on an analysis of economic laws but upon the qualities Marx attributed to the proletariat. But before turning to this topic, it is pertinent to summarise what Marx meant by science and his claim that his analysis of industrial capitalism, history's penultimate stage, had a scientific character.

First, Marx's social science is empirical in that it begins with, confronts and tries to explain the observable facts. But, second, it tries to go beyond the facts to discover the fundamental economic and other structures that are both revealed and concealed by the facts. Third, it attempts to identify these structures by means of a historical analysis of their origins and uniqueness. Fourth, Marx's empirical, structuralist and historical science is not value-neutral but has the pragmatic (revolutionary) purpose of forwarding the construction of new social structures based on the principles of freedom and co-operation. Marx regarded his magnum opus, Capital, as scientific because it met all these standards. It purported to provide a knowledge of the essential features and structures of modern capitalism, derived from the study of its observable phenomena; it compared capitalism with past and potential societies; and the knowledge it provided furthered the revolutionary liberation of humanity's suppressed potential for freedom and co-operation.

Class and the Proletariat

Marx took the social category of an economic class, that is to say the idea that large and influential groups of people share interests and aspirations as a result of their place in the economic organisation of their society, from historians and economists who were not socialists. In an 1852 letter Marx wrote that

> no credit is due to me for discovering the existence of classes in modern society nor yet the struggle between them. Long before me bourgeois historians had described the historical development of this class struggle and bourgeois economists the economic anatomy of the classes.[15]

What was distinctive to Marx's work on class was its emphasis on the early nineteenth-century socialist idea that one particular class, the proletariat, was a potential agency for the socialist revolution.

> What I did that was new was to prove: (1) that the existence of classes is only bound up with particular, historic phases in the development of production; (2) that the class struggle necessarily

15. Marx to J. Weydemeyer, 5 March 1852, K. Marx and F. Engels, Selected Correspondence, 2nd edn (Lawrence and Wishart, London, 1936), p. 57.

leads to the dictatorship of the proletariat; (3) that this dictatorship itself only constitutes the transition to the abolition of all classes and to a classless society.[16]

The term proletariat, which can be traced back to Ancient Rome and which was revived in the eighteenth and nineteenth-century historical discussions of the Roman Empire, was given a new meaning by Marx. For the Romans, it meant the propertyless: people who lacked resources and skills and who could serve their states only by the procreation and rearing of children. Politically, it meant people whose property was insufficient to make them independent of the will of others and who, therefore, were debarred from citizenship rights. The term referred to the unemployed and unemployable for whom the state provided bread and circuses. Marx first displayed an interest in the proletariat, in his writings of 1843, for precisely the reason that had made previous political thinkers uneasy. Proletarians, though dependent upon their state, lived on its margins and were not integrated into it. By turning to the proletariat, therefore, Marx and other nineteenth-century socialists gave notice that they were proposing previously-undreamed-of revolutionary changes that could appeal only to people who had nothing to lose.

Marx originally used the term proletariat, in his writings of 1843 and 1844, to refer to the most suffering and the most alienated members of society, the people who were most separated from an independent and cultured existence. But his use of the term became more complex and ambiguous when, in the *Communist Manifesto* of 1848, he used it to refer not to the unemployed and the outcasts, often the people who had been dislodged from their previous occupations by industrialisation, but to the increasing numbers of industrial workers. One reason why Marx emphasised this new proletariat (the industrial working class) was that he came to see it as the productive class, *par excellence*, which made possible the economic and other achievements of capitalism. In addition, Marx believed that the industrial workers, unlike former proletariats, would in industrialised nations constitute a majority of the population. But there were problems in applying the term proletariat, with its earlier associations, to the new class. The industrial workers, certainly the more skilled and better paid, saw themselves not as outcasts but as economically productive and as the equals of the members of other classes. They believed that they were entitled to voting and other political rights. Their objective was political and social equality with other classes - not a war to the death.

Marx ascribed to nineteenth-century industrial workers qualities which do not easily co-exist. As well as portraying them as (1) a majority class, and therefore able to rule democratically, and (2) a productive class with the capacity to establish a socialism that would maintain and surpass the economic achievements of capitalism, the necessary basis for a rich culture, Marx saw them as also being (3) an

16. Ibid.

alienated and exploited class, and for this reason potentially revolutionary. The first two claims clash with the third. This is because if the members of the proletariat comprise a majority of the population, and are indispensable to the economy, then, at least in liberal democratic nations, they are likely to achieve political rights and economic advances without revolution, as was already occurring during Marx's lifetime. The claim that proletarians are alienated, exploited and potentially revolutionary is, therefore, to attribute qualities to them that rest upon a philosophical conception of an ideal human existence. It does not rest on anything they are likely to feel, their objective situation, or their likely response to it. The tension between the first two claims and the third becomes even more evident if a further issue is raised. If the proletariat is dehumanised and exploited because it is denied a cultured and civilised existence, how is such a class to create a superior culture and civilisation to that of capitalism? Conversely, if, under capitalism, it is able to educate itself to become such a creative class, why should it revolt? Marx's reply, that in the process of its revolutionary struggle against capitalism the proletariat will transform itself, for all its rhetorical force, is more an act of faith than a solution to the problems of reconciling the different qualities Marx attributed to the proletariat. As it is in Marx's economic writings, his analysis of modern capitalism, that Marx, inter alia, tries systematically to develop his conception of the proletariat as a majority, productive, exploited, universal and revolutionary creative class, it is time to discuss this part of his work.

Political Economy

Marx is rightly regarded as the foremost critic of the dominant branches of nineteenth-century economic thought. But it is often forgotten that he incorporated into his rival economics many of the assumptions and objectives of Adam Smith, David Ricardo, and their co-thinkers and successors. Further, as the classical economists were both influences on and influenced by modern industrial capitalism, this is another way of saying that, via Marx, the Marxist revolutionary movement inherited many of the objectives of the economic system it opposed. But precisely what did Marx take from the political economists?

One idea he took has already been mentioned. This was that science, technology and industry could abolish economic scarcity and create a society of abundance. The quarrel between Marx and other economists was not primarily about the objectives of economic life but the means for their achievement. Whereas orthodox economists believed that the necessary conditions were a framework of law and order, in which the private ownership of economic resources was upheld and competition between buyers and sellers allowed to flourish, Marx insisted that the public ownership of economic resources and the co-operation of producers were the means. This, of course, was what made his proposed new society socialist and eventually communist. Its economic principle was the public rather than the private ownership of economic resources. But Marx was rather vague about the precise form public ownership should take and how co-operative production should be organised. His attitude was that he could neither dictate to the future free citizens and producers of socialism nor predict their decisions. The result has been that, in the twentieth century, his professed followers have filled in the details for him.

Marx was more precise and detailed in his analysis and criticism of capitalist production. According to Marx, capitalism could not fulfil its promise to create economic plenty because it was dependent upon the existence of proletarians who would always live in conditions of want and be denied the fruits of their labour. Unless they were economically deprived, they would have no motive to work; if they were paid the equivalent of their labour, there would be no profit for their employers. Further, not only was capitalism inescapably exploitative, but its need to extract an increasing surplus from the proletariat - its vampire-like thirst for profit - made it subject to increasingly severe economic slumps. Marx also believed that competition would lead to ever-increasing investment in machinery and technology, thus reducing the size of the economic surplus and producing a falling rate of profit.[17]

A further idea taken by Marx from the political economists was that economic efficiency and growth required the breaking down of national barriers and the substitution of an international economy . In one of the Communist Manifesto's many eulogistic passages on the achievements of capitalism, Marx wrote that

> [t]he bourgeoisie has through its exploitation of the world-market given a cosmopolitan character to production and consumption in every country. To the great chagrin of reactionists, it has driven from under the feet of industry the national ground on which it stood.... National one-sidedness and narrow mindedness becomes more and more impossible.[18]

But, though Marx applauded capitalism for its assault on national and continental isolation, and for 'liberating' people from the 'idiocy' of rural life, and though he supported the political economists in their promotion of free trade, he denied that capitalism - a socially disruptive economic system - could be the basis for a stable

17. For introductions to Marx's analyses of modern capitalism and its economic crises, and the part they played in his political thought, see B. Brugger and B. Probert, 'Classical Socialist Theory: Nineteenth-Century Marxism' in N. Wintrop (ed.), Liberal Democratic Theory and Its Critics (Croom Helm, London, 1983); G.D.H. Cole, A History of Socialist Thought, vol. 2, Ch. 11, Marx and Engels (Macmillan, London, 1954); and Kolakowski, vol. 1, Chs. 12 and 13, Capitalism as a Dehumanised World and The Contradictions of Capitalism. The pertinent original texts are the three volumes of Marx's Capital.

18. Marx-Engels, Selected Works, vol. 1, p. 36.

international economy or peaceful community. For these purposes, international socialist revolution was necessary.

Marx was an internationalist who opposed the nation state being the main political unit to which political loyalty should be given. He believed that the only worthwhile political loyalty, in the world of industrial capitalism, was that which was given to the international working class and socialist movement, and he urged workers and socialists to be aware of their responsibilities to the workers and socialists of other nations.[19] A frequent criticism of his conception of socialist revolution, and a widely-held explanation of the contrast between his conception of revolution and the actual Marxist revolutions of the twentieth century, is that he - in common with the other political economists of his day - underestimated the strength of national sentiment.

Revolutionary Pragmatism

Marx took both philosophy and empirical study seriously. Neither his early philosophical encounters with Greek philosophy, Hegelianism and left Hegelianism, his later attempts to put economics upon new foundations, nor his detailed historical work and multi-volume study of capitalism can be dismissed as merely propaganda, ideology or exercises in mythmaking. Marx tried, first through philosophy and then history and economics, to acquire a comprehensive understanding of his age - in which the first traumas of industrialisation occurred - and to develop, in a new way, moral and political standards for himself and others. He tried to replace a traditional ethics and normative political philosophy, which speculated upon the nature or essence of man, with a set of standards derived from the study of a capitalist industrial society. He rejected traditional philosophy for *praxis*, a supposedly integrated empirical theory, normative theory and political-revolutionary practice. The empirical theory purported to provide a knowledge of history and industrial capitalism, the normative theory urged the proletariat to create a socialist society, while the practice consisted of socialist and revolutionary class struggle. The theory was intended to guide the practice, and the practical experience of revolutionary class struggle was expected to enrich and modify both the empirical and normative parts of the theory. Theory was to inform practice, and practice to enrich the theory.

Praxis was a radical departure from traditional ethics and political philosophy. Ethics and political philosophy distinguish between right and wrong personal conduct and between just and unjust

19. See, for example, Marx's advice to German and French socialists during the 1870-1871 Franco-Prussian War, K. Marx and F. Engels, *On the Paris Commune* (Progress Publishers, Moscow, 1971); *Writings on the Paris Commune*, ed. H. Draper (Monthly Review Pr., New York, 1971); and K. Marx, *The First International and After*, ed. D. Fernbach (Penguin Books, Harmondsworth, 1974). The last selection contains other examples of Marx's internationalism.

political conduct irrespective of the extent to which individuals, citizens and rulers follow the norms of ethics and political philosophy. They assume that there will always be a gap between the ideal and reality, between how life should be lived and how it is lived, no matter how hard moral persons, citizens and rulers try to reduce these gaps. Marx and other left Hegelian philosophers of praxis, with their desire to make society fully correspond to the ideals of theory, break from this tradition. The problem is that a revolutionary praxis, such as Marx's, which begins with the attempt to make the social world correspond to ideals derived from philosophy, when modified by practical experience, is likely to become little more than an ideology justifying the immediate interests, objectives and policies of revolutionaries. Much of the history of Marxism illustrates this tendency. Beginning with the project of constructing a new world in accordance with the ideals of philosophy - the 'philosophers have only interpreted the world in various ways; the point is to change it'[20] - it has led to dozens of rival Marxisms, each serving the particular needs and goals of Marxist individuals, groups, parties and states.[21]

But this move from ideals to expediency began not after Marx's death but during his lifetime and in his own activity. Partly because his general theory about the deficiencies of capitalism and the need for socialism could provide no precise guidance for socialist strategy and tactics, and partly because he always urged that strategy and tactics be based on particular circumstances, Marx advocated a wide variety of strategies for the many nations he hoped to influence. In particular, he oscillated between reform and insurrection, and between a reliance on the industrial workers and a concern with leadership. From 1847, when he joined the Communist League, to 1850, when he split from most of his fellow communist emigres in London, his strategy was an insurrectionary one with a Jacobin-type minority dictatorship as its objective. From 1850 to 1870 he favoured, where economic growth and national constitutions made it possible, a gradualist and parliamentary strategy. But in 1870 and 1871, after first opposing the setting up of revolutionary, self-governing communes in France, he gave his support to and eulogised the Paris Commune in its challenge to the newly

---

20. 'Theses on Feuerbach', Marx-Engels, Collected Works, vol. 5, p. 5.

21. The view that 'contemplative' philosophy had to be replaced by praxis was shared by Marx with other Young Hegelians. To understand his particular version of praxis, therefore, it is helpful to understand the issues that led to his parting from his former intellectual associates. With Engels, Marx wrote two sets of criticisms of the leading Young Hegelians, The Holy Family, Collected Works, vol. 4 (1975) and The German Ideology. Comparisons between Marx and other Young Hegelians are made in W.J. Brazill, The Young Hegelians (Yale Univ. Pr., New Haven, 1970); K. Loewith, From Hegel to Nietzsche (Constable, London, 1963); and D. McLellan, The Young Hegelians and Karl Marx (Macmillan, London, 1969).

formed Third Republic. Immediately after the destruction of the Paris Commune, however, he abandoned this civil-war strategy to return to a reformist one.

There are also many other oscillations and uncertainties in Marx's practical politics. For example, he was unsure about whether the bourgeoisie were a revolutionary force in nineteenth-century nations that were still pre-capitalist; the extent to which the peasantry were a potential ally of the proletariat; and the likelihood of armed resistance by the enemies of socialism in nations with liberal democratic constitutions and conventions. He was also ambivalent about whether the main enemy of the working-class and socialist revolution was the modern capitalist class or a Bonapartist-Bismarckian state which tried to exercise domination over both capitalists and workers. He was similarly ambivalent about the kind of state that revolutionary workers should try to construct. It is significant that though in his most famous public discussion of the Paris Commune, _The Civil War in France_, a pamphlet he wrote during the April and May of 1871, he emphasised the libertarian and anti-bureaucratic features of the Commune, - the fact that it expressed the activity of a plurality of socialist and other radical groups, and large numbers of people with no party affiliations - elsewhere he supported a minority dictatorship. In a private letter of April 1871, he wrote that a major mistake, and a reason for the eventual defeat of the Commune, was that the 'Central Committee of the National Guard gave up its power too soon, in order to make place for the Commune'.[22]

This analysis of Marx's theory of revolution began with an emphasis on the liberal-democratic origins and character of his thought. But it must now be conceded that Marx could become so intoxicated by the possibility of immediate revolution that the liberal and democratic features of his project could be overwhelmed by a revolutionary pragmatism bordering on opportunism. Nevertheless, there was a theory for the guidance of revolutionaries, with at least a superficial coherence and plausibility, consisting of the ideas that have been outlined.[23] The following is a brief summary of this theory.

---

22. Marx to L. Kugelmann, 12 April 1871, K. Marx, _On Revolution_, ed. S.K. Padover (The Karl Marx Library, vol. 1, McGraw Hill, New York, 1971).

23. On the issue of the relations between Marx's theory and practice, for a sympathetic study of Marx's politics which argues that he subordinated theory to his main concern, the promotion of socialist revolution, see Gilbert, _Marx's Politics_. But for a more comprehensive, balanced and detailed account of both Marx's writings on and participation in revolutionary activity, see H. Draper, _Karl Marx's Theory of Revolution_, vols. 1 and 2 (Monthly Review Pr., New York, 1977 and 1978). See also G. Lichtheim, _Marxism_, 2nd edn (Routledge, London, 1964); J.M. Maguire, _Marx's Theory of Politics_ (Cambridge Univ. Pr., Cambridge, 1978); and B. Nicolaievsky and O. Maenschen-Helfen, _Karl Marx: Man and Fighter_, 2nd Eng. edn (Allen Lane, London, 1973).

Marx's Revolutionary Theory

The revolutionary theory constructed by Marx out of a range of nineteenth-century philosophical, economic and political ideas was also a philosophy of history, a social and political philosophy, and an analysis and diagnosis of modern industrial capitalism. The theory can best be summarised and expressed in terms of history. For Marx, history - or at least the history of the Mediterranean and European peoples, regarded by him as of world importance - consisted of the rise and fall of economic classes and the societies moulded by those classes which achieved dominance. Because of their economic power and privileges, their control of the economic surplus, slaveowning, aristocracies, feudal nobilities and then the modern bourgeoisie were able to achieve a cultural dominance over their societies and a general control over their states (governments, bureaucracies and military forces). Ruling classes ruled, therefore, mainly as a result of economic power, but partly by their influence on culture and by force. Their rule also rested on the rational and genuine consent of other classes. This was because the economic structures promoted by rising classes were more productive than rival ones, thus possessing the capacity to provide higher economic standards for all classes, richer cultures, and an extension of political rights. Labouring classes remained exploited and deprived, but obtained or could obtain some benefit from each new variety of class rule. Technological and economic change, ideology and culture, political skills and the command of military force all played a part in the historical drama, but they were not all regarded by Marx as having the same causal weight. Marx believed that the main source of power and authority within a society was its economic organisation. Similarly, technological and economic developments were the main disrupters of power relations and precipitators of social change.

But there was more to Marx's view of Western history than an attempt to divide it into class-dominated structures and to explain the relations between the causal factors in the movement from one structure to another. In addition to consisting of the rise and fall of the empires and city states of antiquity, and the institutions of feudalism and modern capitalism, history was the expression of the alienation of men and women. History also provided the opportunities for humans to overcome their alienation. In this more hidden drama, men and women abandoned the social co-operation and solidarity of tribal and village life for class-divided, conflict-torn societies, as a several-millenia preparation for a return to harmony and co-operation, once economic scarcity had been abolished and personal independence and a cultured life made possible. The ending of humanity's alienation from a life of individual and group autonomy and co-operation was the objective of socialist revolution. Depending upon how one regards Marx's philosophy of history, he can be seen as giving history a meaning or revealing the secret meaning of history. History, for Marx, was not aimless. It was a movement towards communism: an international, classless, co-operative society of free individuals, living amicably together locally, nationally and internationally, without the coercion of police forces, prisons or armies.

The agency for socialist revolution and the overcoming of alienation was the proletariat. The modern proletariat, the industrial workers, comprised a class which, in the dominant nations, was or was becoming central to the economy and a majority of the population; it was more alienated from the benefits of its labour than any previous class that had contended for social supremacy, and potentially more creative. This was because it was a new kind of class. Unlike previous classes which had struggled for political power, it was a universal class: it had no other interests than that which ultimately benefited all humanity, the achievement of a human existence. If its struggle were successful, a new kind of life of vision and fulfilment would be opened to individuals and the species; if unsuccessful, there would be unprecedented social disintegration. The role of Marxist revolutionaries was to participate in the local and national manifestations of this international revolution, until, internationally, socialism had demonstrated its superiority to capitalism, making it as absurd for a person to wish to return to capitalism as it was for someone in Marx's day to wish to return to the society of the pharaohs. The theory was about one vast revolution or revolutionary process, surpassing in scale all previous revolutions, but made up of many different, more modest revolutions. Marx's revolutionary project was breathtaking in the possibilities it offered to humanity, and to the faithful it offered a way of life, that of the revolutionary. But it also found a place for detailed and careful economic, historical and other scholarship, and it could encourage patience and gradualism in the approach of revolutionaries to the proletariat and to immediate political issues. Marx's proposed revolution was cosmic in its implications and it countenanced violence; but, at times, Marx believed that it could proceed slowly and gently, by means of liberal-democratic and statesmanlike politics.

LENIN

The tension in Marx's work between the breathtaking vistas of socialist revolution and, in comparison, the mundane organisational and parliamentary activities that were necessary preparations for the establishment of the new society was inherited by his followers. The first group to confront it were the organisers and leaders of the predominently Marxist, social-democratic parties of the Second Socialist International, established in 1889, six years after Marx's death. One result of this tension was that most socialist parties of the years from 1889 to 1914 were divided into radical factions, which emphasised the revolutionary purposes of their parties, and moderates, or revisionists as they came to be called, who emphasised the gradualist means of industrial development, trade union growth, and constitutional, parliamentary and reformist politics. Though the disputes between the radicals and the moderates were frequently bitter, until World War One the factions usually managed to live together within the one Labour or Social Democratic party. One of the exceptions was the Russian Social Democratic Party which, in 1903, split into its Bolshevik and Menshevik factions. The conflicts between radicals and moderates came to a head earlier in Tsarist Russia, than in most nations, because a critical issue was the kind of party organisation that should be constructed by revolutionaries who operated in conditions of political absolutism and persecution. In the rest of Europe there were few similar splits until World War One raised the question of whether the parties of the International, which had previously proclaimed an international solidarity against 'imperialist' wars, should support the military struggles waged by their respective governments.

A few years after 1914, these conflicts were exacerbated when an epochal event occurred which, for the Marxists and socialists of Europe and elsewhere, was to prove of even greater consequence than the issues of war and peace. In the Russian Empire, in October 1917, in the names of Marxism, socialism and international revolution, Lenin and his Bolshevik Party captured governmental power. Their seizure of power was opposed by other Marxists, including Menshevik leaders George Plekhanov and Julius Martov. The Mensheviks protested that Russia lacked the economic, cultural and political conditions for a socialist development, they emphasised the small numbers of industrial workers in a predominently peasant society, and they favoured co-operation between all socialist and liberal democratic parties to promote a parliamentary political development and to further industrialisation. According to Lenin, theirs was an incorrect, dogmatic and pedantic view of Marxism and socialist revolution. But whatever the intellectual merits of the arguments of his Russian Marxist opponents, and the political merits of his policies, Lenin, by successfully consolidating Communist power in a largely pre-industrial society, pioneered a form of Marxist socialist revolution that was to inspire revolutionaries in pre-industrial and partly-industrialised nations throughout the world.

Lenin, christened Vladimir Ilyich Ulyanov, was born in 1870 into an upper-middle-class professional family. He began his career as a revolutionary writer, agitator and leader in the 1890s, as a member of the recently formed Russian Social Democratic Party. He died in 1924, living long enough to become anxious over the poltical direction of the regime he had been instrumental in creating. During and after the 1903 Party split, Lenin inspired and organised its Bolshevik faction. In 1917, in the months that followed the February revolution that overthrew Tsar Nicholas II and made possible open political activities by all parties, the Bolsheviks operated as an independent party. In October they organised the Petrograd (Leningrad) insurrection that gave them control of what remained of the bureaucratic state apparatus of the Tsars. By that date they had already achieved dominance within the soviet (council) institutions of self-government that had been set up in February 1917. Lenin's government proclaimed a new kind of revolutionary state, committed to the extension of revolution to other nations. To forward this policy, it established the Third, Communist, International and the modern Communist Parties, and it encouraged socialists to reject Social Democratic and Labour Parties for the national sections of the Communist International.

Lenin's international Communist movement was a coalition between Western revolutionary socialism and Eastern anti-imperialism. Though modern Communism in the final decades of the twentieth century is very different from what it was in Lenin's day, as far as it is one person's creation, it is Lenin's. It is not possible to understand subsequent revolutions, twentieth century socialism and political developments in what is now called the Third World without an understanding of the fundamentals of his political thought and practice. The following discussion will highlight what, it will be argued, were the distinctive and novel features of his form of Marxist revolutionary theory and practice.[24]

Lenin's Revolutionary Theory

Military approach to politics and revolution In 1915, in his pamphlet Socialism and War, Lenin quoted and emphasised, as he did in other writings of the final decade of his life, the maxim of the nineteenth-century German military historian and theorist, Karl von Clausewitz: 'War is the continuation of politics by other [and Lenin inserted between parentheses] "violent" means'.[25] The corollary of this statement is that politics is the conducting of war by other, peaceful, means.

For Lenin, politics and war were similar and continuous rather than contrasting activities. In common with all Marxists, Lenin rejected as a bourgeois illusion the idea that politics in a class-divided

---

24. In addition to an English translation of Lenin's Collected Works (45 vols., Lawrence and Wishart, London, 1960-70), there are two much shorter selections which provide a balanced introduction to his political thought, The Lenin Anthology, ed. R.C. Tucker (Norton, New York, 1975); and Selected Works in Three Volumes (Progress Publishers, Moscow, 1967). For a briefer introduction, see Lenin in His Own Words, ed. E. Fischer (Allen Lane, London, 1972). Political biographies include T. Cliff, Lenin (4 vols., Pluto Press, London, 1975, 1976, 1978 and 1979), a largely uncritical work; L. Fischer, The Life of Lenin, 2nd edn (Harper and Row, New York 1965); and, a more critical study, A.B. Ulam, Lenin and The Bolsheviks (Secker and Warburg, London, 1966). A large amount of material on Lenin's participation in the Russian Revolution is to be found in E.H. Carr, The Bolshevik Revolution (3 vols., Macmillan, London, 1950, 1952 and 1953). For studies of Lenin's political thought, see N. Harding, Lenin's Political Thought (2 vols., St. Martin's Pr., New York, 1977 and 1980); Kolakowski, vol. 2; and A.G. Meyer, Leninism (Harvard Univ. Pr., Cambridge, Mass., 1957). See also M. Liebman, Leninism Under Lenin (Cape, London, 1975); and B.D. Wolfe, Three Who Made a Revolution, 3rd edn (Penguin, Harmondsworth, 1966).

25. Lenin Anthology, p. 188.

nation could be characterised by a genuine, social dialogue and an attempt to establish common values, purposes and policies within a framework of law. Yet he went much further than most Marxists in seeing all politics as never anything more than a form of warfare. Both warfare and politics were seen by Lenin as exercises in the most effective use of force - the force of the spoken and written word, the pen, and the force of violence and coercion, the sword. For Lenin, politics and warfare were simply two ways of engaging in the same activity: achieving and maintaining the maximum amount of power by acquiring and using the maximum amount of force. Whereas for Marx, revolution was primarily a form of social education; for Lenin, it was primarily a form of warfare.

Lenin went much further than Marx, Engels and his other Marxist predecessors in seeing politics and socialist revolution in military terms. Lenin looked at class struggle the way a field marshal looks at a military campaign. It is not accidental that his writings are full of military metaphors. Marxist theory was described as the <u>most powerful weapon</u> possessed by the Russian revolutionaries and masses, and the Russian urban and peasant masses were described as the <u>battalions</u> to be used by Russian revolutionaries against the enemy. Whereas Marx saw himself as an intellectual and political participant in a historical struggle, Lenin saw himself as the equivalent of a commanding officer, an attitude he expressed in his frequent references to the Bolshevik leaders as the revolution's <u>general staff</u>. This military style of thought pervaded Lenin's writings well before World War One and the October 1917 insurrection which plunged Russia into civil war. It was linked to what is sometimes called a <u>crisis theory of revolution</u>.

<u>Crisis theory of revolution</u> Though Lenin claimed and probably believed himself to be a historical determinist, and though he saw the Marxist theory that was supposed to guide him as a science, providing a knowledge of inevitable and inexorable historical laws and stages of development, his real view of revolution was rather different. By his <u>real view of revolution</u> is meant the one he acted upon when there was a possibility of insurrection. This real view, however, was not always hidden; at times, Lenin made it explicit. It was a voluntarist theory of revolution which relied on the will and determination of revolutionaries and their skilful use of social crises for revolutionary purposes.

For Lenin, revolution depended upon two simple conditions: (1) a revolutionary party prepared to organise for and seize governmental power, and (2) a social and political crisis that weakened the governmental class that was being challenged and gave the support of the masses to the revolutionaries. It was a simple but effective theory, widely adopted by subsequent revolutionary parties. It lacked anything specifically Marxist, but could be attached to Marxism. When formulated in a neutral language, it can be described as a sociology of revolution. Lenin's classic formulation of it is in <u>Left-Wing Communism: An Infantile Disorder</u> (1920).

> The fundamental law of revolution, which has been confirmed by all revolutions, and particularly by all three Russian revolutions in the twentieth century, is as follows. It is not enough for revolution that the exploited and oppressed masses should understand the impossibility of living in the old way and demand changes; it is essential for revolution that the exploiters should not be able to live and rule in the old way. Only when the '_lower classes' do not want_ the old way, and when the 'upper classes' _cannot carry on in the old way_ - only then can revolution triumph. This truth may be expressed in other words: revolution is impossible without a nation-wide crisis (affecting both the exploited and the exploiters).[26]

I shall now turn to the kind of revolutionary party which Lenin advocated and led, and which eventually used a national crisis to acquire political power.

The revolutionary party Lenin introduced into Marxism a party organisation that had been pioneered by rival revolutionary traditions. Lenin advocated and organised a centralised party of fulltime, active revolutionaries, dedicated to the achieving of governmental power. Earlier, in the nineteenth century, attempts had been made to construct such parties elsewhere in Europe, by Blanqui, Mazzini and others, and in Russia by Peter Tkachev and his supporters among the populists (peasant socialists). But Lenin's was both the first Marxist party of this kind and the first to succeed in its objectives.

Lenin's first and most complete statement of his theory of party organisation, _What is to be Done?_, was published in 1902. The main premiss of the theory was that, if left to themselves, the industrial workers (Marx's proletariat) acquired only a 'trade union consciousness'. Though the workers were an exploited and suffering class, Lenin maintained that they responded to their exploitation and suffering by engaging in reformist rather than revolutionary politics. For a Marxist-type revolution to occur, therefore, a revolutionary consciousness had to be taken to them by intellectuals who, initially, would be largely of bourgeois origin. Lenin noted that this development had characterised the formation of the modern European socialist movement, and that Marx and Engels were prominent examples of such intellectuals.

Though the founder of Russian Marxism, George Plekhanov, and some other Marxist critics objected that Lenin's assumption about the workers was non-Marxist and idealist, because it denied that working class consciousness was the product of economic and other material circumstances, Lenin had taken the idea from other Marxists. It had, in fact, been a commonplace among many of the leaders of the German and other European Social Democratic Parties. The novelty was the conclusion that Lenin drew from this view of the origin of socialist

---

26. Lenin, _Selected Works_, vol. 3,. p. 430.

ideas. Whereas Karl Kautsky and other German and European leaders had concluded that educational work had to be conducted both within and by a mass socialist party, Lenin's conclusion was that socialist revolution required not a mass, pluralist party in which all Marxist and socialist viewpoints were represented but small, centralised, hierarchical and disciplined parties, consisting of fulltime revolutionary intellectuals, organisers and agitators. Ideally, a majority of party members should come from and have strong ties with the working class, but this was not a necessary part of the project. In *What is to be Done?*, Lenin urged that a revolutionary party should be concerned with the grievances and revolutionary potential of the peasantry and middle classes, not just those of the urban workers. It was the related issue of the restrictions Lenin wished to put on party membership that brought about the 1903 split in the Russian Social Democratic Party, and the formation of its Bolshevik and Menshevik factions.

It has been argued by some writers on Lenin that he broke from his 1902 theory of the party when, in the Russian revolutions of 1905 and 1917, he recognised and enthused over the fact that, spontaneously, millions of urban workers and poor peasants acquired a revolutionary consciousness.[27] A difficulty for this interpretation of Lenin's views on the revolutionary party is that during and after the revolutionary years of 1905 and 1917, despite his discovery of spontaneity, Lenin continued to urge the need for a centralised and disciplined party, now for the purpose of directing the spontaneity of the masses. The only significant modifications to his 1902-3 view on the revolutionary party were his beliefs that (1) rank-and-file independence should be encouraged to combat conservative leaders, and that (2) the party should be opened to large numbers of people and not confined to a few. (Indeed, after 1918, the Communist Party had a membership of hundreds of thousands and then millions rather than the hundreds and thousands of most of the pre-governmental period.) But, within the party, effective power remained in the hands of a small revolutionary elite, the *old guard* as it came to be called after 1917. Lenin, in other words, modified the premisses of the theory when he recognised that, spontaneously, workers could acquire a revolutionary consciousness, but he was never prepared to substitute this spontaneity for the party or to make the party merely an institution for the expression of this spontaneity. His party remained an instrument for the directing of workers, peasants and others by a revolutionary elite.

Exploitation of grievances Whenever and wherever there were anti-government grievances, protests and militancy in the Russian Empire, between 1903 and 1917, Lenin and the Bolshevik party tried to exploit them. Lenin's party supported religious dissenters against the Tsarist church and state, despite the party's atheism. The party supported

27. The argument pervades Liebman's study. It is stated more concisely by Cliff, vol. 1, pp. 168-83 and 231-3, and R. Dunayevskaya, *Marxism and Freedom*, 4th edn (Pluto Pr., London, 1975) pp. 178-85.

liberal and constitutional struggles, though its objective was a revolutionary dictatorship. It supported the factory, neighbourhood, village and barracks-based system of soviet participatory democracy directed against the Tsar, in 1905, and against the provisional revolutionary governments of 1917, despite the intention to construct a centralised state dominated by the Bolshevik Party. Similarly, Lenin, more than any other leading pre-World War One Marxist, supported the slogan of national self-determination and the right of the nations of the Russian empire to establish independent states. This was despite the fact that his party was a unitary and not a federated one, recruiting from within the whole of the Russian empire, and having as its aim a unified socialist republic, co-operating with other socialist nations in a regional or international socialist community. A similar revolutionary opportunism characterised Lenin's attitude to the peasantry.

Both before and during the revolutionary years of 1905 and 1906, Lenin maintained that, as a result of the economic weakness and political spinelessness of its bourgeoisie, there were only two revolutionary classes in Russia: the industrial workers and the peasantry. From 1906 to 1917, his revolutionary strategy was directed toward the formation of a revolutionary government that would represent both classes and their respective political parties, but be subject to the hegemony of the workers and their political party - the Bolsheviks. In 1917, when he concluded that the majority of the leaders of the main peasant party, the Social Revolutionaries, were not prepared to break from the Russian bourgeoisie, Lenin and the Bolsheviks made a bid for peasant support in opposition to the Social Revolutionaries. In contrast to the Social Revolutionaries who procrastinated on the issue, the Bolsheviks encouraged village soviets to seize and distribute agricultural land. Marxist critics, including Kautsky and Rosa Luxemburg in Germany and Martov in Russia, charged Lenin with opportunism and irresponsibility. They argued that Lenin was abandoning the socialist objective of a socialised and co-operative agricultural system for a capitalist rural economy. They warned Lenin against the dangers of trying to combine a socialist industrial and urban development with a rural market based on the private ownership of land, smallscale farming and the profit motive. They further argued that this opportunist bid for peasant support would make the peasantry, and not Marx's industrial workers, the social agency for and principal support of revolution.[28] Lenin's attempt to reconcile a socialist urban with a capitalist rural development was

---

28. K. Kautsky, The Dictatorship of the Proletariat, 2nd Eng. edn (Univ. of Michigan Pr., Michigan, 1964); R. Luxemburg, The Russian Revolution and Leninism or Marxism (Univ. of Michigan Pr., Michigan, 1961); and, for Martov's criticisms, I. Getzler, Martov (Melbourne Univ. Pr., Melbourne, 1967), pp. 168-203; and Kolakowski, vol. 2, pp. 517-20. See also A. Ascher ed., The Mensheviks in the Russian Revolution (Thames and Hudson, London, 1976), especially pp. 89-136.

eventually to give way to the horrors of Stalin's forced collectivisation, at the end of the 1920s, and to the agricultural problems that have since plagued the USSR. But to understand how Lenin convinced himself and tried to justify what appeared to be flagrant examples of opportunism, on nationalism and the peasantry, with Marxist internationalism and socialism, it is necessary to examine his theory of imperialism.

Analysis of imperialism Whereas Marx had seen capitalism as the power that socialist revolution had to destroy, and the revolutionary agency as the urban working class of the advanced capitalist nations, Lenin, after researching and writing his study of *Imperialism* (1917), came to see imperialism as the main enemy, and the revolutionary forces as comprising not only the industrial workers of Europe and North America but the peasantry and the bourgeois nationalist movements of Asia, Africa and South America. After his 1917 analysis of imperialism, Lenin operated with a view of the world in which a small number of industrially developed capitalist nations exploited, by means of political empires and the activities of giant economic combines, the whole of the planet. According to Lenin, the profits from this worldwide exploitation sustained capitalism, partly by enabling it to grant economic concessions to an 'aristocracy of labour' within the imperialist nations. But precisely because capitalism had become a worldwide system of exploitation, it could be weakened not only by proletarian class struggle within the metropolitian nations but by peasant unrest, nationalist protest and colonial uprisings abroad. Partly because of the discontent that would be provoked by imperialist activity in the colonial and semi-colonial countries, and partly because of the inevitable conflicts among the exploiting nations and combines for greater shares of the spoils, capitalist imperialism would inevitably be accompanied by civil, national and international wars, for which World War One was the harbinger.

It was his analysis of imperialism which, more than anything else, gave Lenin his justification for seizing power in the name of Marxist socialism in a territory that, according to anti-Leninist Marxists, lacked the economic and other conditions for a socialist development. Similarly, it provided a rationale for Lenin's national and peasant policies. Lenin's argument, in the months and days preceding the October 1917 capture of power, was that as well as beginning a socialist development in Russia, a socialist capture of power in Russia would weaken imperialism (world capitalism) by removing Russia and her territories from its sphere of exploitation. To use a remark that was much quoted by Lenin, Leon Trotsky and other Bolshevik leaders and publicists, socialist revolution was possible in a backward part of the world, lacking the material means for socialism, because Russia and her territories were the *weakest link in the chain of world capitalism*. It was also possible because a socialist revolution in Russia was not primarily a national revolution but the first part of a worldwide revolution against imperialism.[29]

Lenin's approximately one-hundred-page pamphlet, Imperialism, is probably the most influential, twentieth-century revolutionary text. But in addition to its influence on both Communist and nationalist revolutionary movements throughout the world, it was also the means whereby Lenin transferred to international relations and diplomacy his military approach to politics. Relations between nation-states were seen as parts of a planetary, quasi-class struggle between imperialist and anti-imperialist forces. This is a view of the world that has, at least for for propaganda purposes, been adopted not only by nationalist and other revolutionaries engaged in trying to capture power but by the governments and diplomats of post-revolutionary nations. In the USSR, it encouraged the principle that the supreme rule for the guidance of Soviet foreign policy was maintaining the security and extending the influence of the first, purportedly, socialist, anti-imperialist nation. As Kolakowski has observed,

> The new state by definition represented the leading force in history; whether attacking or defending itself, it was acting in the name of progress. International law, arbitration, disarmament talks, the 'outlawing' of war - all these were deceptions as long as capitalism existed, and afterwards they would not be necessary, for wars were as impossible under socialism as they were inevitable under capitalism.[30]

Dictatorship of the proletariat   Lenin took from Marx the revolutionary aim of establishing a dictatorship of the proletariat, but he gave this objective an emphasis of his own. For Marx, the dictatorship of the proletariat was the governmental form for the transition from capitalism to socialism. Partly because he expected the transition to vary according to circumstances, Marx never tried to anticipate the legal and institutional features of such a dictatorship. The nearest he came to discussing the institutions of the transitional society was his stress, in the Civil War in France (1871), on the direct democracy of the Paris Commune. Marx emphasised the Commune's regular discussions, debates and elections, its merging of the legislative and executive branches of government, and its anti-bureaucratism. In the decades that followed Marx's death, most leaders of the Second International thought that the dictatorship of the proletariat simply meant rule or domination by the proletariat (industrial workers), and that just as the dictatorship or rule of the bourgeoisie was compatible

---

29. For a brief selection from Lenin's 1917 writings on why and how socialist revolution was necessary and possible in Russia, see the Lenin Anthology, Part 3, The Revolutionary Taking of Power. For a fuller selection, Selected Works, vol. 2.

30. Kolakowski, vol. 2, p. 496.

with liberal democratic and constitutional checks to governments and to the politically powerful so too would the dictatorship of the proletariat. The dictatorship of the proletariat was a term they were uneasy with and tended to avoid, but they upheld what they regarded as its intent: the extension of the power and authority of workers and citizens over governments and rulers by means of the extension of the power and authority of parliamentary institutions. The dictatorship of the proletariat meant for them, therefore, not the end of constitutionalism, law and representative democracy but their further development.

Lenin's view was different. For Lenin, the dictatorship of the proletariat meant not greater control by citizens and especially workers over governments and rulers but the removal from revolutionary movements and governments of all legal, political and other restraints. In 1906, in a pamphlet that praised the spontaneous violence of the masses, Lenin wrote that 'the scientific term "dictatorship" means nothing more nor less than authority untrammelled by any laws, absolutely unrestricted by any laws whatever, and based directly on force'.[31] After 1917, this understanding of dictatorship was restated again and again. In the Proletarian Revolution and the Renegade Kautsky (1918), for example, Lenin declared that 'the revolutionary dictatorship of the proletariat is rule won and maintained by the use of violence by the proletariat against the bourgeoisie, rule that is unrestricted by any laws'.[32] But not only did Lenin and the Bolsheviks interpret the term dictatorship differently from other Marxists, they also used the term proletariat in novel ways. In addition to frequently using it to include the peasantry, and interchangeably with the toilers, after October 1917 they used it as a euphemism and code-word for the one-party, centralised and terroristic state of a revolutionary elite.[33]

In his emphasis on the lawlessness of proletarian dictatorships, Lenin was saying something more than that a transition to socialism required radical changes to inherited constitutions and laws that had institutionalised a capitalist economy and society. His guiding principle, if it can be called that, was that it was not the function of a socialist revolution to establish new constitutions and new laws, that is to say new rules by which individuals and groups can voluntary co-operate in founding a new civilisation, but to liberate the revolutionary party and government from all restraint. The will of the governmental

---

31. Lenin, 'The Victory of the Cadets and the Tasks of the Workers' Party', Collected Works, vol. 10, p. 246.

32. Lenin, Selected Works, vol. 3, p. 82.

33. It is instructive to constrast Lenin's State and Revolution, Selected Works, vol. 2, written during the summer of 1917, which advocates and eulogises direct democracy of the Paris Commune type, with his defence of an oligarchical, terroristic state written less than eighteen months later, The Proletarian Revolution and the Renegade Kautsky, ibid., vol. 3. See also Lenin's 1919 lecture on 'The State', ibid.

elite was thus made the supreme law of the Russian Revolution. Not even industrial workers let alone anyone else could claim rights and liberties against the state, independently participate in the making of policy, or recall and replace rulers. There were no formal or informal institutions that provided the means for the urban workers, with or without the peasantry, to decide who should represent them, to check, or to engage in a genuine dialogue with the Communist Party which claimed to embody their ultimate interests. Lenin, himself, demonstrated an awareness of the implications of this view of dictatorship when, a few months before his final illness, he became concerned about the excessive arrogance and bureaucratism of both his party and state.[34]

Lenin's dictatorship of the proletariat left the Russian workers, in common with other classes, without rights, liberties or formal checks on whoever governed in their name. In practice, Lenin relied on the good will of the leaders of the Communist Party. The result was that whoever possessed and exercised party and governmental power in a post-revolutionary Leninist state could pass off whatever they did, no matter how brutal, inefficient, corrupt, non-Marxist or anti-socialist, as an expression of Marxist theory and the latest model of socialist development.

Lenin's military approach to politics could and did generate effective strategies and tactics for a successful capture of power. What it failed to do, and what it could not do, was to provide political and legal standards for, and checks and limits to, revolutionary and post-revolutionary rulers. Lenin's thought and practice is limited to revolution in the insurrectionary sense of the term. It is irrelevant if not opposed to Marx's conception of revolution as the self education of the industrial workers, and the creation of a new and superior civilisation. Lenin's political thought and practice also make nonsense of Rosa Luxemburg's much-quoted remark that the choice before twentieth-century men and women is between socialism or barbarism. Lenin's revolutionary politics combined socialism and barbarism.

REVOLUTION SINCE LENIN

Just as there are many differences between the Marxism of Marx and that of subsequent Marxists, both Leninists and anti-Leninists, so there are significant differences between the Leninism of Lenin and that of subsequent Leninists. The six sets of Leninist ideas which have been discussed have been adopted and applied by subsequent Leninists. But subsequent Leninist leaders have given these ideas emphases of their own and added to them ideas distinctive to themselves. Stalin, Trotsky, Bukharin, Khruschev, Tito, Mao Zedong, Che Guevara and Castro are among the many prominent Leninists who have developed

---

34. See Lenin Anthology, Part 7, The Fate of the Revolution; and M. Lewin, Lenin's Last Struggle (Faber, London, 1969).

unique and rival forms of Leninist theory and practice. In the Third World, the many varieties of Leninism have attracted communist and nationalist intellectuals and politicians convinced that they know the social development and organisation that is best for their peoples. Unlike the original Marxism of Marx, with its belief that socialism arose out of and was the natural heir of an advanced industrial-capitalist and liberal-democratic civilisation, Leninist Marxism can be used to mobilise populations and later to legitimise powerful state apparatuses in semi-industrialised nations lacking a constitutional tradition.

But in the West, even in nations with large Communist Parties, Marxist revolution, either in Marx's original proletarian form or Lenin's vanguard-party form, appears to be remote. Yet, since the 1930s, there has never been a time when Marxist and Leninist ideas have attracted so much sympathy among journalists, broadcasters, academics and other intellectuals. In recent years, what has been called the Marx renaissance and, more cynically, the Marx industry has flourished, and it has been accompanied by a considerable interest in the work of Western Marxists and neo-Marxists who have tried to develop twentieth-century forms of classical and/or Leninist Marxism applicable to Western nations. Examples include Rosa Luxemburg, George Lukács, Antonio Gramsci, and the Frankfurt School.[35] On the other hand, in contrast to the early 1920s and late 1930s, when there was also considerable intellectual support for Marxist ideas and politics, there has never been so much disagreement about the precise character of Marxist revolution or what exactly a Marxist ought to do. The political problem for Marxists and their sympathisers is that there is little in Western nations that resembles a Marxist revolutionary agency, either in the sense of Marx's proletariat or Lenin's revolutionary-elitist party. Even the large Communist Parties of France, Italy and elsewhere are more the relics of past hopes and struggles than an expression of present aspirations.

Though the revolutionary projects of Marx and the Second International were the products of Western society, and Lenin's the product of Russia's very different history and conditions, paradoxically, if a Marxist project is to have a future in the West, it is more likely to be Lenin's. This is because, whereas there is no social class or social coalition which corresponds to Marx's original proletariat - a universal, majority, economically productive, and cohesive class - if there is a further deterioration of Western economic and cultural life, and if political problems become even more difficult to solve, then there will be fertile grounds for Lenin's elitist, power-centred and opportunist form of revolutionary politics. But it will not only be Marxists,

---

35. For attempts to discover an independent post-Lenin, Western Marxist tradition, see D. Howard and K. Klare (eds.), The Unknown Dimension: European Marxism Since Lenin (Basic Books, New York, 1972); and D. Howard, The Marxian Legacy (Macmillan, London, 1977).

Leninists or opportunists with Lenin's vision, breadth of culture and genuine concern about the suffering of human beings who will try to till these fields. Lenin's revolutionary party and strategy, and the theory which provided a rationale for them, are, to use his military terminology, powerful weapons. But, as subsequent revolutions have shown, suitably modified, they are weapons which can be used by people who are very different from Lenin and who possess different purposes. Though Lenin would have disowned them, in their various ways, Stalin, Mussolini, Hitler and the post-World War Two nationalist demagogues of the third world are all Lenin's pupils.

Chapter 7

MODERNISATION AND REVOLUTION

Bill Brugger and Kate Hannan

This chapter will explore the connection drawn by various writers between modernisation and revolution. The chapter is a considerably condensed version of a previous work which discusses four ways of looking at modernisation and three senses of revolution.[1] The first approach to modernisation, described as ethnocentric, takes a particular society to epitomise modernity and what are felt to be the necessary features of modernisation are simply generalisations from that particularity. This approach is often combined with the second - the technological determinist - in which technology and industrialism are portrayed as having a dynamic of their own; the developed capitalist (or socialist) states of today are seen as the underdeveloped world's tomorrow. A third approach, described as multilinear, posits a number of different routes to modernity and sometimes a number of different modernities. Finally a fourth approach sees the whole of human history as exhibiting the working out of a universal principle such as reason or freedom. Because the key to history is not to be found in the material world, we describe this as idealist; yet it does not assert that human history is merely an amalgam of what goes on in individual human minds (i.e. subjective); rather human minds participate in history inasmuch as they reflect a universal world spirit - such a position claims to be objective.

Clearly the above positions are not mutually exclusive. In recent years the first two approaches are usually combined and represent the developmental orthodoxy of both the United States and the Soviet Union. The third approach may be cast in a technological determinist vein or combined with the fourth. The final view, though less popular than the others, was revived in the 1970s as a response to disillusion with the grandiose claims of science to solve all the world's problems; yet obviously it must be combined with the important role of science and technology in shaping our lives.

The three senses of revolution used here are firstly cultural - a fundamental change in the value system which informs a society. Secondly, revolution might be seen in terms of a change in the

---

1. B. Brugger and K. Hannan, Modernisation and Revolution (Croom Helm, London, 1983).

dominant mode of production and hence the nature of the ruling class - a definition in terms of political economy. Thirdly, revolution might be seen in terms of the overthrow of a regime by collective violence; this narrowly political definition, by focusing on the overthrow of a regime, would exclude palace coups which overthrow particular governments but is not so broad as to encompass the overthrow of a political order.

Ethnocentric Views

Social thought in all societies at most times has been ethnocentric. The world has been divided into the 'civilised' and the 'barbarians' and it was never too clear which would triumph.

The Roman Empire did quite well for a time by granting Roman citizenship to 'barbarians' and by convincing local rulers (by persuasion and conquest) that economic prosperity depended upon the institutions which upheld Roman law. The word 'progress' existed, but in its verbal form it was what armies did and as an abstract noun applied to history it was no more than the march of events. Yet there was a sense in which marginal societies were seen to be developing towards the *pax Romana*. There was no notion of social revolution (even though the origin of that word also was Latin) and even the Greek view, of a revolving sequence of forms of government (monarchy/tyranny, aristocracy/oligarchy, polyarchy/democracy) had paled before a system which seemed there to stay. Revolution, in Aristotle's sense of *stasis*, there indeed was, and the central government in Rome was overthrown several times - but after the advent of Augustus the regime did not change for several hundred years.

If there was an implicit notion of development in ancient Rome, it had no place for revolution - except perhaps the one which had brought the Augustan state into being. At the other end of the world, the Han Empire was legitimised by a similar set of beliefs. But the collapse of the Roman Empire and the Han dynasty in China revived in the West the notion of revolution as the Greek cycle of birth, death and rebirth and in China the similar notion of a dynastic cycle. The 'dark ages' in the West were defined as such in terms not only of Christian but also of Roman values and 'barbarian' empires sought legitimacy in Roman symbols. Similarly, in China, the repeated 'barbarian' conquests of the next millenium-and-a-half resulted in the establishment of agrarian bureaucracies modelled on those of the Han dynasty and legitimised by Han Confucian values. In both east and west there was much cultural diffusion. Europe absorbed the valuable products of Islamic culture (e.g. in mathematics) whilst still despising the 'barbarian'. So also did China which added the riches of Buddhist and other cultures whilst maintaining cultural chauvinism. Both civilisations remained, in their own eyes, the centre of the world. In both cultures there was a significant development of science and technology (with China doing much better than Europe at least until the eighteenth century) yet a linear view of history necessary to a theory of modernisation remained absent. The dominant view was cyclical and the only alternative was millenarian revolt.

Yet, in the West, the seventeenth century saw the beginnings of a fundamental change. The discovery (or invention) of the 'individual' as a political actor needed a new theory of political obligation. For Aristotle, who in Hobbes's day was still required reading in most western universities, the fundamental political unit was the politically-determined citizen not the pre-social individual with rights independent of society. For the early Christians what was pre-social was the human soul. As Howell's contribution to this volume has noted, this belief was reconciled with the Aristotelian view by St. Thomas Aquinas and it was not until the seventeenth century that the state came to be interpreted as a mechanism to preserve pre-social human rights, namely life, liberty and estate. There is much argument concerning what brought about this change. But all agree it was the product of revolution. For crude Marxists it was essentially the product of the early bourgeois revolution which demanded a theory which would legitimise the pursuit of individual wealth whilst discouraging expenditure. The 'Protestant ethic', therefore, was a way of maximising investment so necessary to primitive capitalist accumulation. At the same time individualism broke down affective ties (kinship etc.), making for a transferable labour force. Others, however, in the Weberian tradition, argue that two revolutions proceeded simultaneously. The first of these, the Puritan revolution (what we have referred to earlier as a cultural revolution), antedated the bourgeois revolution but provided a behavioural disposition which was able to serve the ends of capital accumulation. In other words the bourgeois (political-economic) revolution did not cause the cultural revolution, nor was the reverse the case; what occurred was a happy coincidence.

In both of these views there is an element of ethnocentricity. There are many ways whereby savings may become investment, and a market orientation may be fostered other than by developing a theory of individual human rights. One has only to look at the history of Song China (960-1280), or for that matter Chinese communities in Asia in more recent times, to document that. It is true that capitalism (in the Marxian sense of a mode of production which had at its core a class which had nothing to sell but its labour power and a ruling class which lived off surplus value) did not develop in China until after the impact of the West. But then neither did it develop in Europe until at least a century after the doctrine of individual human rights was put forward. One suspects that the crude Marxist view results from a projection backwards from the Britain described in Marx's Capital. Because Britain was the most advanced capitalist country in the mid-nineteenth century, then surely it had been further on the way towards developing capitalist ideas in the seventeenth century. Such might be the case but it is not necessarily so, and the answer can only be reached by an exercise in comparative economic history. As for the Weberian view, it has to be demonstrated why the orientation towards investment was more likely to follow from the Puritan cultural revolution than any other change in ideas in the seventeenth century. Indeed the Catholic ideas promoted in the cities of the Italian Renaissance were equally conducive to productive investment.

By casting 'modern' society in terms of that capitalist behaviour which has pertained in England and Northern Europe since the Industrial Revolution the views of the seventeenth century discussed above may be seen as ethnocentric. They focus on revolution in two of the senses outlined in our Introduction. What may be said about the seventeenth century in terms of the third narrowly political definition to which we have referred? The English revolution of mid-century was certainly quite violent and did result in a lasting change of regime; this is quite clear when one considers that the attempts to restore the status quo ante in the reigns of Charles II and James II were to result in the relatively non-violent 'revolution' of 1688. That revolution was celebrated as the successful reconciliation of the essence of natural law based on pre-social human rights with a social contract establishing a sovereign to which all owed obedience. At the core of the system was a process of representation and the institutions of limited government. It was as if 1688 was the summit of human history, and accordingly generations of Whig historians rewrote history to show why the historical developments of preceding centuries all pointed to the Whig achievement. At first the 'glorious revolution' of 1688 was seen as largely an English affair but, within a century, it was seen as having universal application. Despite his comments on the specificity of national traditions, this was the model which the French theorist Montesquieu took as epitomising a 'balance of powers' (legislative, executive and judiciary) which might be emulated by other countries.[2] Montesquieu was engaged in what political scientists of the 1950s and 1960s called the study of 'political development'.

Such an exercise is perhaps the most ethnocentric of all. The procedure is to establish a model of what a developed polity looks like and then to show how other polities diverge from it and what they need to do to 'catch up'. In the 1950s the models which were created looked suspiciously like the United States though some of the more unsavoury elements of American political life might be dispensed with and replaced by features of an idealised Britain. But it was not only the Americans and Britons who engaged in this ethnocentric exercise. Soviet writers also were at pains to show their satellites and clients a glimpse of their political future.

Diffusion and Modernity in the Less Developed World

Among the practitioners of the ethnocentric approach there is usually an affirmation and idealisation of the political revolution which brought the 'advanced' system into being, be it the 'glorious revolution' of 1688 or the American revolution after 1776. In the Soviet Union the idealisation of the Bolshevik revolution is usually joined to the belief that other countries will have to go through a similar political

2. C. Montesquieu, The Spirit of the Laws, revised edn (2 vols., Hafner, New York, 1965).

upheaval. But woe betide any which attempts to do so without Soviet guidance! The relatively independent revolutions in China and Yugoslavia have not fared well amongst Soviet commentators. At least, that is how the situation used to be. Since the 1960s new elements have entered Soviet thought about the process of development and the notion of a 'non-capitalist path to development' prescribed for India might suggest that theoretically Soviet ideologists are moving closer to a multilinear view of development.

In the west on the other hand, despite an idealisation of the political revolution which brought the 'advanced' state into existence there is usually a deprecation of revolution today. This may be because theorists believe that the 'wretched of the earth' are too poor not to let the 'social question' (economic demands) distort the political act of creating a 'new beginning'.[3] Or theorists believe that social change might be managed in such a way as to avoid violence. This latter position was clearly that of W.W. Rostow in his classic work The Stages of Economic Growth.[4] Rostow saw less developed countries as participating in a kind of air-race in which they moved to a 'take-off' position, after which self-sustained growth became possible. Such a view suggested that investment by advanced capitalist countries in the less developed world helped provide the conditions for 'take-off', and that revolution directed against foreign domination was economically irrational. This work, subtitled A Non-Communist Manifesto, was immensely influential amongst those who considered that revolution in poor countries was the work of malevolent communists. Such communists, it was believed, exported revolution to the underdeveloped countries and seduced local people with Lenin's view that it was only by sending capital to the colonies that developed capitalist countries maintained their high standard of living. Both the air-race model and the idea that revolution is exported seem dubious. Countries do not just take off after the appropriate infusion of technology and then remain flying. Some take-off and then crash (e.g. Poland). Others never reach the end of the runway and are denied entry into a crowded sky, whilst a few provide models of growth for economists committed to 'the magic of the market' (e.g. Taiwan and South Korea). Doubtless revolutions in some less developed countries (in the narrowly political sense) were provoked by foreign intervention (e.g. in the three countries of Indo China) but the receptiveness of those countries to revolutionary ideas depended to a large extent on the domestic situation and the prospect of a revolution in the wider political economy sense. In any case, it is extremely difficult to argue that foreign influence was at all significant amongst the revolutionaries who overthrew the Shah of Iran.

The above picture is one of diffusion. Technology is diffused

---

3. For an explanation of this way of thinking see H. Arendt, On Revolution (Penguin, Harmondsworth, 1973).

4. W.W. Rostow, The Stages of Economic Growth: A Non-Communist Manifesto (Cambridge University Press, Cambridge, 1962).

from the west to facilitate the conditions for take-off. But diffusion of technology from the west is accompanied by the spread of 'modern' western cultural values which might be resisted in less developed countries. It is possible, therefore, that revolutions in the narrowly political sense of the word might actually be the product, not of external subversion, but of that very resistence. Attempts to explain such a phenomenon often draw upon a structural-functionalist framework of analysis. The structural-functionalist framework starts from the assumption that human beings rationally pursue their common human needs within structures dictated by the environment. Those social structures develop to perform a number of functions necessary to reproduce the social system. They do this by fostering 'orientations to action' on the part of individuals. When the environment changes due to the diffusion of goods, values, etc., from more advanced societies, the necessary social functions may only be fulfilled by the attainment of a new equilibrium between social institutions and orientations to action. Revolution, therefore, will occur when the gradual attainment of the new equilibrium is frustrated. This is the position taken by Chalmers Johnson the author of two very influential books in the 1960s.[5] Johnson's focus is on what he terms a 'disequilibrated social system'. This is one of which has experienced 'multiple disfunctions'. These include a failure in socialisation (the way values are transmitted), disagreement over basic social goals and a lack of synchronisation of social roles. Such multiple disfunctions may be internally generated due to environmental change or the rise of new ideologies or externally generated due to war, imports of technology etc. The key variable, however, is not the number and scope of the multiple disfunctions but the response of the governing elite. A revolution will occur when a governing elite fails to remedy the situation and loses legitimacy. It may try to compensate for this legitimation crisis by coercive measures but it might also lose control over the instruments of coercion. In short, revolutions are cases of failed systems management.

Stripped to its bare essentials, Johnson's account is not a theory of revolution at all. It is an elaborate, and at times highly sophisticated, taxonomy of factors one needs to take into account if one is to explain revolution, assuming of course that the basic axiom about social functions holds. Such a taxonomy could only become a theory if one was told what determines the successful or unsuccessful response of the governing elite. Alas, all we have is a blueprint for the social machine and the hope that the engineer will be intelligent enough to know how to operate it. Presumably the modernisation which engenders multiple disfunctions also improves the ability of an elite to overcome them. The trouble arises when one considers that the engineer is, in fact, part of the blueprint. Further problems occur once

5. C. Johnson, Revolution and the Social System (Stanford University Press, Stanford, Calif., 1964) and C. Johnson, Revolutionary Change (University of London Press, London, 1968).

one considers that functions have meaning only in terms of stability. Revolutions are seen as aberrant cases of mal-adaptation to the inexorable dictates of diffused modernisation; or to put it another way revolutions in the narrowly political sense of the word are merely the consequences of badly-managed cultural evolution.

Here cultural evolution is defined ethnocentrically. Thus Lucien Pye, talking about the pace and scope of social change in South East Asia, argued that it was dependent upon the extent to which colonial rulers established:

1. rationalised administrative practices.
2. fixed and standardised taxation in place of tribute in kind, corvee labour etc.
3. secular and codified legal systems.
4. liberal economic policies.
5. a westernised education system.[6]

The 'new images of authority' which derived from the above were clearly of western origin as indeed was the very conception of rationality itself. What was usually meant by 'rational' in such discussions was the choice of means appropriate to ends which were self-evident. It seemed obvious that promotion of persons on the basis of technical achievement was better than on the basis of family relationships[7]. What was ignored was the fact that economic development was often better served by ties of kinship or quasi-kinship. This had surely been the case among Jewish, Lebanese or overseas Chinese communities. Indeed, part of Japan's economic 'miracle' was achieved within networks of quasi-kinship. What was ignored in the whole debate was a very different kind of rationality oriented towards values which might derive from an ideal society or perhaps from the stock of cultural symbols rooted in particular local traditions. It was by no means self-evident, therefore, that religious ties between local elites and the masses would disappear as industrialisation proceeded. They might actually be reinforced as people became oriented towards different aspects of traditional cultural symbols. This is what happened in the Protestant Reformation in the west (God, the author of a rational and well ordered universe, was transformed into God the unknowable who might only be approached by faith). Why shouldn't the same kind of process occur in countries like Iran? It is quite ethnocentric to argue that the recent religious revivals are simply throwbacks to a tradition which ought to have been discarded. Religion is not always the opium of the people. It may be a powerful stimulant.

Failure to predict the recent Islamic revolutions, it seems, stems

---

6. L. Pye, 'The Politics of Southeast Asia', in G. Almond, and J. Coleman (eds.), The Politics of the Developing Areas (Princeton University Press, Princeton, N.J., 1960), p. 84.

7. Pye, pp. 82-152.

from a fundamental flaw in the diffusionists' approach. They all acknowledge that change and adaptation proceeds unevenly. But the problem is not just one of a lack of fit between social structure and 'orientations to action'. Fundamental dislocation may occur within both social structure and 'orientations to action'. Thus, as Pye noted, one of the consequences of westernisation was the drive for administrative centralisation. The growth of cities in many less developed countries was not the result of industrialisation, as in the west, but of a change in administrative activities. The growth of urbanisation at a rate much faster than industrialisation was to generate social tensions which frustrated another goal of westernisation - the efficient deployment of resources to achieve a rise across the board in the standard of living. The adoption of one form of structural change from the west, therefore, militated against another; and it was not much use castigating local leaders for being 'unsystematic'. Should one be surprised, therefore, at the recent urban revolution in Iran, which combines a rational rejection of the source of frustration (the domination of a parasitic elite) with what westerners claim to be an irrational affirmation of Islamic fundamentalism? Surely only an armchair academic could complain that Islamic revolutionaries should be more discriminating in what was being rejected.

The fact that different aspects of the western notion of modernisation may come into contradiction with each other makes it extremely difficult for the diffusionist to evaluate the degree of modernisation achieved. A country might rank quite high on one western scale of modernisation (e.g. 'economic development') and quite low on another ('political development'). Such a country, we might suggest, is South Korea. Within each scale of development, moreover, there are insuperable contradictions. Is an oil-rich state, with amongst the highest per capita GNPs in the world but with minimal social services, developed economically? And when it comes to political development, the problems seem even greater. Some two decades ago Gabriel Almond, a pioneer in that field, attempted to develop a list of functional categories within which to chart the progression of a polity from tradition to modernity. These included political socialisation (making people aware of politics), interest articulation (the ability to voice particular interests), interest aggregation (the formation of parties, pressure groups etc.) and political communication. It should be possible, he believed, to chalk up progress in each of these 'input' functions and then look at the 'output' functions of rule-making (legislative), rule-application (executive) and rule-adjudication (judicial). A developed polity would be one which displayed a high degree of structural differentiation within a bureaucracy which processed the input functions and serviced the output functions.[8] Almond's pioneering work spawned many books which used these functional categories. But the problem remained! If one accepts the ethnocentric view how does one explain how a low score on one

8. Almond and Coleman (eds.), pp. 3-64.

functional category might be combined with a high score on another, especially when both scores might be generated by the same process? The Indian revolution, for example (if that is what it was), produced a polity which performed quite well in terms of input functions but displayed a completely contradictory performance in terms of output. It now possesses a rather inept legislature which periodically passes acts that it does not expect to see enforced, a well differentiated bureaucracy, and an executive which from time to time overwhelms both legislature and judiciary and usually gets away with it.

Cultural Diffusion and Revolution

Nowadays little is said about the functional categories pioneered by Almond. What is left of the structural-functionalist paradigm is the argument concerning adaptation to what is diffused from the west, though now much greater sophistication may be found in explicit discussions of revolution. Take for example the work of Samuel Huntington who argues that revolution as a form of collective violence is one product of the diffusion of modern ideas into a situation where the regime is incapable of developing institutions adequate to contain the strain.[9] Where institutionalisation does occur and collective violence is avoided we have 'development'; but where modernisation fails to be complemented by institutionalisation, we have 'political decay'. For Huntington:

> The political essence of revolution is the rapid expansion of political consciousness and the rapid mobilization of new groups into politics at a speed which makes it impossible for existing political institutions to assimilate them.[10]

Thus, revolution as a form of collective violence is not a product of 'traditional' society, nor of 'modern' industrialised society, but of societies in the early stages of modernisation. Such a view, it is said, contradicts the picture painted by Marx who supposedly saw revolution as the product of mature capitalism.[11] Modern revolutions in the 'east', moreover, take a form very different from those which occurred in the west during its early modernisation. In the 'east', new groups mobilise outside the old order and then move in to overthrow it; whereas in the west the old institutions had to disintegrate before new groups mobilised and entered politics.

Whatever the level of sophistication reached, it seems impossible

---

9. S. Huntington, Political Order in Changing Societies (Yale University Press, New Haven, 1968). Also see S. Huntington, 'Political Development and Political Decay, World Politics, vol. 17, no. 3 (April 1965), pp.386-430

10. Huntington, Political Order..., p. 266.

11. R. Tucker, The Marxian Revolutionary Idea (Norton, New York, 1969), pp. 136-7.

to escape from tautological thinking. Huntington's tautology is quite apparent; revolution and modernisation are defined in terms of each other. Thus, despite his sophisticated discussion of the characteristics of political order in different types of society, all Huntington is saying is that revolutions occur except when existing institutions prevent them. The very word 'institutionalisation' is defined in terms of the absence of revolution. Secondly we are never quite sure which elements of modernisation are decisive in causing instability. Could it be rapid urbanisation which we advanced earlier as a factor in the Iranian revolution? Huntington, it appears, does not seem to think so since the lumpenproletariat which lives on the fringes of modernising cities is hardly ever a force for radical change.[12] Could it be disorientation caused by unfamiliarity with industrial routine? Surely that also cannot be the case; at most such a condition causes machine breaking and other Luddite activities which hardly ever constitute a challenge to the political regime. Could it be the poor working conditions which normally pertain in the early stages of industrialisation? Again, such an explanation is unlikely since major upheavals usually occur after the promulgation of some factory legislation. We are left, therefore, with no explanation as to why political mobilisation becomes effective other than the point, made long ago by Marx, that modern industry collects people together in numbers larger than ever before.

As for the claim that Marx has been refuted by the observation that revolutions occur in the early stages of modernisation, one must underline that Marx was talking about proletarian revolution in the political-economy sense. Under most circumstances, Marx gave reasons as to why this would be violent, but did allow for the possibility of non-violent revolution in Britain, Holland and America. Such could be achieved because of the cultural traditions of those countries and the weakness of the military-bureaucratic apparatus within them.[13] In any case, no revolution in the contemporary less developed world might be described as proletarian in the sense in which Marx understood the term. Neither was the Russian revolution of 1917 nor the Chinese revolution, which culminated in 1949, proletarian. As Lenin saw it, socialism or even state control over a capitalist economy was something to be established in the future[14] and, as a subsequent chapter will make plain, the Chinese revolution was predicated on the leadership of a 'four class bloc' (workers, peasants, national bourgeoisie and petty bourgeosie). Huntington's mistake is to conflate Marx's broader (political economy) conception of revolution with the narrow

12. Huntington, p. 278.

13. K. Marx, (1872) in H. Gerth (ed.), The First International: Minutes of the Hague Congress of 1972 with Related Documents (University of Wisconsin Press, Madison, 1958), p. 236.

14. V. Lenin, '"Left Wing" Childishness and the Petty Bourgeois Mentality', May 1918, in Lenin, V., Selected Works, 3 vol. edn. (Progress Publishers, Moscow, 1976), vol. 2, pp. 631-7.

political definition in terms of the overthrow of a regime by collective violence. Secondly he ignores Marx's argument that the tradition of particular countries will affect the possibility of violence.

Finally, Huntington's conclusion about the 'eastern' and 'western' types of revolution is highly questionable. The 1911 revolution in China, for example, conforms more to the western pattern whereas that which culminated in 1949 is a clear case of the eastern type. Using Huntington's formula one could also conclude that the American revolution after 1776 was of the eastern type. A Marxist might, of course, disqualify the Chinese revolution of 1911 and the American revolution of 1776 on the ground that in neither did the mode of production change. Huntington, however, is not a Marxist, and since he defines revolution in the narrow (collective violence) and cultural senses of the word, he is obliged to take such revolutions seriously.

Cultural Diffusion and Social Psychology

What is missing from Huntington's analysis is an adequate theory linking the political, the economic and the psychological. Huntington attempts to establish a linkage by starting from the political dimension. W.W. Rostow, on the other hand, starts from the economic dimension. In the first case the result is tautological thinking, and in the second a rather crude economic determinism. A third, and at first sight more attractive, approach is to start from considerations of social psychology.

The late development of social psychological approaches to revolution often blinds us to the fact, noted in Chapter Two of this volume, that attempts have been made in this direction since the time of Aristotle. In modern times, long before people began to think in terms of revolution in the underdeveloped world, Alexis de Tocqueville offered us an interesting psychological dimension in his analysis of the great French Revolution.[15] As Howell has suggested in Chapter Three, in Tocqueville's eyes revolution in the political economy sense was well under way before the events of 1789-95. Under the royal absolutism of the Bourbon regime there had already taken place a massive transfer of economic and political power to the bourgeoisie. What remained was aristocratic privilege without much power. The general rise in affluence in the eighteenth century consequent upon the transfer of power to the bourgeoisie, moreover, produced a rising horizon of expectations which allowed those who already had considerable power to see that they could easily destroy aristocratic privilege. To this Tocqueville added the general psychological postulate that greater resentment is felt by those who have some power and little privilege than by those who have no power and no privilege.

The psychological consequences of a lack of fit between power and privilege, we would suggest, are quite apparent in countries in the

---

15. A. de Tocqueville, The Ancien Regime and the French Revolution (1856) (Collins/Fontana, 1966).

early stages of westernisation. In Latin America, the phenomenon of 'the middle-class military coup' occurs when a powerful westernised section of an army comes to resent the government of traditional caudillos (military leaders) based on the privileges of land ownership. Such also has been the pattern of the Egyptian and other Middle Eastern revolutions. The need, however, is to specify the link between social position and psychological orientation.

In recent years attempts to achieve this have taken the form of a number of theses about 'relative deprivation'. An early attempt was that of James Davies the originator of the 'J curve' thesis.[16] This holds that a growing awareness of the benefits of economic growth produces a 'rising horizon of expectations'. This horizon of expectations continues to rise even when an economic slump occurs. The result is a gap between expectations and achievement which causes resentment. When that resentment is directed at a regime, revolution is likely.

Though one may argue that the French and Russian revolutions might be seen in terms of frustrated expectations, one cannot fail to observe that the 'J curve' phenomenon was evident in most countries in the world during the great depression of the 1930s: yet few revolutions in fact occurred. Davies' attempt to explain this situation casts doubt on his whole approach. A revolution did not occur during the 1930s in the United States, he tells us, because of 'the vigor with which the national government attacked the depression in 1933'.[17] Does that mean that a revolutionary response to the 'J curve' occurs only when governments are too weak to take any remedial action and are held responsible by people for their economic plight? If such is the case, the 'J curve' thesis is no more than one factor amongst many which might explain why people and groups become disaffected with governments. There is also a problem of evidence. Many cases might be cited of societies in the 1930s which avoided revolutions even though significant portions of the population blamed their weak governments for failure to respond to the depression. A similar position, we would contend, pertains today in both the advanced industrial and less developed worlds. In the latter, the overwhelming majority of countries are currently in a 'J curve' situation; yet world revolution seems remote.

Perhaps one of the most telling arguments against Davies' formulation of the 'J curve' thesis, when applied to the less developed world, is provided by Wertheim. He argues that in developing countries the horizon of expectations tends to be class-specific. Though the horizon of expectations of bourgeois groups might rise with the beginnings of economic growth, peasant expectations can remain static or decline. In any case, the question of expectations is much more complex than the 'J curve' thesis allows. In Java, for example, the depression of the

---

16. J. Davies, 'Towards a Theory of Revolution', American Sociological Review, vol. 27, no. 1 (February 1962), pp. 5-19.
17. Ibid., p. 16.

1930s caused a decline in the expectations of the Indonesian bourgeoisie, which was only reversed when the Japanese occupying power replaced Dutch officials by Indonesians, to whom it offered a kind of independence. It was the return of the Dutch which brought about the decline in achievement and the 'J curve' phenomenon. Meanwhile the expectations of peasants, declining during the depression, continued to decline throughout the whole period of Japanese occupation.[18] No theory which attempts to reconcile expectations with achievement is much use unless one takes into account class division. In other words one has to link social psychological explanations with arguments about social structure.

We can think of no single study where that link between a sociological and a social psychological approach has been adequately forged. In fact the tendency has been for the two approaches to diverge; though, to be sure, both have become much more sophisticated since Davies' first article and the work of Chalmers Johnson. In the field of social psychology the Feierabends and Nesvold have created a number of interesting variations of the 'J curve' thesis,[19] Ted Gurr has enumerated a typology of relative deprivation which specifies two basic categories of relative deprivation additional to Davies' initial model.[20] The first of these describes the potential for collective violence stemming from the gap between a rising horizon of expectations and a capability (that which can be achieved) which remains static (aspirational deprivation). Such a situation is extremely common in newly independent countries which expect far too much from the independent regime. The second form of deprivation (decremental) arises when people become increasingly unable to satisfy stable expectations. In the less developed world, it is felt typically by a 'traditional' elite displaced by a colonial authority. An additional pattern, suggested by Hagopian, occurs when rising expectations outstrip rising capabilities (accelerated deprivation). Such a situation may have held at the time of the Meiji restoration (1869) in Japan. Indeed, anyone with imagination may create further models specifying the relationship between expectations and capabilities. Suppose, for example, that declining capabilities outstrip declining expectations. Could this have been the motivation of the pro-Vietnamese groups in Pol Pot's Kampuchea? To all this one might add the methodology pioneered by the Feierabends which poses hypotheses about the rate at

---

18. Wertheim, Evolution and Revolution: The Rising Waves of Emancipation (Penguin, Harmondsworth, 1974), pp. 191-7. When referring to the bourgeoisie, Wertheim speaks of a 'reversed J curve'.

19. I. Feierabend, R. Feierabend and B. Nesvold, 'Social Change and Political Violence: Cross-National Patterns' in H. Graham, and T. Gurr (eds.), The History of Violence in America: Historical and Comparative Perspectives (Praeger, New York, 1969), pp. 637-44.

20. T. Gurr, Why Men Rebel (Princeton University Press, 1970), pp.46-56. Gurr refers to Davies' pattern as 'progressive deprivation'.

which the relative deprivation gap appears and the degree of fluctuations of both capabilities and expectations. But however complicated the picture becomes, the methodological problems of forging an adequate link between the sociological and the social psychological approach are immense.

First, how is it possible for the social psychologist to explain the conditions under which the potential for collective violence becomes translated into revolution rather than anything else? Second, it seems useless to talk about relative deprivation unless one specifies just what one means by capabilities and expectations. Various schemes have been put forward. The crudest simply measures actual income, makes guesses about potential income and asks a sample about expected income. At a more sophisticated level, variations of Abraham Maslow's hierarchy of needs are employed. Maslow listed five categories of universal needs with the following priority, (1) physiological needs, (2) safety needs, (3) affection needs, (4) esteem needs and (5) self-actualisation or self-development needs.[21] Each of these need areas become activated only when the prior needs are met; but once a higher need becomes activated it is not necessarily extinguished when the individual suffers deprivation of a prior need. It is according to Maslow's scheme that Davies argues that the satisfaction of physical needs may lead to a feeling of deprivation with regard to other needs and so on.[22] A revolution, therefore, may depend upon frustration at any of the above levels. Such a theory sounds quite plausible until one considers how one could ascertain at the social level when needs 3, 4 or 5 are contributing to violence. Alexis de Tocqueville tied together the lack of bourgeois esteem and the French Revolution, and Frantz Fanon saw violence as a precursor of self-development. But how one could find evidence for such assertions is a problem. The situation is even further complicated when one considers what causes expectations to rise. Perhaps a fruitful line of enquiry is to examine the various expectations of modernising groups (bureaucrats, merchants) who are apparently in a position to appropriate the wealth or power of traditional elites or classes. But if that is our scenario, we have no need for social psychology. Perhaps a simple explanation of group conflict based on rational calculation might suffice.

---

21. A. Maslow, Motivation and Personality, 2nd ed. (Harper and Row, New York, 1954). pp. 35-47.
To the five needs listed Maslow then added 'the desire to know and understand' and 'aesthetic needs'; see pp. 48-58.

22. J. Davies, 'The J-curve of Rising and Declining Satisfaction as a cause of some great Revolutions and a contained Rebellion', in Graham and Gurr (eds.), pp. 690-730.

The Methodological Problem

The problem here is a basic question of social science methodology. Should our starting point be individual expectations (as in social psychology), rational calculation on the part of individuals (in the tradition of John Stuart Mill), rational calculation on the part of groups (as in modern game theory) conflicting value systems (in the tradition of Weber), the integration of society (in the tradition of Durkheim) or objective interests which may not fully be perceived by the actors (as in Marxism). Indeed, how should we conceive collective action? We have discussed the problems of linking expectations and society. When it comes to the rational calculation of individuals or groups it seems that in most circumstances the average group member's estimated additional return from participation in revolutionary activity will be less than the cost of the effort itself.[23] Collective revolutionary action, therefore, must either lie outside rational (means-ends) self interest or must be in accord with a different notion of rationality (Weber's substantive or value-rationality). If we take the latter view, we slide into an analysis which takes collective values as its starting point. The problem then becomes explaining the origins of and changes in dominant values. If our approach then proceeds to explain values in terms of integrative functions, we are back to the tautologies we noted in discussing Huntington. Perhaps then we should focus on objective interests but then we are faced with the problem of identifying which are real and which are false. Ideally the scholar should attempt to integrate all the above and Charles Tilly has suggested one schema whereby this may be done.[24] We suspect, however, that the problem of priority (at which level one begins) will remain forever.

Retreating a little from these methodological problems, we recommend the simple approach adopted by Wertheim to reconcile politics, economics and psychology in an explanation of revolution in terms of collective violence in the less developed countries. As he sees them the regimes created by departing colonial powers are usually based on time-honoured patron-client relations. The basic ideology of such regimes is a form of 'populism' (a petty-bourgeois cum peasant ideology which posits the existence of an undifferentiated 'people', led usually by a charismatic leader). Such was the case in Indonesia and most countries on the African continent. These regimes have a low potential for violent revolution, and the patron-client relations are a powerful conservative force. To accommodate many different groups, however, some of which are Marxist (though similarly based on patron-client relations), the modernising regimes adopt a 'left' posture, which makes them vulnerable to the retaliation of vested interests and the American advocates of counter-insurgency. The result is usually the

---

23. See M. Olsen, The Logic of Collective Action (Harvard University Press, Cambridge, Mass., 1965).

24. C. Tilly, From Mobilization to Revolution (Addison Wesley, Reading, Mass)., 1978.

establishment of military dictatorships which destroy patron-client relations by force. That, Wertheim believes, is what happened in the Indonesian coup of 1965. The masses, destabilised by such a situation, could easily turn to guerrilla groups which provide a new sense of solidarity and offer the only way of furthering emancipation.[25]

Though we are somewhat sceptical about the recent contributions of social psychology towards an understanding of revolutions in the less developed world, we cannot deny that the arguments of social psychologists were taken very seriously by those who wished to prevent violent revolutions. Social psychology was, after all, a major element in Project Camelot - the abortive attempt by the United States government to analyse the causes of violent revolution in the 1960s.[26] Such projects are no longer fashionable nor considered cost-effective. In the meantime, regimes attempt to prevent violent revolution in less developed countries by using policies which Wertheim considers of little use. In his view, economic and welfare measures rarely go far enough: psychological distractions can last only for a short time; and repression by brute force can easily become a revolutionary accelerator[27].

The Dependency Model: A Challenge to the Diffusionists?

The diffusionist model regarded revolution as the result of mal-adaptation to a Western conception of the march of progress. Such maladaptation might be seen as stemming from uneven development (e.g. urbanisation without economic growth, the formation of political parties without institutions to contain them etc.) or from different kinds of 'relative deprivation'. By the mid-1960s, the diffusionist model was challenged by new perspectives in political economy. At that time it was recognised that many less developed countries might not be in a position to 'catch-up' with the advanced industrial nations. There began to develop what were known as 'dependency' theories which held that there was a necessary relationship between development and underdevelopment. A pioneer in this work was the economist Andre Gunder Frank who argued, from a study of Latin America, that part of the economic surplus of countries occupying the 'periphery' of the international capitalist system was extracted by countries at the 'core'. Those 'peripheral' countries, dependent upon the metropolitan capitalist countries, were to be seen as 'passive victims'. Their history was not in the least autonomous. It was determined by their position in a single world capitalist economy. This dependency, however, was not considered to be a one-sided relationship. The metropolitan capitalist countries had needed peripheral countries to assist in the task of capital accumulation in the past and continued to need them to

---

25. Wertheim, pp. 236-64.

26. See Horowitz, I.L., (ed.), The Rise and Fall of Project Camelot revised edn. (MIT Press, Cambridge, Mass., 1974).

27. Wertheim, pp. 265-95.

overcome economic stagnation. The same historical process which had generated development at the core had also generated under-development at the periphery. This process continued into the monopoly stage of capitalism with the third world providing investment outlets for the expanded surplus expropriated by the metropoles.

The picture painted was of an all-pervading capitalist system of control ranging down from the metropoles through the capital cities of satellite nations to regional and local centres, then through the large landowners and merchants to the small peasants, tenants and landless labourers.[28] The extraction of the surplus proceeded in the opposite direction with each level appropriating a portion of the surplus. Such a picture seemed attractive to revolutionaries in the 1960s in that a revolutionary dislocation at any point in the system could be seen as contributing to a global revolution in the political economy sense. It helped to explain why the United States was prepared to spend countless times more money on suppressing the Vietnamese revolution than it could ever recover from that area; what was at stake was the entire system of capitalist control. Yet at the same time, in the absence of 'many Vietnams' (a constant theme of Che Guevara) the theory pointed to the futility of a revolution aimed at nationalising foreign assets in an economy skewed to the export of one or two crops or mineral resources. Whatever regime might take power would find its economic activities constrained by the international system. Frank's diagnosis, therefore, seemed to suggest that nothing short of instant world revolution would achieve very much. In the 1970s, when that eventuality seemed very remote, Frank's views became accepted by very respectable elites in less developed countries as a rationale for their inability to achieve the economic growth they had promised on taking power.

While we would not want to deny the distorting and blocking effects of foreign penetration in less developed countries, we are not convinced of the utility of Frank's arguments about the drainage overseas of capital necessary for development. Even if it can be demonstrated that there is, in fact, a net outflow of capital from such countries to the industrialised capitalist world, it is probably much too small to have any significant effect on the prospects for development. What is important, from an economic point of view, is not so much the international flow of profits but the productivity of capital which remains in less developed countries.

A second major criticism of Frank's original thesis is that arguments about the international division of labour tended to crowd out considerations of the class structure of individual countries.

---

28. See A.G.Frank, Latin America: Under-Development or Revolution (Monthly Review Press, New York, 1969), pp. 3-17; 'On the Mechanisms of Imperialism: The Case of Brazil', Monthly Review, vol. 16, no. 5 (September, 1964); 'Services Rendered', Monthly Review, vol. 17, no. 2 (1965); Capitalism and Underdevelopment (Monthly Review Press, New York, 1969).

Responding to such criticism, Frank was later to attempt an integration of class analysis with his thesis about the international division of labour. An analysis of the class structure of Latin American countries, he concluded, pointed to the fact that objective conditions did not exist for any nationalist or autonomous solution to the problems of development. All over the continent one saw the growth of what he called a lumpenbourgeoisie - a class formed in response to the needs of foreign industry and commerce which was interested in keeping the people in a state of wretched backwardness. Instead of all-round development one had lumpendevelopment which reproduced the conditions whereby that class remained dominant.[29]

In a situation characterised as lumpendevelopment revolutions would only occur when the hold of the metropolitan capitalist powers was weakened. Such had been the pattern in past revolutions in Latin America. The revolutions which had brought many of the various states into existence at the beginning of the nineteenth century had become possible when the power of Spain collapsed before Napoleon's armies. At that time landed interests utilised the ideology of liberalism to wrest power from colonial authorities. In the twentieth century, the Great Depression of the 1930s and the war in Europe provided opportunities for revolutions led by indigenous bourgeois elements. Here Frank was talking about revolutions in the political economy sense of the word. They were clearly different from the incessant coups d'etat which had dogged most of recent Latin American history. Such political-economic revolutions did not necessitate the violent overthrow of regimes as is exemplified in the most famous Mexican revolution led by Cardenas. In fact, as we noted with Wertheim's analysis, the manifestation of widespread violence quite often resulted not from revolutionary insurrections but from interests allied with foreign powers practising counter-insurgency. Such has been a repeated occurrence in Argentina where, paradoxically, the one regime, which did offer prospects of an autonomous revolution in the political economy sense (the first Peronist government) came to power expressing sympathy for European fascism.

The above arguments about Latin America, it would seem, have relevance for recent revolutions in other parts of the world. Few would deny that the decline of European power in Asia during the Second World War fostered the development of revolutionary forces in many countries, though in Africa south of the Sahara the situation was very different - due perhaps to the lack of development at that time of a bourgeoisie committed to autonomy. In the 1950s and 1960s, however, the assertion of American power made such 'national capitalist' revolutions highly unlikely. In Latin America there was only Velasco's Peruvian revolution (1968) which was unable to carry through the seizure of power into a revolution in the political economy sense. In Asia, U Ne Win's Burmese revolution seemed only to condemn that

---

29. See A.G. Frank, Lumpenbourgeoisie, Lumpendevelopment (Monthly Review Press, New York, 1972).

country to perpetual stagnation. For Frank and many dependency theorists like him, autonomous capitalist development through revolution seems no longer on the agenda.

The work of Frank pointed to the need for development thinkers to look at the world as a whole and, amongst the dependency theorists, the most outstanding achievement in this regard was the work of Immanuel Wallerstein.[30] Wallerstein began by asking why the European core was able to develop before the rest of the world. The conventional diffusionist view held that the commercialisation of agriculture in Britain, which drove peasants off the land, provided both capital for industrial investment and a proletariat to work in industrial enterprises. The growth generated by this development then served as a model for the rest of the world. Wallerstein accepted the first part of this view but severely modified the second. As he saw it the commercialisation of agriculture in the seventeenth century coincided with a period where a reintroduction of serfdom east of the Elbe had tied peasants to the land. Soon the west was in a position to sell industrial goods at relatively high prices to the east in return for lower-priced grain. Thus the 'core' capitalist countries profited at the expense of Russia and Eastern Europe which at that time constituted the periphery. The same process has continued to this day with the periphery getting bigger and bigger. Such development has resulted in a complicated global division of labour in which a new category - the 'semi-periphery' - has appeared. Each of these three zones performs different economic roles in maintaining the global capitalist system. Each zone is characterised by a different mode of labour control, a different pattern of profit generation and a different class structure. With the growth of this division of labour, there has developed a system of state power in which core states appear very strong due to the need by capitalists for 'extra-economic assistance' to secure favourable terms of trade. At the periphery, on the other hand, the strength of states ranges from negligibility (in the colonial situation) to a very low level (under conditions of neo-colonialism). Such a global division of labour and geographical division of power, which has developed over four centuries, is extremely stable and might be expected to remain stable so long as the market is able to expand into areas in which pre-capitalist forms of economy exist.

Wallerstein's account is based on a very selective reading of history. He argues that successful market relations at the 'core' led to the development of strong states to protect and further develop market relations. In the periphery, however, the failure successfully to develop market relations precluded the development of strong states. Such an argument ignores the pre-existing state structures in the periphery. There is considerable literature which argues that a very strong state (in what Wallerstein calls the periphery) was required to

---

30. I. Wallerstein, The Modern World-System: Capitalist Agriculture and the Origins of the European World - Economy in the Sixteenth Century (Academic Press, New York and London, 1974).

bring about the 'second serfdom' in the first place.[31] With such evidence, how is it possible to argue that the unequal strength of state structures is necessary to sustain the global division of labour? It may be argued that the strength of the eastern states was a decisive force in bringing about an alternative path to modernisation. With Wallerstein we are back to the same ethnocentric and unilinear view as that offered by the diffusionists. In Wallerstein's thesis revolutions in the narrow political sense are merely the consequence of the mal-adaptation of peripheral societies to the demands of the metropoles. Though Wallerstein's picture does allow for a more sophisticated analysis of class formations, classes are reduced merely to categories in a world market system. There is an absence of pressure or action from below. All change has ultimately to flow from the preferences of the dominant classes in 'core' capitalist nations.

Are not dependency theories the mirror image of the diffusionist model? All that has changed is the observer's moral evaluation of the consequences of a top-down view of progress. The trickle-down benefits are now reinterpreted as patterns of exploitation. The plusses of the diffusionist view have simply become the minuses of the dependency view. And what of revolution in the political economy sense? Can one conceive of a set of occurrences which will bring the system to an end? Could it be that the same structure of world power, established in the sixteenth century, will be maintained so long as the market can expand? And when the market covers the whole globe and there are no more traditional producers to fleece, will the system collapse and usher in a revolutionary age?

A Multilinear View

We have looked so far at ethnocentric and technological determinist interpretations of modernisation and revolution in all three senses outlined earlier. For the classical diffusionists revolution was aberrant for it blocked the benefits of progress which would trickle down from centre to periphery. In inverting this view, the dependency theorists called for a revolution in the political economy sense which could only be effective if it were global. In affirming this latter position many tired regimes could rationalise their inability to do anything or could explain the failure of socialist experiments. Gertzel will return to this problem in the chapter on Guinea-Bissau. In the meantime we might anticipate one of the arguments of Amilcar Cabral that the first task of development in many less developed countries is for those countries to recover their own history. Clearly history is not all of one piece and there are many different paths to development. Such an obvious point was made long ago by Marx and Engels who would

31. See G. Konrad and I. Szelenyi, The Intellectuals on the Road to Class Power: A Sociological Study of the Role of the Intelligentsia in Socialism (Harcourt, Brace and Jovanovich, New York, 1979).

have been shocked to see their writings pressed into a unilinear scheme by Stalin and other Marxist-Leninist writers who came after him.

In the work from which this chapter is taken we have outlined views of Marx which are very different from the Soviet orthodoxy. Space forbids repetition here. We will focus, therefore, on only one modern writer in the multilinear genre - Barrington Moore Jr., whose book Social Origins of Dictatorship and Democracy earned much acclaim in the 1960s.[32] This study projected backwards from three end-states - bourgeois democracy, fascism and communism and dealt with the relationship of revolution in the narrow political sense to revolution in the political economic sense. Modernity, for Moore, was promoted by the development of market relations in agriculture within a rational centralised state. Unlike many other studies his focus was not simply on the groups which carried out a successful revolution but on the relationship of those groups to the classes which were seen to have been crowded off the face of history - in particular the peasantry. Having noted 'the curious fact' that by the sixteenth and seventeenth centuries royal absolutist states or agrarian bureaucracies had been established in all the major countries he studied (England, France, the Prussian part of Germany, Russia, China, Japan and India) Moore approached the question: were there structural features which may be identified in agrarian societies which facilitated, hindered or even made impossible the development of parliamentary democracy? Moore concluded that Western feudalism contained certain conditions which distinguished it from other societies. It was only in Western Europe that a delicate balance occurred between too much and too little royal power. In the west (unlike Russia) there was no need for an Ivan the Terrible to break the back of the independent nobility, nor was there a central authority supervising the activities of the society as a whole. For Moore the first route to modernity - that of bourgeois revolution - was traversed in England, France, and in the United States. In pursuing revolution in the wider (political economy) sense, each of those countries went through a bloody revolution in the narrow political sense. In England this was the Puritan Revolution of the mid-seventeenth century. In France it was the Great Revolution of 1789-95 and in the United States it was the Civil War of 1861-65. In each case a strong bourgeoisie was able to rise to power. Its choice of allies, however, determined the nature, scope and direction of violence.

In England, the bourgeoisie allied itself with a sizeable section of the landed gentry to oppose an absolutist monarch who was concerned to prevent the destruction of the peasantry as a class. The victory of this alliance against Charles I in the Civil War was seen by Moore to have hastened the destruction of the peasantry. This was a key element in agricultural modernity since it enabled England to adopt a commercial form of agriculture which linked up town and country in a

---

32. Barrington Moore Jr., Social Origins of Dictatorship and Democracy: Lord and Peasant in the Making of the Modern World (Beacon Press, Boston, 1966).

system of complementary markets. At the same time the 'eliminated' peasantry could be absorbed into a completely new kind of social formation.

The landed upper classes had split in their attitude towards the policies of Charles I, in particular with regard to the peasants. The elimination of the peasantry, however, did not lead to a unified reassertion of landed interests. On the contrary, the post-Civil War period was characterised by the continuation of shifting coalitions between various groups of landed interests and the urban bourgeoisie. This provided the basic framework for interest-group politics characteristic of bourgeois parliamentary democracy. Moreover, with the defeat of royal absolutism and with the peasantry on the way to destruction there was no need for a strong state to maintain the extraction of the agricultural surplus.

In France, on the other hand, the landed gentry resisted the commercialisation of agriculture and opposed the bourgeoisie. The bourgeoisie, therefore, sought allies amongst the peasantry to overthrow the <u>ancien regime</u>. The result was the bloody revolution of 1789-95 which shattered the landed gentry and left the bourgeoisie and the peasantry holding the field. The identity of interest between those classes was sufficiently great to allow for a bourgeois democracy but not great enough to allow for the same kind of weak state structure as England. There remained problems of extracting the agricultural surplus and the peasants, fearing for their survival, were given to political extremes which from time to time threatened the stability of the new regime. In short, the result was an unstable bourgeois democracy.

In the United States two types of economy existed in two different parts of the country. Neither the north nor the south possessed a peasantry. In the north there was a class of independent farmers already assimilated into commercialised agriculture with no conflict of interest with the bourgeoisie. In the south there was, of course, a landed gentry and slaves working in a plantation economy which had been commercialised along lines completely different to the north. The clash was to occur over which kind of economic system would dominate the newly opened west. The result was a protracted period of violence which took the form of a civil war between regions. This civil war, Moore considered, constituted a revolution more profound than that commenced in 1776. The outcome was the destruction of the landed gentry as a class and the freeing of the slaves. Since there was no major conflict of interest between the dominant classes in the north - the bourgeoisie and the independent farmers - bourgeois democracy prevailed and there was no need for a strong state to extract the agricultural surplus.

The second route from pre-industrial society to modernity was, according to Moore, exemplified by Germany. Here the bourgeoisie was much weaker than in the west. For such a bourgeoisie to challenge the landed gentry would be to invite disaster. Consequently sections of the relatively weak commercial and industrial bourgeoisie sought dissident elements of the dominant landed gentry to put through the changes required for industrial society. For basically military reasons it was possible to find such elements and this fraction of the landed gentry took the initiative in promoting the development of industry and the commercialisation of agriculture.

There was, however, a clash of interests between, on the one hand, the dominant allies which tried to maximise the extraction of the rural surplus and, on the other, a peasantry which feared for its future. Instead of surplus extraction through the market which aided the development of parliamentary democracy in the west, a labour-repressive agrarian system grew up which depended on political mechanisms (and here the term is used very loosely) to ensure that a large number of people worked the land to provide a surplus to be consumed by other classes. The route to parliamentary democracy, as experienced in the west, was blocked in Prussia when the Prussian nobility expanded its holdings at the expense of the peasantry, just as that class was about to be emancipated under the Teutonic Order. Together with the reduction of the peasantry to a new form of serfdom, a process was initiated where towns were reduced to dependence upon the rural-based nobility by curtailing the export of their products in favour of the direct export of agricultural produce in the form of grain. The throttling of the market between town and country was to inhibit any alliance between landowners and townspeople and this was further exacerbated by the Hohenzollern policy of destroying the independence of the nobility and playing off nobles and bourgeoisie one against the other. Consequently, rather than strong parliamentary democracy, there took shape the militarised fusion of bureaucracy and landed aristocracy which was to take the initiative in the modernisation process. The parliamentary forms which did develop in Germany were never strong enough to solve the economic and social problems which confronted them. Upon their collapse in the 19th century, the peasants were dealt with by a mixture of repression and mobilisation behind symbols which stemmed not only from the militarist values of the old aristocracy but also from a rural tradition. This process culminated in fascism or 'revolution from above'.

The Japanese sub-alternative to the above model was also to result in a 'total commitment to authority' and, like Prussia, the fascist route was initiated once a weak industrial and commercial bourgeoisie sought elements of the landed classes to take the lead in the process of industrialisation. But where such a situation was impossible, either because the bourgeoisie was too weak or suitable allies in the dominant class could not be found, the result was not fascism but a 'peasant revolution' leading to communism. Such, Moore tells us, is what happened in Russia and China. This was his third route to modernisation.

In Russia and China, society was dominated by a huge agrarian bureaucracy which served to inhibit the impulse to modernisation more than in any of the countries discussed so far. Yet even Russia and China were not insulated from modernisation in other countries and foreign influence began to be felt in parts of the two empires. Such influence produced strains amongst the peasantry which was to provide the main force for overthrowing the old order under the leadership of Communist parties. The key to the effectiveness of peasant revolution in those countries was to be found in the way the agricultural surplus was extracted. Again the western pattern of extracting the rural surplus through the market was absent. The extraction of the surplus in Russia and China depended upon the power of the centralised agrarian bureaucracy. In the west the power of the central government was not particularly relevant to the peasants, whereas in Russia and China the peasants were conscious of the fact that the strength of the central government affected directly the amount of the agricultural surplus they had to surrender. In such a situation they had a strong motivation to overthrow the agrarian bureaucracy.

The peasant revolutions of recent times changed fundamentally the idea of the peasant as merely an object of history, as 'a form of social life over which historical changes pass but which contributes nothing to the impetus of those changes'. But here there is a cruel irony! At the point in Moore's account where the peasantry became a major element in historical change, it ceased to exist as a class. The peasantry which made revolution has in every case become its major victim. It appears that peasants were capable only of destroying an old regime but not of inventing a new one. In Russia and China, collectivisation has been carried on by a state made even stronger than before in order to maximise the rural surplus. This has spelt doom to the peasants as a class.

Immediately upon its publication in the mid-1960s, Moore's book was greeted with much acclaim amongst social theorists and a barrage of criticism from historians of each of the countries he discussed.[33] It was pointed out that the English peasantry took a long time to disappear and that the English Civil War could hardly be considered part of the 'bourgeois revolution'. As for France, many historians refused to accept that France before 1789 was feudal at all. Similarly historians of Germany and Japan confronted Moore with their

---

33. See S. Rothman, 'Barrington Moore and the Dialectics of Revolution', *American Political Science Review* vol. 64, no. 1 (March 1970), pp. 61-85, 182-3; T. Tilton, 'The Social Origin of Liberal Democracy: The Swedish Case', *American Political Science Review* vol. 68 no. 2 (June 1974), pp. 561-71; T. Skopcol, 'A Critical Review of Barrington Moore's Social Origins of Dictatorship and Democracy', *Politics and Society*; vol. IV, no. 1 (Fall 1973), pp. 1-34; D. Lowenthal, review in *History and Theory*, vol VII, no. 2 (1968), pp. 257-78; J.V. Femia, 'Barrington Moore and the Pre-conditions for Democracy', *British Journal of Political Science*, vol. II, part 1 (January 1972), pp. 21-46; L. Stone, 'News from Everywhere', *New York Review of Books*, vol. IX, 24 August 1967, pp. 31-5; R. Dore, 'Making Sense of History', *Archives Europeenes de Sociologie*, vol. X, no. 1 (1969), pp. 295-305; J. Weiner, 'The Barrington Moore Thesis and its Critics', *Theory and Society*, 2 (1975), pp. 301-30.

objections. Was fascism not just a temporary twentieth century aberration? Others could not see how the Russian revolution could be described as 'peasant'. Doubtless more peasants took part than any other class but that was also true of the English revolution. Moore's answer was that one should define a revolution not in terms of who takes part nor in terms of its leaders but in terms of the interests served (which is how he characterises the 'bourgeois revolutions' in England and France). But if that is the case and if it is true that the peasants have been destroyed as a class, was either the Russian or the Chinese revolutions 'peasant'? In any case it is extraordinarily difficult to argue that the peasants in Russia and China have disappeared as classes except in the sense of becoming kolkhoz (collective farm) workers or commune members who as individuals no longer legally own most of the land.

A further set of criticisms centre on the universality which Moore claims for his scheme. Having outlined his typology, Moore then attempts to see how one may deal with India. The results are inconclusive. What, one wonders, would he do with Switzerland and Sweden? An appeal to the old diffusionist viewpoint that smaller countries follow large ones ignores the fact that those two countries were more autonomous than Germany at the time of its unification. The problem remains as to how one might utilise Moore's approach to history in considering all those parts of the world where the overwhelming majority of the population are peasants and which have only recently begun to transform their argicultural systems. Do the fascist and communist routes offer the only alternatives?

An Objective Idealist View

Any taxonomy of world history, such as that offered by Moore, is open to the criticisms of historians who tend to stress the specifics of their particular field of study. More often than not such historians over-emphasise the particularity of different cultural tradition in a manner similar to Burke who has been discussed earlier in this volume. Pre-eminent here was the nineteenth century German historical school which stressed the uniqueness of the German national spirit (Volksgeist). When Max Weber broke from that tradition to engage in a more sociological endeavour he was felt by many of his colleagues to have let the side down. Yet even Weber who saw the world converging into a bureaucratised modernity remained a cultural relativist. But how is it possible to give due weight to the world of ideas and still avoid relativist thinking? Back in the early nineteenth century Hegel offered an answer in his portrayal of a universal world spirit (Zeitgeist) becoming more conscious of itself as history unfolds towards greater freedom. A century later, as Weberian sociology pursued its relativistic path, as Marxist political economy eschewed 'idealism' and as historians ploughed ever narrower furrows, Hegel's views became very unfashionable; at least until the 1970s. By that time the re-emphasis on the early Marx and the attempted reconciliation of Marx and Hegel saw a recrudescence of what we referred to in our Introduction as objective idealism.

Our brief in this chapter lays outside the Marxist tradition so let us consider one writer in the objective idealist school who makes no claims to reconcile Marx and Hegel and may not even realise the extent to which he belongs to the Hegelian tradition. This is W.F. Wertheim whose work we have referred to earlier in this chapter. Wertheim's Evolution and Revolution was written at the tail end of the radical period of the late 1960s and early 1970s. In his view, evolution is governed by a principle of emancipation which comes more and more to realise itself. In his own words he is a finalist - an approach which is usually called teleological. This is the formulation of a process according to where it will lead to, as opposed to determinism - the formulation of a process according to where it starts. This teleological view and a claim to be able to predict future events Wertheim attempts to reconcile with voluntarism - the belief in free will.

It is not at all clear whether Wertheim's attempted reconciliation succeeds; nevertheless his attempt is extremely stimulating. Human history, he claims, is proceeding from the emancipation of humankind from nature to emancipation from other human beings. In this process, revolution is no more than accelerated evolution and counter-revolution is simply a decline in the opportunities for emancipation. To this schema is added the concept, borrowed from Clifford Geertz, of 'involution' which signifies a process of emancipation which will lead to a dead end. Thus the events in France after 1789 were indeed a revolution, not just in the sense of the overthrow of a regime by collective violence but in Wertheim's sense of contributing towards the emancipation of the French people. What happened after 1933 in Germany was a counter-revolution in that the opportunities for emancipation declined. Finally the Indonesian developments are seen as 'involutionary' because they are leading to a dead end.

The problem with the above typology is that we are never quite sure whether what is claimed to be a revolution actually furthers the cause of human emancipation until long after the event. Just how do we know that involution has taken place until the dead end is reached? What do we do with the Bolshevik Revolution which, according to Wertheim, was followed by a 'Thermidor' (a shift to more conservative policies and values)? For Wertheim, the Soviet people are much more emancipated now than in 1917; thus the Bolshevik Revolution was indeed a contributor to emancipation. But suppose that regime becomes more and more repressive, does that alter the status of what happened in 1917 or do we decide long after the event that a counter-revolution has occurred? Who can say, moreover, just what the status of the Iranian revolution might be at the present? In making his concept of emancipation twofold - emancipation from the forces of nature, and emancipation from domination by privileged individuals, Wertheim has charted a course that leaves him with a dilemma. If emancipation and its attendant human progress is to be from the forces of nature, then the most efficient development of the productive process can be equated with human progress. At the same time such efficiency could militate against his social criterion of progress - emancipation from domination and greater co-operation.

The tension between these two concepts becomes evident when Wertheim attempts to discuss the uprising against Soviet dominance in Hungary in 1956. In the light of his notions of revolution and counter-revolution it is not surprising that for Wertheim the events in Hungary in 1956 are best described as 'ambiguous'. From the position of his twofold notion of emancipation he must argue that if the anti-Soviet movement associated with Premier Nagy was an attempt efficiently to develop the productive forces, in terms of emancipation from the forces of nature it was progressive and thus revolutionary. On the other hand, Nagy's movement had as a part of its platform the reversal of rural collectivisation with an attendant decrease in human co-operation. Such a programme can be seen as counter-revolutionary. Even with the benefit of the hindsight necessary for assessing revolution in Wertheim's terms, it is extremely difficult to assess the general tendency of revolutions (or counter-revolutions) which cross Wertheim's twofold categorisation of emancipation. This difficulty is not helped at all by the fact that, though the Hungarian uprising was abortive in terms of its stated immediate aims, events in Hungary in 1956 can be seen to have contributed to the subsequent adoption of policies for economic reform. These on the one hand have promoted the development of the productive forces, and on the other have decreased co-operative human action in the work place by stressing competition between industrial enterprises and between individual workers.

The picture becomes even more complicated when we consider Wertheim's view that progress is not linear but occurs in dialectical leaps with 'the poor and blank' (a term borrowed from Mao Zedong) leaping ahead of the most advanced. This is supported by the arguments of people such as Romein (who talks about the 'law of the retarding lead'), Service (who talks in terms of a 'leapfrog effect'), Sahlins' point that backward feudalism had the potential to leap ahead of the more advanced Roman Empire, and similar arguments deriving from Engels, Lenin, rotsky and, of course, Mao Zedong. But what are the conditions under which a backward country leaps ahead? It is never, according to Wertheim, the most backward country which does so. How then do we spot the potential front runner?

The notion of 'leap-frog' is beset with enormous problems for the social scientist. Nevertheless, as a description of what happened to certain societies in the course of their revolutions, it does have much empirical validity. The problem is how to move from a description of particular histories to a social science generalisation.

More fruitful, perhaps, for the social scientist, is Wertheim's discussion of 'counterpoint values'. Wertheim maintains that every dominant value system in a society depends for its success on the point to which it can incorporate counterpoint values. An example here will help. The legitimisation of papal hierarchy in the Roman Catholic Church depends for its success upon the incorporation into its legitimising ideology of the notion that the rich person can as easily enter the Kingdom of God as the camel pass through the eye of a needle. The domination of a bourgeois elite in liberal society, moreover, depends upon the incorporation of the idea of equality before the law. It is wrong, therefore, to see society always in terms of competing value systems. Rather one should look at the institutionalisation of counterpoints. Once that institutionalisation breaks down, there are preconditions for revolution. Finally, revolution consists in the situation where the deinstitutionalised subordinate values become the new dominant values.

What are the preconditions which make for the deinstitutionalisation of counterpoint values? Here Wertheim distinguishes between two types of revolution. The bourgeois revolution in the West comes about when economic growth and increasing vertical mobility is met by an intransigent elite and occurs always in an authoritarian system. Peasant revolutions in the east, however, occur in conditions of extreme poverty, where there is a lack of opportunity for vertical social mobility for the masses but considerable horizontal mobility (between regions and between jobs) and finally where there is a harsh political system. This latter set of conditions, however, needs to be activated by what he calls an accelerator. This term, borrowed from Chalmers Johnson, signifies a set of features which become important only when the basic preconditions are present. They may include a crisis in government finances, a lost or losing war etc. But the problem remains in deciding whether or not those accelerators are in fact basic preconditions.

The presence of the preconditions for peasant revolution in many countries today suggests that Wertheim sees revolution as a basic feature of modernisation (which must involve emancipation). He believes, moreover, that these revolutions will take the political form of the overthrow of a regime by collective violence. The two cases of non-violent revolution which he cites, India and the Chinese Cultural Revolution (which were both apparently revolutions from below led from above), only qualify as non-violent by a considerable stretch of the imagination.

Conclusion

Though Wertheim's book appeared just one decade ago, it has a somewhat outdated air. The present is a more disillusioned age and few people express much faith in any principle of emancipation. Wertheim was extremely enthusiastic about the possibilities for emancipation offered by the Chinese Cultural Revolution but not many today would share his views. A subsequent chapter in this book will return to that subject. In the meantime let us note that in the 1980s any discussion of emancipation must take into account the fact that limitations of natural resources place severe constraints on either the liberating potential of technology or the ability of humankind indefinitely to subdue nature to its will. It seems increasingly that the global revolution which we might face will be a desperate fight for an equitable share of a shrinking cake. The energy crisis of the 1970s pointed to an accretion of wealth by elites in a few fortunate 'developing' countries whilst the saddest effects were experienced by less developed countries with no petroleum. Such considerations conjured up vistas of conflict among the less-developed countries as well as what became increasingly known as north and south. The demise of dependency theory at that time left a real gap in thinking about development. Many scholars turned to piecemeal social reforms while others saw such reforms as merely leading to involution. Meanwhile the libertarian right pointed to a handful of 'newly industrialising countries' (such as Taiwan, Malaysia, Singapore and South Korea) as evidence to support their desire to return to the laissez faire ideas supposedly propagated in the revolutions of the late eighteenth century.

Over the general atmosphere of left pessimism and right libertarian dogmatism there hangs the shadow of the bomb. Indeed the outcome of super-power rivalry will probably be not the revolutionary recapture of one's own history but a return to a history that Hegel would not recognise as history - the history of the stone age. Contrary to Wintrop, we believe that the only alternative to be posed is socialism or barbarism. What is needed is a fundamental change in the global political economy; where in Aristotle's words the unequal no longer have to strive to be equal and the equal no longer have the opportunity to achieve a new inequality. The first task involves a greater revolution than we have ever seen - the global redistribution of resources; to achieve this 'new beginning' the Soviet experiences are not relevant. The second tasks involves a cultural revolution. Some in China in the mid-1960s believed in such a cultural revolution but, as a subsequent chapter will show, employed methods which culminated in what might be seen as a disillusioned counter-revolution. If barbarism is to be avoided a prime task of social scientists is to work out the means to realise the human aspects of Wertheim's principle of emancipation. To do that we need to think of the future in terms which should be unashamedly utopian. To be sure, utopian thinking may produce unintended violence. 'Realism', on the other hand, can be guaranteed to perpetuate an existing situation where the routine violence generated by existing social structures becomes more acute. One may never prove Barrington Moore's point that the major violent revolutions which brought about a change in regime all involved less suffering than the structures of the old regime which were swept aside. But intuitively we feel he has a point.[34] We may, however, no longer generalise about the future from the great revolutions of the past. The possibility that a major revolution might bring about a nuclear holocaust demands a new beginning in our thinking about any new beginning in our social life.

---

34. In a review of the work on which this chapter is based, Peter Calvert points to our criticism of Moore's 'unqualified felicific calculus' and his 'suspect theory of what constitutes human suffering'. Be it noted we wish merely to point out methodological problems rather than substantive errors. See Third World Quarterly, vol VI, no. 1 (January 1984), pp. 227-9.

PART 2

CASE-STUDIES OF RECENT REVOLUTIONS

Chapter Eight

THE SOVIET UNION - A DEFUNCT REVOLUTION

David Close

The construction of a new order is just as much a part of revolution as the destruction of an old one, and all the more worth studying because it is a comparatively neglected aspect of the phenomenon. As an example of such construction the Soviet Union is especially informative. The social change that has been carried out by its leaders since their seizure of power in 1917 has been extraordinarily sweeping. Their present successors claim to be continuing the work of building communism according to the founders' precepts; and enough time has elapsed to enable one to make a reasonably fair assessment of their claim. The aim of this chapter, then, will be to enquire how far the state, economy and society created by the Communist Party of the Soviet Union have fulfilled the ideas of Marx and Lenin. To answer this question is to trace the spiritual demise of a revolutionary ideology.

The almost religious character of this ideology is embodied in State and Revolution, where Lenin boldly repeated the utopian aims of Marx just before coming to power in 1917.[1] Lenin set before his party the goal of creating a humane, egalitarian, prosperous society, characterised by Marx's slogan 'from each according to his ability, to each according to his needs'. Political organisation would be extremely democratic, with all citizens learning 'how to govern the state themselves'. Any form of political or police coercion would be rendered unnecessary by the disappearance of social conflict and anti-social activities. In these senses the state would 'wither away'. Communal ownership and cooperative administration of the economy would (somehow) stimulate technological progress, and avoid the waste caused under capitalism by competition and the inequitable distribution of wealth. Consequently society would be so prosperous that everyone's needs would be easily satisfied, and money would be unnecessary. There would be little distinction in status and wealth between individuals, and none between sexes. Presumably Lenin, like Trotsky, agreed with Marx that there would be complete cultural

1. (International Publishers, New York, 1932), Ch. 5.

freedom, so that 'the free development of each will be the condition of the free development of all'.[2]

Lenin predicted realistically that the 'socialist' phase of transition from the pre-revolutionary order to communism would be long, and unavoidably accompanied by a continuance of political coercion and material inequality. To this day, the CPSU describes its regime as socialist. The persistence of utopian aspiration is revealed in the remarkably optimistic forecasts of the 1961 programme. Communism would be substantially achieved within 20 years, in which time per capita production would far outstrip that of the USA; wage differentials would shrink; the range of free services would widen; and various state functions, including the enforcement of law and order, would be transferred to voluntary bodies.[3]

The contradiction, which had also faced the leaders of the French revolution, was that dictatorial methods were needed to create the democratic utopia. But to Lenin and his colleagues, dictatorial rule was more than a distasteful necessity. They were moulded more than they realised by Russia's autocratic tradition, and specifically by the need for autocratic methods to control the peasant masses and the subject nationalities. And through ideological convictions which have been examined in an earlier chapter, Lenin believed in authoritarian leadership of his party, while his party saw itself as an elite corps uniquely possessed of vital truths. The manifest oppressiveness of his party's rule caused Lenin anguish, but was a result of his own determination to impose his policies on the Russian people. His followers were also torn by contradictory impulses - in their case between the desire for open debate within the party, and psychological dependence on Lenin's leadership.[4] The triumph of dictatorial tendencies was made inevitable by the hostility of the environment which the Bolsheviks[5] faced after 1917, hostility greater than that endured by any later communist regime. The weakness of their appeal to Russian society is shown by the fact that they secured only a quarter of the seats in the constituent assembly which met in January 1918, so that they felt obliged to disperse it at gunpoint. They had then to defend their regime against White armies supported by the Western powers. When they had accomplished this task, they still faced the latent hostility of the peasant majority of the population. From 1929 the regime subordinated all else to the rapid development of heavy industry, a task demanding dictatorial methods and obviously necessary for its survival in the face of a resurgent Germany and a passively

2. K. Marx & F. Engels, Manifesto of the Communist Party (Progress Publishers, Moscow, 1952), p. 75 (last words of Ch. 2).

3. The Programme of the Communist Party of the Soviet Union (Soviet Booklet no. 83, London, 1961), pp. 44-73.

4. A.B. Ulam, Lenin and the Bolsheviks. The Intellectual and Political History of the Triumph of Communism in Russia (Secker & Warburg, London, 1966), pp. 468-474, 531-5.

5. As the CPSU was nicknamed in its early years.

hostile West. The kind of regime that appeared in the 1930s - with its personality cult, wholesale purges and labour camps - can be partly accounted for by the personal preferences of Josef Stalin. But his rise can itself be attributed in part to the fact that his insularity and pragmatism appealed to the unsophisticated workers and peasants who flooded into the party after 1917. Indirectly, then, the CPSU was moulded by the backwardness of the society which it had conquered.

In the 1930s Stalin carried the authoritarian strain in Bolshevism to an extreme, and used that authority to jettison wholesale (in practice if not always in theory) the ideals of 1917. The exiled Trotsky described the process vividly in The Revolution Betrayed, his denunciation therein of Stalin's 'monstrous .... intensity of repression'[6] being perhaps made all the more penetrating by the fact that he himself had helped to lay its foundations. Like the Tsarist state, Stalin's set out, in the name of a quasi-sacred authority,[7] to control all important social activities, and suppress all initiative from below. By directing the party - through his policy of 'socialism in one country', adopted in the 1920s - to stop working and waiting for world revolution, Stalin had encouraged it to ignore also the prerequisites for revolution within Russia. To lessen further the risk that the ideals of 1917 might be asserted against himself, he had most of the 'old guard' of the party executed, and also purged drastically the parties outside Russia. The industrial proletariat, in whose name the revolution had occurred, was (quoting Trotsky) subjected to a 'corps of slave-drivers' imposing 'piece-work payment, hard conditions of material existence, lack of free movement, with terrible police repression penetrating the life of every factory.'[8] As Trotsky again observed, the strict censorship that was imposed on creative arts and every intellectual pursuit, including the natural sciences, negated Marxist ideals of spiritual self-fulfilment, and prevented the kind of experimentation that was especially needed in a revolutionary society.[9]

By the time of Stalin's death in 1953, little was left of the circumstances in which his police-state had originally been created. The Soviet Union's international isolation had ended, and its military position was comparatively secure. The presumptively hostile classes within Russia (peasants, pre-revolutionary businessmen, professionals and aristocracy) had been wiped out. The population as a whole now accepted the legitimacy of the regime, as was shown by the fact that even exiles and dissidents tended henceforth to accept basic features of it, such as one-party rule, state control of the economy and comprehensive welfare services. By Lenin's criteria of 1917 the time

---

6. The Revolution Betrayed. What is the Soviet Union and Where is it Going? (Pathfinder Press, New York, 1972), p.108 (Ch. 5, section 3).

7. S. Rothman & G.W. Breslauer, Soviet Politics and Society (West Publishing Co., New York, 1978), p. 309.

8. Pp. 241-2 (Ch. 9, introductory section).

9. P. 180 (Ch. 7, section 3).

was ripe for a move towards democratic communism. Of course nothing like this happened because dictatorial rule was firmly institutionalised. What did change was that this rule became less personal and arbitrary. Stalin's successors as General Secretary could not aspire to his personal authority; and the party's leading organ, the Politburo, became again the real centre of power. Consequently the apparatus of party officials strengthened its position in relation to the General Secretary, the state machinery, and the people outside the party. It resisted the attempts by Nikita Khrushchev, General Secretary from 1953 to 1964, to weaken its increasing security of tenure.[10] And in the latest version of the Soviet constitution, that of 1977, the party's dominance is for the first time made explicit.[11] Only token moves have been made towards the 'withering away of the state', in the transfer of petty administrative, police and judicial duties to volunteer organisations.[12]

The methods by which the party and state controlled the population changed after 1953. Stalin's successors quickly abandoned much of his arbitrariness and brutality, partly because they had suffered from it themselves, partly because they had not the nerve or stomach to inflict it on others, and partly because it was no longer appropriate. Now that party cadres with specialist knowledge had penetrated all corners of society, their steady supervision was more effective than spasmodic terror. A more trained and indoctrinated workforce no longer needed, or was willing to accept, as much coercion as before. And in an increasingly stable society, some autonomy, and capacity to resist party interference, naturally developed in many sectors. It has been found, for example, that Soviet intellectuals tend to give their professional ethic increasing precedence over party loyalty.[13] On the other hand, party officials have come to recognise that some freedom for others to criticise their policies is necessary for efficiency. For example, reforms in the secondary school curriculum, designed to encourage critical thought and independent study, were prompted by the complaints of educational specialists that the old curriculum was not preparing students for work at higher levels. (The argument that critical or creative thinking was necessary for the citizen of a revolutionary society would naturally have cut no ice with the political authorities.)[14] Dissent with broad aims, however, such as the relaxation of press censorship, or the enlargement of liberties for religious groups or national minorities, has been suppressed with

10. Rothman & Breslauer, pp. 166-7.
11. Rothman & Breslauer, pp. 223-4.
12. D. Lane, Politics and Society in the USSR, 2nd ed. (M.Robertson, London, 1978), p. 161.
13. L.G. Churchward, The Soviet Intelligentsia. An Essay on the Social Structure and Roles of Soviet Intellectuals during the 1960s (Routledge & Kegan Paul, London, 1973), pp. 54, 84.
14. Rothman & Breslauer, pp. 42-3, 105, 173, 182-3.

consistent severity since the regime's reaction in the mid-1960s against 'the thaw' which Khrushchev allowed.[15]

Consideration of the way in which the Soviet Union was industrialised will reinforce the conclusion that the revolution was betrayed, in ways which even Trotsky failed to notice. The Bolsheviks, as good Marxists, believed that rapid industrialisation was essential both for their own continued tenure of power and for the creation of a communist society - hence Lenin's famous dictum, 'communism is Soviet power plus the electrification of the whole country'.[16] That central planning would make industrialisation more efficient was a socialist commonplace in the early twentieth century. That planning should include control, and that the pace of industrialisation should be forced by coercive methods, conformed with the general style of government which Lenin and Stalin adopted. The outcome was the command economy, which has survived to the present, and is characterised by extreme centralisation on a national scale, and emphasis (in the interests of rapid growth as well as defence) on armaments, heavy industry and energy at the expense of agriculture, housing and consumer goods. In the 1930s and 1940s the achievements of this system were prodigious. A large and increasing mass of the population was transferred from a primitive and wretched rural existence to an urban industrialised one in which steady improvements in living standards were possible. But the defects of this system became increasingly apparent thereafter.

These defects have often been described.[17] There is a bureaucratic nightmare of overcentralisation, which overloads ministries in Moscow with decisions which need to be made at enterprise (i.e. factory or collective farm) level, and suppresses initiative at all levels below the top. There is the vain attempt by central planners to take the myriad decisions which in capitalist economies are left to market forces. Overcentralisation has proved especially damaging to agriculture, which is further weakened by a constant drain of able people to the cities, and to technologically advanced industries (e.g. chemicals and pharmaceuticals), which are further weakened by the political barriers that the regime imposes to the international exchange of ideas. The interests of agriculture, and of consumer interests generally, are chronically underrepresented among central policy-makers, so that plan targets in these areas have been constantly underfulfilled.

15. Rothman & Breslauer, pp. 219-220.

16. Quoted in Ulam, p. 481.

17. Rothman & Breslauer, pp. 238-240, 288; A. Nove, 'Agriculture' and P. Hanson, 'The Import of Western Technology', in A. Brown & M. Kaser (eds.), The Soviet Union Since the Fall of Khrushchev, 2nd ed. (Macmillan, London, 1978), pp. 1-18; A. Katz, The Politics of Economic Reform in the Soviet Union (Praeger, New York, 1972), pp. vii, 179, 197.

The costs of these defects are grievous, in economic efficiency and consumer satisfaction. Recent studies have shown that civilian industries tend to lag technologically behind their counterparts in the West. Manufactured goods, because of their generally poor quality, are meagrely represented in export markets outside the Soviet bloc. The living standards of most citizens - in respect for example of housing, clothes, food and consumer durables - are still bleak by Western standards, and have not shown an improvement commensurate with the growth of the economy since the 1930s. The Soviet Union is forced into a humiliating and (given the inconvertibility of the rouble) costly dependence on imports from the West of grain and technology.

The attempts made by successive Soviet leaders to tackle these problems have been thwarted by the institutions which Stalin created and the values which he inculcated.[18] Thus a policy adopted in 1965 of transferring responsibility to the enterprise manager failed, for reasons which included the reluctance of managers to take such responsibility, and the fear by *apparatchiks* (or party officials) that any move towards market relations might slip out of their control. The regime has not found incentives for wage-earners that can replace the authoritarian combination of carrot-and-stick applied under Stalin. The only effective substitutes are beyond its power to offer: massive increases in material rewards and democratic control over enterprises. The basic problem is that Soviet leaders cannot afford to attack the command economy seriously, because their system of government is identified with it. Yet, as we now see, it has proved ill-equipped to provide the technological progress and consumer affluence which have always been vital Communist aims.

The Soviet leaders' choice of political and economic system determined to a large extent their choice of social system. Even so, they arguably had somewhat more freedom of choice in moulding social relations than in other spheres of policy. This possibility makes their social policies especially interesting. At first, after 1917, they made considerable effort to put their egalitarian principles into practice. They took measures to limit the income and status of officials, to reduce wage differentials, and to raise the status of women in various ways. They recognised at the same time that great differences of income would have to be tolerated during the socialist period. Thus the scarce skills of bourgeois specialists of various kinds were rewarded with relative generosity. The attempts made to limit the influx of middle-class children into tertiary institutions and increase that of working-class children had only limited success. In secondary schools

---

18. Rothman & Breslauer, pp. 105, 243-5; Katz, pp. v-vii.

however, curricula and teaching methods were, it seems, designed to encourage broad interests and democratic attitudes among pupils.[19]

Such egalitarian tendencies as existed in the 1920s were systematically reversed by Stalin from 1929 onwards. He attacked egalitarianism with amazing openess, declaring it flatly to have 'nothing in common with Marxist socialism'.[20] Elite privileges were increased at a time when the living standards of the mass of the people were being forced down. The result was that elites of diverse kinds - such as leading party officials, state officials, military men, enterprise managers and scientists - enjoyed an exclusive life-style, which included domestic servants, the rare privilege of foreign travel, and access to special educational institutions, medical services and shops providing a wide variety of scarce goods. These rewards have survived, in large part, to the present.[21] Commanding these elites were (and still are) the leading _apparatchiks_, represented in the Politburo and Central Committee. While open to influence by other elites, who were of course strongly represented in the party, they retained considerable power to determine the distribution of material rewards in Soviet society as a whole. In the later 1930s, Trotsky wondered whether this 'commanding stratum' might become a new exploiting class, entrenched in property rights.[22] As he acknowledged, this was not yet happening: its privileges depended on Stalin's favour, which was notoriously fickle, and owed little or nothing to inherited advantages. The forms in which wealth could be accumulated were severely restricted in law and to a large extent in practice. Since the 1940s, however, some grounds for Trotsky's forebodings have appeared. The _apparatchiks'_ tenure of posts has become comparatively secure, and they are therefore better able to ensure vital educational advantages for their offspring. Taxes on inheritance of wealth were reduced to very little in 1943. Recently there have been signs that higher _apparatchiks_ have reinsured themselves against the risk of demotion by illegally buying land, gold or academic degrees.[23]

The elites under Stalin occupied the peak of a steeply graduated hierarchy, distinctions in which came to consist increasingly of educational qualifications. Those possessing a tertiary degree (whom we may like Lloyd Churchward describe as the intelligentsia) have,

19. M. Matthews, _Privilege in the Soviet Union_ (Allen & Unwin, London, 1978), pp. 61-70; Rothman & Breslauer, pp. 64, 77; G.W. Lapidus, 'Educational Strategies and Cultural Revolution', in S. Fitzpatrick (ed.), _Cultural Revolution in Russia 1928-31_ (Indiana University Press, Bloomington, 1978), pp. 82-4.

20. Quoted in Lane, p. 385.

21. Matthews, _Privilege_, pp. 33, 47-9, 127-130. According to Matthews' definition (pp. 29-33) the elite groups comprise 0.2% of the workforce.

22. _Revolution Betrayed_, p. 249; _In Defence of Marxism_ (Pathfinder Press, New York, 1973), pp. 9-11.

23. Matthews, _Privilege_, p. 102; Rothman & Breslauer, p. 118.

with their families, reached a proportion of the population (6-8% around 1970) far higher than in western Europe and second only to that in the USA.[24] While its higher ranks form a large part of the elites, its lower ranks, which include schoolteachers, GPs and most lawyers, tend to earn less than skilled workers. Even so the demand for tertiary education among the latter has exceeded the supply; and meanwhile there has been a shortage of recruits to skilled manual occupations, which has recently made it necessary for the regime to increase their attractiveness.[25] Thus the traditional Marxist aim of abolishing the status-distinction between mental and manual work has not been fulfilled, although admittedly this distinction is less than in capitalist countries. It is also significant that tertiary institutions have a marked status ranking, and that the intelligentsia's offspring, while they have always occupied a disproportionate share of places in tertiary education as a whole, have dominated especially the higher-ranking institutions. Their dominance was deliberately increased in the 1930s and 1940s by the introduction of student fees and school-leaving certificates. They appear since to have maintained their position and to have fought off Khrushchev's attempts to increase, for egalitarian reasons, the quota of children of manual backgrounds.[26]

The manual workforce in the 1930s became steeply stratified, with wage differentials related to skill, and also, through piece-rates, to production. The traditionally low status of peasants (in their new role of collective farm workers) was continued by their exclusion from minimum wage and social security provisions, by restrictions on internal travel, and by their low share of the amenities available to urban workers, including education. These disadvantages - which, although diminished, remain substantial - are made more serious by the fact that agricultural workers, even now, form one-sixth of the population.[27]

The measures which were intended in the 1920s to weaken the family - by, for example, facilitating divorce and abortion, and removing the disabilities of illegitimate children - were reversed in the 1930s. Although Soviet leaders have since Stalin partly restored the measures of the 1920s, they seem to have lost interest in the goal of weakening the family, now that parents belong to a generation that has been socialised into Soviet communism. Consequently the family has, as in capitalist countries, remained an important means of preserving status distinctions.[28] In secondary education, also, traditional attitudes were revived in the 1930s. There was a return to authoritarian relations between teachers and pupils, and to pedagogic

---

24. Matthews, Privilege, Class and Society in Soviet Russia (Allen Lane, London, 1972), p. 146.

25. Rothman & Breslauer, p. 122; Matthews, Class and Society, p. 292.

26. Ibid., pp. 286, 296-305.

27. Rothman & Breslauer, pp. 94-96, 103-4.

28. Lane, pp. 345-9.

techniques, such as lectures, exams and rote-learning, which encouraged obedience and conformity. Even after the recent reforms, these features still characterise Soviet education. The general aim of higher education has been to train specialised servants of the state, not to encourage individual self-fulfilment, and still less criticism of the social order.[29]

With regard to women, the main concern of the regime in the 1930s was to utilise their economic potential to the full. As a long-term result, their participation in the workforce, including the intelligentsia, has been far higher than in capitalist countries, a fact which has presumably made them more economically independent of parents or husbands. But men's assumptions of superiority have proved at least as durable as they are under capitalism, and the regime has done little effective to attack them. Thus it has been found that women tend to hold poorer-paid jobs than men in all occupational categories, and are thinly represented in all elites including the political. Moreover, women with jobs still tend to do the housework; and the regime has consistently neglected to alleviate the latter burden by adequate investment in creches, domestic gadgets and housing. While there is, as Stanley Rothman and George Breslauer remark, much scope for a feminist movement, no sign of one has appeared.[30]

Inequality of income in Stalin's Russia (as measured by the ratio of the top to the bottom decile, taking into account taxation and social welfare) was quite possibly greater than in any other industrialised society in this century.[31] It was however combined with an exceptionally high rate of upward mobility, because of the mass movement from agriculture to industry, and the creation of new managerial and professional classes. Since Stalin's death the decline in income differentials has been extraordinarily rapid. It has clearly been caused by the regime's repeated measures to increase the living standards of poorer, manual workers, measures which seem to have been motivated mainly by concern for the regime's popularity, and secondarily by egalitarian considerations. Yet even today, inequality seems to be much greater than in other Communist countries, and as Peter Wiles has shown, may well be as great as in Great Britain. Meanwhile, with the consolidation of the social system, the rate of upward mobility of manual workers has declined to a point not obviously greater than in the USA (where the proportion of the population with tertiary education is similar). Industrial workers may still have better opportunities than in the latter of ascending the social ladder, especially through the hierarchy of party officials, where they are favoured for ideological reasons. But in the main, the various social strata of today are perpetuating themselves: for example,

---

29. Rothman & Breslauer, pp. 77-81.
30. Ibid., pp. 68-70.
31. Matthews, <u>Class and Society</u>, p. 42.

tomorrow's intelligentsia can be expected to consist largely of the children of today's.[32]

The motives of Soviet leaders in maintaining inequality have been their determination to preserve their privileges, and their need to provide the workforce with the incentives to work steadily and improve their skills. Although these imperatives have weakened since 1953 - in that the regime has become less dictatorial and the workforce better trained - they are continuing to mould the social hierarchy. Thus Soviet society today displays widespread and marked status distinctions, which show no sign of declining. Isaac Deutscher has argued that the spread of higher education, and the egalitarianism of official ideology, can be expected to erode inequalities progressively.[33] The validity of this contention is far from self-evident. As a force for greater equality, the spread of higher education seems to be offset by the growth of educational prerequisites for better-paid jobs. For example, the opportunities for manual workers to rise into managerial ranks are diminishing for this reason.[34] And there seems no reason to assume that the contradictions, with regard to inequality, between official theory and official practice will cause critical problems for the regime. On the contrary, the Soviet Union seems to illustrate Wertheim's argument that contradictory values may be quite consistent with the long-term stability of a political system.[35]

We can now see that Soviet leaders have effectively abandoned the ultimate, utopian aims of the 1917 revolution, except in the limited sense that they seem to be influenced by these aims in their modest attempts to improve the living standards and educational opportunities of manual workers. The 1961 programme soon became an embarrassment, to be ignored; and the traditional practice was resumed of relegating communism to the remote future.[36] Soviet leaders do not encourage discussion about any ways (other than technological) of achieving the Marxist-Leninist utopia, and indeed tend to treat such discussion as subversive. The cost to the political system is a generally low level of idealistic and emotional commitment to it. Party members seem to lack the fervour which characterises revolutionary creeds at their zenith, and the mass of citizens, especially the poorer or less educated, tend to regard the authorities' exhortations with passive cynicism. The idealistic appeal on which the

---

32. P. Wiles, Distribution of Income: East and West (North-Holland Publishing Co., Amsterdam, 1974), pp. 1-12, 23-5; Lane, p. 141; Rothman & Breslauer, pp. 120-3.

33. The Unfinished Revolution. Russia 1917-1967 (Oxford University Press, London, 1967), pp. 58-9.

34. Rothman & Breslauer, p. 121.

35. Evolution and Revolution, p.109.

36. A.B. Evans, 'Developed Socialism in Soviet Ideology', Soviet Studies, vol.29, no.3 (July 1977), p. 417.

regime chiefly relies in its exhortations is nationalism,[37] which is in Marxist terms a retrograde ideology. Still more telling is the Soviet Union's failure, which has grown increasingly apparent during the last generation, to win converts or imitators outside its sphere of dominance. Communist parties outside this sphere have chosen to interpret Marxism-Leninism quite differently from the Soviet leaders, as we see for example in Tito's break with Stalin from 1948 onwards, and in the rise of Eurocommunism in western Europe since the 1960s. Nor do underdeveloped countries appear to look for inspiration to the Soviet model of economic development. The ideological ossification of the regime is symbolised by the dull, aged bureaucrats who lead it.

It seems then that the Soviet revolution has reached a dead end. Some commentators, like Wertheim, have drawn a parallel between Soviet developments and Thermidor (the conservative counter-movement which began in France in 1795), so implying that at some point the revolution deviated to the right. But as Wertheim inadvertently shows, such a point cannot be convincingly identified.[38] The reason why not is that, as we have seen, there have been strong elements of continuity in Soviet policy since the Bolsheviks' seizure of power. The allegedly right-wing tendencies in the Soviet regime surely originated earlier: in Lenin's concept of an authoritarian party, and in his decision to seize power in a traditionally autocratic and economically backward country.

---

37. Rothman & Breslauer, p. 80.
38. Evolution and Revolution, pp. 221, 331-2.

Chapter Nine

CHINA - AN INTERRUPTED REVOLUTION

Bill Brugger

For many years the Chinese revolution which culminated in 1949 was taken as an ideal against which many other revolutions were measured. For Huntington, the Chinese revolution exemplified the 'Eastern' type in which an alternative regime is created before the *ancien regime* disappears, as opposed to the 'Western' type in which a new regime is born consequent upon the disintegration of the *ancien regime*.[1] For Wertheim, the Chinese revolution, was a clear example of a backward country (in Mao Zedong's words 'poor and blank') leaping ahead of others in the global drive towards emancipation.[2] For Chalmers Johnson, in structural-functionalist mood, the Chinese revolution was a paradigm case of elite incapacity to manage multiple disfunctions[3] or, in a less obscure vein, a clear example of a social revolution precipitated by Japanese-induced peasant nationalism.[4] Indeed many commentators take the Chinese revolution to be the peasant revolution par excellence. For a while many Third World revolutionaries used that description admiringly whilst Trotskyists and eventually the leaders of the Soviet Union saw in it a source of un-proletarian deviation.

This tendency to take China as an ideal has a long history. In the eighteenth century the *philosophes* of the Enlightenment, whilst seeing China as the antithesis of revolutionary, still idealised that country as typifying an administration more in tune with the 'Age of Reason' than anything in the European despotisms (enlightened or otherwise). In the late eighteenth and nineteenth century the mood changed. In different ways Montesquieu, Smith, Hegel and Marx pieced together a new model, which was equally unrevolutionary but this time characterised by 'oriental despotism' or the 'Asiatic mode of

1. See p. 128.
2. See p. 146.
3. See p. 125.
4. C. Johnson, *Peasant Nationalism and Communist Power* (Stanford University Press, Stanford, Calif., 1962).

production'.[5] Such a society could never be revolutionary and change would have to wait upon the transformation of the rest of the world. As the nineteenth century wore on, all that could be hoped for was the incorporation of China into the rest of the world through opium, the gunboat, modern urban administration in the treaty ports, a small foreign-trained corps of intellectuals and missionaries trying in vain to staunch the 'Niagara of souls crashing down to perdition'. China the source of all virtue had become the source of all evil (even though many of the ascribed evils such as opium had been imported from the West). The mood had indeed changed but the tendency to create ideal types had not.

Yet eighteenth-century China never had the ideal rational bureaucracy attributed to it. Nor was nineteenth-century China the source of such unparalleled evil. Nor indeed were the categorisations of the Chinese revolution as pure as they have been painted as was noted in Chapter 7. If the Chinese revolution which culminated in 1949 was 'eastern' in Huntington's sense then the revolution of 1911 was 'western' in that the Imperial regime did in fact crumble from within before any new order was created. In fact, a new order was not created, and the 1911 revolution was interrupted by the chaotic warlord era. And as for Wertheim's dialectical leaps towards emancipation, the vantage point of 1983 offers much less sanguine a picture than the period of the early Cultural Revolution in which he wrote. In this post-functionalist age, moreover, the idea that a revolution might be explained largely in terms of elite mismanagement is seen as somewhat naive. To be sure the Chinese revolution was nationalist but the work of Selden[6] and others points to a positive social appeal exercised by the policies of the Chinese Communist Party which goes far beyond a simple nationalist appeal to the peasants to resist the Japanese (a conclusion no doubt influenced by the bulk of Johnson's sources which derived from the Japanese military authorities). Even the notion of the Chinese revolution as being overwhelmingly of a peasant nature must confront the evidence about the activities of the urban underground which was quite able to administer cities such as Shanghai before the People's Liberation Army entered the urban areas. Indeed, much of the faction-fighting in the Cultural Revolution might be understood in terms of the different urban and rural origins of those different factions.[7] The Chinese revolution is much more complex than the creators of ideal types have depicted.

To understand the nature of the Chinese revolution, I shall try to describe how various members of the Chinese Communist Party

---

5. See P. Anderson, Lineages of the Absolutist State (New Left Books, London, 1974), pp. 477-8.

6. M. Selden, The Yenan Way in Revolutionary China (Harvard University Press, Cambridge, Mass.), 1971.

7. See D. and N. Milton, The Wind Will Not Subside: Years in Revolutionary China 1964-1969 (Pantheon Books, New York, 1976).

understood it. The Party was born in the wake of the May Fourth Movement of 1919 - a time of great intellectual ferment in which Marxists rubbed shoulders with Liberals and Anarchists and in which intellectuals expressed sudden political conversions. Those intellectuals were not always coherent in their beliefs nor altogether sure about how to relate to the peasantry and the fledgling working class. At the time of the Party's formation in 1921, its leaders had only hazy and confused ideas about the revolutionary nature of their aims. Indeed at that time it was actually proposed that the relative merits of the Russian and German revolutions be examined before any concrete strategy was worked out - a very un-Leninist view.[8] The initial aim of the Party was simply to organise the working class; but the Comintern, informed by Lenin's theses on the national and colonial question, made it quite clear that the Chinese party was to engage in an essentially bourgeois democratic revolution and added the task of helping to mobilise the national bourgeoisie. After initial flirtation with a central Chinese warlord, Wu Peifu, the Comintern eventually forged an alliance with Sun Zhongshan's (Sun Yat-sen's) Guomindang (Kuomintang) which Russian advisers sought to reorganise. The aim was to unify the country, to sever China from the embrace of imperialism and to dispossess the landlord class. The alliance was short-lived. Strikes aimed at foreign business soon spilled over into Chinese business and the sons of land-owners would only support radical land reform when it was someone else's land which was being redistributed. Following the death of Sun Zhongshan (1925) and during a Northern Expedition to unify the country (1926), the Guomindang split into a right and left wing in which the former triumphed following the purges led by Jiang Jieshi (Chiang K'ai-shek) in 1927.

As Jiang attempted to crush it in the late 1920s, the Communist Party lurched from one putschist strategy to another. The initial aim was to recapture urban bases to ensure the continuance of the supposed proletarian-peasant alliance. By 1930 that strategy had failed due to inept leadership, uninformed advice from the Comintern (rent by the leadership struggle marking Stalin's rise to power), naive faith in the increasingly small 'left Guomindang' and an impatient optimism which bore no relation to the reality of the situation. By that time Mao Zedong, who had built up revolutionary base areas first in Jingganshan (Ching-kan-shan) and later in Jiangxi (Kiangsi), was learning how to ignore the instructions or advice from the Party centre in Shanghai and had begun to develop a revolutionary strategy of his own.

The Chinese revolution, interrupted in the late 1920s, achieved a new lease of life during the period of the Jiangxi Soviet in the early 1930s. At that time Mao, anxious to rectify the damage done by the earlier obsession with capturing cities, began to develop a set of policies known as 'people's war'. He advocated a protracted war in the countryside, integrating regular troops with guerillas and a popular

8. B. Schwartz, Chinese Communism and the Rise of Mao (Harvard University Press, Cambridge, Mass.), 1966, p. 34.

militia. The strategy of that time was expressed in the slogan: 'the enemy advances, we retreat; the enemy camps, we harass; the enemy tires, we attack; the enemy retreats, we pursue'. Large bodies of Red Army troops were concentrated to pick off enemy units and war along fixed fronts was avoided; the aim was to drown an urban-based enemy in what was referred to as 'a sea of people'.[9] In this process peasant activism was to be promoted by a very radical programme of land reform in which the property of both landlords and rich peasants was distributed. The costs of Mao's strategy were quite high. In retrospect it seems that land reform was too radical, alienating potential sources of support. The flexible strategy of 'people's war', moreover, involved abandoning peasants to their fate whenever the enemy advanced in strength; fear of reprisals, therefore, dampened peasant activism. Considerations such as these led to Mao being removed from a position of military leadership in 1933 and the adoption of what was referred to as the 'forward and offensive line'. As a response to Jiang's fourth and fifth encirclement campaigns, the Red Army stood its ground and was defeated. There followed the abandonment of the Jiangxi Soviet and the epic Long March of 1934-5. Once again the revolution was interrupted.

The Long March consolidated Mao's leadership over the Chinese Communist Party and vindicated his military strategy. Its culmination was the establishment of new base areas which eventually centred on the country town of Yan'an (Yenan). Following the outbreak of full-scale hostilities with Japan in 1937, a new United Front with the Guomindang was forged, though by 1941 tensions between the two 'allies' had deteriorated to the point of armed conflict. By that time the bulk of resistance to Japan in North China was being carried on forces led by the Communist Party and followed the old people's war strategy. To be sure, savage 'mopping up' operations, carried out by Japanese forces which were always numerically too few to occupy the countryside, did strengthen the Communist cause. Yet the Yan'an model of leadership and administration was also a powerful factor in peasant identification with the Communist Party.

The Yan'an model was worked out within the context of a much more explicit formulation of the type of revolution promoted by the Communist Party. The Party was not engaged in a 'proletarian' revolution or even a socialist revolution. The model of socialism announced by Stalin in 1936 was seen as a very distant project. The Party was engaged in a species of bourgeois revolution known as 'new democratic'.[10] According to this formulation, the Party was to promote the interests of a 'four class bloc' of workers, peasants, petty bourgeoisie and national capitalists to oppose landlords (conventionally though, in my view, wrongly referred to as 'feudal') and comprador

9. See J. Girling, People's War (George Allen & Unwin, London, 1969), pp. 49-114.

10. Mao Zedong, Selected Works, vol. II (Peking Foreign Languages Press (PFLP), Beijing, 1965), pp. 339-84.

capitalists (those with close connections with foreign imperialist powers). This formulation, much broader than Lenin's 'democratic dictatorship of workers and peasants' aimed initially not to overthrow capitalism but to control it and direct it towards national as opposed to imperialist ends.

In the Yan'an model, the fluid pattern of military administration was linked to an equally fluid pattern of highly simplified civil and economic administration which operated according to the principle of 'concentrated leadership and divided operations'. Overall general policies were made at the centre (Yan'an) but considerable operational leeway was given to dispersed units of administration throughout the area. The system was highly decentralised with operational leadership vested in a peculiar leadership type - the 'cadre'. Such cadres were required to be conscious of the overall goals of developmental policies and political movements and to this end were subject to an on-going process of 'rectification' whereby heterodox views were criticised and commitment reinforced. In the field, however, cadres were given considerable freedom in interpreting policy and in working out operational instructions. They were required to forge close links with the people amongst whom they operated and, in the manner of Rousseau's 'legislator', were to 'persuade rather than command'. Leadership policy was summed up in a set of principles known as the 'mass line' which demanded the fullest discussion of central policies by ordinary people and the processing of mass demands and support for the formulation of subsequent policy.[11] The mass line demanded that the cadre walk the narrow path between, on the one hand, 'commandism' (issuing instructions based on centrally-determined policy without any regard for popular sentiment) and, on the other, 'tailism' (courting public opinion by not making any decision related to interests wider than those which the peasants perceived immediately). Both military and civilian cadres were required constantly to demonstrate their altruism, commitment to community goals and repudiation of the centuries-old vice of parasitism of which civilian officials and military officers in China had been guilty. Such commitment was best demonstrated within an egalitarian ethos. In theory official Party policy was not egalitarian; it could not be so long as Stalin, who had some, if rather remote, theoretical influence on Party policy, condemned egalitarism as 'a reactionary petty-bourgeois absurdity worthy of some primitive sect of ascetics'.[12] In practice, however, Stalinist influence was negligible and the egalitarian ethos did much to foster very close links between civilians and military, cadres and peasants.

Within the framework of a United Front policy, land reform was discontinued and the stress laid on rent reduction and the development of rural co-operatives which were required to demonstrate a high degree of self-sufficiency. Such self-sufficiency was seen not only as

---

11. Mao Zedong, 1 June 1943, Selected Works, vol. III, p. 119.
12. J. Stalin, 26 January 1934, J. Stalin, Works, vol. XIII (Foreign Languages Publishing House, Moscow, 1955), p. 361.

worthwhile in itself, but as necessary in a cellular economy with bad communications subject to penetration by Japanese forces. Indeed the efforts of the Japanese to mop up Communists did much to foster a degree of group cohesion that made the egalitarian ethos more effective. It was not only co-operatives that were required to be self-sufficient; some military units achieved up to 50% self-sufficiency in agricultural production upon land which they had newly reclaimed. In this situation agriculture and light industry were expected to develop side by side and to generate savings for the armaments industry so necessary at that time.

With decentralised mass mobilisation, education tended to be directed to immediate tasks.[13] The achievement of literacy was essential in an area where the literacy rate was some one percent in the mid-1930s, and courses were naturally oriented towards practical requirements. The educational reforms of that time were directed to changing the attitude of teachers ignorant of peasant life who had come from the coastal cities to the base areas to take part in the resistance struggle. There was a tendency also to de-emphasise the formal school system in favour of a decentralised informal system which spread the literacy base at the expense of quality in training. The emphasis was on creating conditions for large number of people to take modest steps towards community goals rather than selecting a highly qualified elite - a necessary policy but one which was later to be criticised by professionals.

The Yan'an period, in the early 1940s, was radical in the sense that very new organisations were created and new patterns of commitment were fostered even though United Front policies inhibited the process of land reform. It is significant to note that, in the history of the Chinese Communist Party, periods of radicalism have always been accompanied by criticism of foreign developmental models but after 1949 decisions were taken gradually to emulate the current Soviet developmental model. It is true that in some sectors, during limited periods, policy was far from moderate compared with the Yan'an situation. Land reform had been implemented vigorously after 1946[14] and, although the tempo slowed down after 1948, rural policy remained relatively radical until 1953. Similarly, in 1951-2 a number of mass movements were instituted to control the private sector of industry, to improve security during the Korean War and to correct a tendency for cadres to relax. By 1953, however, attempts were made to copy the Soviet system of planning and economic organisation.[15]

The full-scale emulation of the Stalinist model only really got

---

13. See P. Seybolt, 'The Yenan Revolution in Mass Education', The China Quarterly (CQ), 48, (Oct.-Dec. 1971), pp. 641-69.

14. For an excellent account of this see W. Hinton, Fanshen (Vintage Books, New York, 1966).

15. The best account of this is H. Schurmann, Ideology and Organization in Communist China (University of California Press, Berkeley, 1966).

under way after the death of Stalin in 1953. In the economic field the Soviet model stressed a concentration on heavy industry and very rapid industrialisation. Predictably such a concentration produced an investment crisis by the middle 1950s when it was seen that other sectors of industry were not generating savings sufficient to keep up heavy industrial development; nevertheless, such a programme was probably necessary when economic blockade and threatened invasion made a stress on the defence industry paramount. Commenting in 1962, Mao observed that this period dampened the creativity of the Chinese people but had been indispensable.[16]

Concentration on centralised planning led inevitably to a process of bureaucratisation. The new culture-hero of the period was not the multi-competent cadre but the manager and engineer, not the self-sacrificing peasant-soldier but a Chinese equivalent of the Stakhanovite worker. Egalitarianism was now sharply criticised as a manifestation of the 'guerrilla mentality' or an 'agrarian socialist' deviation. The armed forces had fought through the Civil War and the Korean War without ranks; yet in 1955 the whole paraphernalia of the Soviet ranking system was brought in with highly 'progressive' salary grades. A private drew some Y6 per month whereas the newly created rank of Marshal drew in excess of Y500. (One cannot, of course, express this as a ratio since privates and non-commissioned officers received free board and uniform etc.). In civilian administration there existed up to 30 bureaucratic grades with salary ranging from under Y30 to Y560.[17] In industry the primary concern was for individual material incentive expressed according to the 'socialist' formula of 'from each according to labour, to each according to work' and measured 'scientifically' in terms of individual piecework, long criticised by socialists in capitalist countries as 'sweated labour'. Any demand for payment according to need was criticised as 'idealist' since it implied a desire to implement 'communist' forms of remuneration at a time when material conditions were as yet not even fully commensurate with the demands of socialism.

As urban 'rationalisation' was speeded up, so rural transformation was slowed down. Land reform tended to stop at the point of land redistribution and mutual aid. The removal of landlords saw the growth of a 'kulak' class which utilised traditional connections to fill the gap vacated by the former rural elite.[18] The privileged economic position of rich peasants put them in a position to buy out poorer peasants whose share in the land redistribution had often been too small to be economically viable especially when harvests were bad. The inadequacy of state banking facilities in the countryside

16. Mao Zedong, January 1962, in Mao Zhuxi Wenxuan, n.p.n.d. (Red Guard source), p. 74.

17. E. Vogel, 'From Revolutionary to Semi-Bureaucrat: The "Regularisation of Cadres"', CQ, 29 (January-March 1967), p. 51.

18. See T. Bernstein, 'Problems of Village Leadership After Land Reform', CQ, 36 (October-December 1968), pp. 1-22.

meant that poorer peasants frequently turned to the richer peasants for loans against which land holdings were mortgaged. Clearly land concentration would become serious unless measures were taken to prevent the right to alienate land and unless rich peasants were compelled to join the fledgling agricultural producers' co-operatives which, at that time, tended to be less productive than the richer private sector.

By 1955 it became clear to Mao that once again the revolutionary impetus had been interrupted. New class polarisation in the countryside and the investment crisis caused by an over-concentration on heavy industry led to a renewed drive for collectivisation. This was carried out with some loss of production but with nowhere near the chaos which accompanied the Soviet drive in the late 1920s.[19] The success of the movement owed much to the fact that landholdings were smaller but it was also due in large measure to the continued peasant commitment to the Communist Party generated during the years of war. At the same time the private sector of industry and commerce was socialised and Chinese leaders could contemplate the beginning of a new stage of development.

Despite the fact that, by 1956, the Chinese Communist Party was rethinking its implementation of a model of organisation copied from the Soviet Union, it nonetheless still adhered to a notion of socialist construction laid down by Stalin in the mid-1930s and slightly modified in 1952. By the time of the introduction of the Soviet Constitution of 1936 Stalin had transformed the notion of socialism as a developmental process into a description of a discrete mode of production. I have argued elsewhere that in doing this Stalin saw socialism as something akin to a Weberian ideal type rather than what Marx saw as a mode of production.[20] In practice what was presented was the skeleton of a system called 'socialism', and the task of socialist construction was to flesh it out. Most of the agenda for the immediate future consisted of economic items. In as much as class struggle existed it was seen as a residue of the past or the result of foreign influence. By 1936 Stalin could talk of the disappearance of

---

19. T. Bernstein, 'Leadership and Mass Mobilisation in the Soviet and Chinese Collectivisation Campaigns of 1929-30 and 1955-56: A Comparison', CQ, 31 (July-September 1967), pp. 1-47; P. Nolan, 'Collectivisation in China: Some Comparisons with the USSR', Journal of Peasant Studies, vol. III, no. 2, January 1976, pp. 192-220.

20. B. Brugger, 'Soviet and Chinese Views on Revolution and Socialism - Some Thoughts on the Problems of Diachrony and Synchrony', Journal of Contemporary Asia, vol. XI, no. 3, 1981, pp. 311-32. Weber defines an 'ideal type' as 'the synthesis of a great many diffuse, discrete, more or less present and occasionally absent concrete individual phenomena which are arranged according to...one-sidely emphasised viewpoints into a unified analytical contract', M. Weber, The Methodology of the Social Sciences (New York, The Free Press, 1949), p. 90. Marxists usually criticise these 'ideal types' as static.

the peasants (they had been transformed into kolkhoz or sovkhoz workers) and the transformation of the proletariat into 'the working class'. Such a view did not stop Stalin invoking the notion of the 'dictatorship of the proletariat' during the bloody purges of the late 1930s; nevertheless the conception of socialism which was transmitted to China in the 1950s was far from revolutionary.

Following the initial collectivisation of agriculture and the socialisation of industry and commerce in the mid-1950s, the Chinese leadership began to view its own new stage of development in the above Stalinist form. Thus at the Eighth Party Congress in 1956 the main contradiction in Chinese society was no longer seen in terms of 'class struggle'. Now the main contradiction was said to be between the 'advanced socialist system' and 'the backward productive forces'.[21] The primary task was economic development within the newly created planning structure. Before long, however, Mao, who had begun to see the existing planning structure as a cause of inertia, became increasingly unhappy with the line of the Eighth Party Congress and added a more dynamic notion to his views on socialist construction. Commenting on the events in Hungary in late 1956, Mao observed that they had been due in large measure to the 'incorrect handling of contradictions' in society. 'Non-antagonistic' contradictions (capable of resolution by persuasion and discussion) had been allowed to become 'antagonistic' (requiring one aspect of the contradiction to annihilate the other).[22] The recognition that non-antagonistic contradictions, incorrectly handled, might become antagonistic built upon Stalin's views of 1952[23] but went beyond them. The cosy view that a socialist future was guaranteed and the major tasks were simple and economic was severely questioned.

Nor was it at all clear that the moderate policies adopted by the Eighth Party Congress would stimulate economic development at sufficient speed. Mao's early attempts to 'handle contradictions' during the movement to 'let a hundred flowers bloom' in 1957 soon grew over into a full-scale attack on conservatism in economic construction and repeated revisions of China's Second Five Year Plan. The result was the Great Leap Forward of 1958-59 which aimed to achieve a rapid economic breakthrough by the simultaneous promotion of heavy industry, light industry and agriculture, completely outside the parameters of the national plan. The massive feats of endeavour during the production drive of 1958 are legendary. The successes were on a grand scale but so were the failures. As the economy was thrown out of gear the planning machinery broke down, statistics were

---

21. Chinese Communist Party, 27 September 1956, Eighth National Congress of the Chinese Communist Party (PFLP, Beijing, 1956), p. 116.

22. See Mao Zedong, 27 February 1957, in Selected Works, vol. V, pp 384-421.

23. J. Stalin, Economic Problems of Socialism in the U.S.S.R. (1952), PFLP, Beijing, 1972.

falsified and much chaos ensued. The commune system which emerged at that time was designed amongst other things to achieve an agricultural breakthrough though heavy industry still developed at a quite disproportionate speed. The initial strategy was one which aimed to improve the rural-urban terms of trade in favour of the peasants and to boost consumption; but as things turned out the rate at which funds were reserved for investment was higher than ever before and eventually this dampened peasant ardour.

Much has been written on the strengths and weaknesses of the Great Leap Forward. This is not the place to rehearse the arguments. What is significant to the theme of this chapter is that Mao and various other leaders in the Chinese Communist Party began to consider the economic push in terms of a social revolution in which structures were created conducive to the advance towards a new 'communist' form of society. Now the process of socialist construction was not just the sober achievement of long-term planned targets but was itself a revolution - an uninterrupted revolution (buduan geming).[24] A stress on balanced planning and orderly book-keeping, Mao felt, could interrupt the revolutionary process. After all, 'imbalance' was the long-term trend; balance was 'temporary and relative'.[25] Society should progress in a wave-like motion with sudden bursts of creative activity punctuated by troughs of consolidation.

By 1959 the Great Leap had met immense difficulties occasioning a good deal of scepticism amongst the Chinese Leadership. After a brief revival following a leadership struggle late in that year, the Leap ground to a halt and the period of consolidation which followed was one in which the Chinese people endured bitter hardships. A significant portion of the Chinese leadership were determined that there should be no new high tide and no more uncontrolled spurts of 'uninterrupted revolution'.

After the demise of the Great Leap, Mao retired to what he referred to as the 'second line' of the Chinese leadership in which he contemplated events in China and more particularly the collapse of revolutionary fervour in the Soviet Union.

In his writings of the early 1960s, Mao seemed above all to be concerned with working out a theoretical explanation of 'revisionism'. Up to that time, the term had been treated merely as a behavioural characteristic amenable to arbitrary interpretation. Now, Mao attempted to depict a number of stages through which the socialist revolution would pass and to define revisionism as the adoption of policies which belonged to a superseded stage.

---

24. See G. Young and D. Woodward, 'From Contradictions Among the People to Class Struggle: The Theories of Uninterrupted and Continuous Revolution', Asian Survey, vol. XVIII, no. 9 (September 1978), pp. 912-33.

25. Mao Zedong, 19 February 1958, from untitled Red Guard Source, p. 33. See translation in Current Background, 892 (21 October 1969), p. 7.

The problem of the stages of revolution has always been a very contentious one among Marxist-Leninists. In telescoping the bourgeois democratic stage of revolution into the socialist stage, Trotsky had incurred the ire of the whole of the Stalinist establishment. Thus, when Mao put forward his ideas on 'uninterrupted revolution' in the Great Leap Forward, he made the point that he was not adopting a Trotskyist position and still conceived of discrete stages.[26] Schram, who translates the term 'uninterrupted revolution' (buduan geming) as 'permanent revolution' (the term used by Trotsky and by Mao in his criticism of Trotsky), is unconvinced by Mao's defence.[27] Levy, on the other hand, who focuses on Mao's writings of 1960-2, is sure that Mao had worked out a coherent 'timing theory'.[28] Though each of Mao's transitional stages established the preconditions for the next, it was quite separate. The first of these in modern Chinese history constituted the bourgeois democratic revolution which ended in 1949 with the seizure of power.[29] Here, Mao revised the earlier view that the bourgeois democratic revolution had continued through the new democratic stage of the early 1950s. The second stage constituted the socialist transformation which was completed by the mid-1950s. Here, Mao was careful to avoid saying that socialism had been achieved[30] indicating that he had come to reject the static model of socialism which Stalin had laid down in 1936. The third stage, which began in the mid-1950s, was marked by the co-existence of 'co-operative ownership' and 'ownership by the whole people', though one is never quite sure which elements of the Chinese economy belonged to which category. The fourth stage, which had yet to be embarked upon, was to be characterised by 'total ownership by the whole people' and the fifth stage was, in fact, communism. After that there would be other stages which no one at present could define.[31]

Having elaborated these stages, it was possible to develop a theory critical of developments in the Soviet Union. As Mao saw it, the Soviet leadership applied principles valid for one stage to completely different stages. Stalin, for example, did not see the different roles played by commodities in the different stages of

---

26. Mao Zedong, 28 January 1958, Chinese Law and Government, vol. I, no. 4, Winter 1968-9, pp. 13-14. This discussion of Mao's views on 'continuous revolution' is taken from B. Brugger, China: Liberation and Transformation (Croom Helm, London, 1981), pp. 248-53. Some passages are identical.

27. S. Schram, 'Mao Tse-tung and the Theory of the Permanent Revolution, 1958-69', CQ, 46 (April-June 1971), pp. 221-44.

28. R. Levy, 'New Light on Mao: His Views on the Soviet Union's "Political Economy"', CQ, 61 (March 1975), pp. 95-117.

29. Mao Zedong 1960 (or 1961-2), in Joint Publications Research Service, Miscellany of Mao Tse-tung Thought (1949-1968), 2 vols., Arlington, Va., 20 February 1974, p. 252.

30. Ibid., p. 268.

31. Ibid., pp. 264 and 273.

socialist transition. Both Mao and Stalin agreed that labour power could no longer remain a commodity once the socialist revolution had begun. Both also agreed that commodity production was necessary so long as co-operative ownership coexisted with 'ownership by the whole people';[32] only that way could exchange between the two sectors be ensured. They differed, however, with regard to the commodity feature of the means of production. As Mao saw it, Stalin regarded the replacement, by planning, of the commodity feature of the means of production as a key element of socialism.[33] Stalin, therefore, applied policies appropriate to the stage of 'total ownership by the whole people' to the stage where that form of ownership still coexisted with co-operative ownership. Thus there was a premature and excessive reliance on the planning machinery and an inefficient centralisation which dampened mass initiative.

Though Stalin had erred by implementing, in the current stage, policies appropriate to another stage, his error was qualitatively different from that of the Soviet leadership in the early 1960s. Stalin, in applying policies appropriate to a future stage, had committed a 'leftist' error. The current Soviet leadership was implementing policies appropriate to a superseded stage. They were thus 'revisionist'. If the above is a correct interpretation of Mao's views, then the implications for Chinese policies were most profound. Unfortunately, Mao was reluctant to draw those implications, probably because he had supported most of the policies of retrenchment in the wake of the Great Leap. It is possible that Mao viewed the situation on two levels. On the one hand, he supported measures designed to restore the economy and foster the norms of inner-Party debate. On the other hand, he surely could not fail to notice that those policies might also be seen as belonging to a superseded stage of development and could be described as 'revisionist'. If Mao had followed through his theoretical discussion, he might have concluded that contracting out publically-owned land to peasant families constituted a retreat to the second or even the first stage. Other policies, moreover, might have been seen as appropriate for the current stage in terms of ownership but in terms of Mao's other two criteria for evaluating a particular stage - the relations between people at work and the reciprocal relations between production and distribution.[34] This was particularly the case with regard to industrial management.

Mao was to go much further than just examining policies. By the early 1960s, it was evident that he was becoming more and more concerned that new privileged groups might provide the basis for the formation of a new bourgeoisie. He spoke of 'vested interest groups' (jide liyi jituan)[35] stemming from the 'three major differences'

32. Ibid., p. 298.

33. Mao Zedong, November 1958 (or 1959), in ibid., p. 130. Discussed in Levy, loc.cit., pp. 103-4.

34. Mao Zedong, 1960 (or 1961-2), loc.cit., p. 270.

35. Ibid., p. 273.

(between town and country; worker and peasant and mental and manual labour). These had taken on a hereditary nature.[36] At a conference attended by 7,000 cadres in January 1962 he was quite explicit:

> In our country, the system of man exploiting man has already been abolished as has the economic basis of landlords and bourgeoisie. Since the reactionary classes are now not so terrible as hitherto, we speak of them as remnants. Yet on no account must we treat these remnants lightly. We must continue to engage in struggle with them for they are still planning a comeback. In a socialist society moreover new bourgeois elements may still be produced. Classes and class struggle remain throughout the entire socialist stage and that struggle is protracted, complex and sometimes even violent.[37]

Thus the slogan 'never forget the class struggle', was to dominate Mao's thinking during the next few years. Though Mao still saw classes as residues of the past, his new formulation allowed for classes to be generated in the process of socialist transition. The implications of this generative view are quite profound. It now became conceivable that newly generated classes might be found in the leadership of the Communist Party itself. Socialism could now be viewed not as a model to be achieved and consolidated but as the whole process of transition from capitalism to communism. It was, moreover, reversible. A restoration of capitalism could now be conceived as taking place not only because of the actions of enemy agents (as it was according to the view of the early 1950s), not only because of the inappropriate handling of contradictions (as it was according to Mao's managerial view of the mid-1950s), but because of inequalities generated in the process of economic development.

But how was the generation of these new classes to be prevented? Here we must look at Mao's discussion of the relationship between the productive forces and the relations of production. Since Mao ignored the old problem in Marxism which stems from Marx's location of the relations of production in both the economic base and the ideological superstructure, his views on his subject tend to be somewhat crude. Nevertheless, following Levy, I am convinced that it is possible to see in Mao's writings of the early 1960s the germs of a theory of cultural revolution. Mao felt that the process, described by Marx, whereby a revolution is caused by productive forces outstripping the relations of production - i.e. when the superstructure lags behind the economic base - was valid only for advanced societies. In more

36. See R. Kraus, 'Class Conflict and the Vocabulary of Social Analysis in China', CQ, 69 (March 1977), pp. 63-4.

37. Mao Zedong, 30 January 1962, Mao n.p.n.d. (probably 1967), pp. 68-9, emphasis added. Slightly different translation in Peking Review, 27 (7 July 1978), p. 12.

backward countries, a revolution begins in the superstructure because that is the weakest link in the chain of capitalist control.[38] Thus the relations of production may be transformed before the corresponding productive forces have fully developed and the superstructure, instead of lagging behind, provides the conditions to push the productive forces forward. A cultural revolution, therefore, precedes a social revolution. What is more contentious, both in interpretation and in substance, is Levy's suggestion that the above conclusion was seen by Mao as valid not only for major revolutions marking a seizure of power but for qualitative leaps in the process of socialist transition. Together, these leaps might be seen as part of a continuing process of revolution and the excessive consolidation of any stage in the transition process would create obstacles for the development of the next.[39] To prevent excessive consolidation in any stage, a number of measures had to be taken which were, in the first instance, superstructural.

The above formulation was markedly different from most Soviet views of the determining role of the productive forces. The official Soviet view was not a mechanistic one where changes in the productive forces automatically produced changes in the relations of production, or where the latter were simply a drag on the former. Indeed Stalin, in 1952, castigated the would-be textbook writer Yaroshenko for absorbing the relations of production into the productive forces and reaching a mechanistic view of communism as rational organisation.[40] Nevertheless, Mao gave a far greater weight to the active role of the superstructure than Stalin; indeed he criticised Stalin on precisely that point.[41]

If the above is a correct description of Mao's position, then he had revised the orthodox view of cultural revolution. This held that changes in ideas lag behind changes in material forces and a revolutionary process is necessary to bring them back into correspondence. This had been the view which had informed Mao's mid-1950s view of uninterrupted revolution and it continued into the 1960s. Indeed, in the same work in which Levy suggests Mao might be arguing in favour of superstructural push, one may still find paragraphs discussing cultural lag.[42] Of course, superstructural push and cultural lag need not necessarily be in contradiction but one cannot use both theories to describe the same period. Yet Mao seemed to be doing precisely that. But perhaps one may understand his reluctance to abandon the theory of cultural lag in favour of initial superstructural push. After all, it could lead to a charge of 'idealism'. It is debatable, however, whether the notion of superstructural push leads inevitably to idealism. Nowhere is it argued that the preconditions for revolution

38. Levy, loc.cit., pp. 107-8, based on Mao Zedong 1960 (or 1961-2), loc.cit., pp. 258-9.

39. Ibid., p. 272.

40. Stalin, 1952, pp. 60-86.

41. Mao Zedong, November 1958 (or 1959), loc.cit., p. 130.

42. Mao Zedong, 1960 (or 1961-2), loc.cit., p. 280.

are created in people's minds, merely that the precipitant is, in fact, located in the superstructure and that the initial role of leadership in that sphere is crucial. Surely this is what Lenin's theory of a Bolshevik Party, where a vanguard leads the proletariat from trade union consciousness to revolutionary consciousness is all about. It is not my intention here to evaluate whether such an argument is tenable or whether Mao's extension of Lenin's idea about the 'weakest link' is valid; nor do I wish to enter the savage polemic about Mao's Marxist credentials.[43] I wish merely to describe Mao's early thinking about cultural revolution which was to play such a major part in Chinese politics for a decade and a half.

It must be stressed that the view that new classes generated during the process of socialist transition should be the object of struggle and that an onslaught in the 'superstructural' sphere should provide the conditions for a radical transformation of the relations of production remained as only one strand of Mao's thought in the Cultural Revolution which began in 1966. Mao was always unwilling to explore the un-Leninist implications of his view that the Communist Party could be a major site for the recrudescence of a new exploiting class. Thus when Red Guards stormed the various headquarters of the Communist Party they repeatedly chanted the first quotation in the 'little red book' to the effect that the Communist Party was the nucleus of the revolution;[44] evidently the Party had been made simply an abstract symbol.

It is idle to speculate on the possible course of the Cultural Revolution had there been no theoretical confusion. As things turned out, the movement resulted in factionalism, repeated military intervention, a disillusionment on the part of many rank and file Party cadres and continued inertia in the countryside where the bulk of the population lived; the Cultural Revolution was certainly not a peasant revolution, however much its leaders may have been guilty of 'peasant deviation'. After 1969 and especially after Lin Biao's alleged attempt at a coup in 1971, attempts were made to put together the pieces once again and the Party structure which emerged differed little from that which had existed prior to 1966. Fears once again that the revolution had been interrupted led to a move 'against the tide'[45] (identified with the 'Gang of Four') though the mass mobilisation of the mid-1960s could not be repeated.

The last attempt to give substance to the idea of 'continuing the revolution under the dictatorship of the proletariat' was to take place in 1975 when Zhang Chunqiao and Yao Wenyuan (two members of the

---

43. See the debate in Modern China, vol. II, no. 4 (October 1976), pp. 421-72; vol. III, no. 1 (January 1977), pp. 101-18; vol. III, no. 2 (April 1977), pp. 125-84; vol. III, no. 4 (October, 1977), pp. 379-508.

44. Mao Zedong, Quotations from Chairman Mao Tse-tung (PFLP, Beijing, 1966).

45. See B. Brugger, China: Radicalism to Revisionism: 1962-1979 (Croom Helm, London, 1981), pp. 170-200.

'Gang of Four') put forward a number of theses on what was called 'bourgeois right'.[46] Taking their cue from Marx's discussion in the 'Critique of the Gotha Programme'[47] (1875) the radicals argued that a society undergoing socialist transition was still characterised by 'bourgeois right'. This had two dimensions. The first dimension was legal; equal rights were given to people made unequal by their economic location. From this it was inferred that unless there was positive discrimination in favour of the underprivileged, inequalities would become entrenched and class polarisation would grow. The second dimension was economic. Because a single standard was used in determining wages (payment according to work), those who could produce more received more and because they received more they were in a better position to produce more. From this it was inferred that more egalitarian policies were required.

The radical analysis of 1975 was most stimulating. Yet the question arose as to what mechanism might be used to 'restrict' this 'bourgeois right'. Zhang and Yao's answer was that restriction might be achieved by the 'dictatorship of the proletariat' which, in practice, tended to be no more than the use of the public security apparatus to remove dissidents. At no stage did the radical campaigns of the mid-1970s produce the mass activity which would have given the term 'dictatorship of the proletariat' any wider content. In any case, memories of the 'high tide' of the Cultural Revolution in the late 1960s and the resentments caused generated so much hostility that the 'Gang' could quite easily be removed from the scene following the death of Mao Zedong in the autumn of 1976.

In the period which followed, the Hua Guofeng leadership sought first to reinterpret Mao's ideas of 'continuing the revolution' in terms of his views of 'uninterrupted revolution' of the mid-1950s which were outside the context of massive class struggle.[48] The return to power of Deng Xiaoping, however, generated an intense inner-party debate which eventually resulted in a new set of policies and theoretical formulations following the Third Plenum of the Eleventh Central Committee in December 1978. After that plenum, revolution both in the sense of the generative view of class of the 1960s and of the wave-like developments of the Great Leap Forward was laid to rest. The line of the Eighth Party Congress was restored and then modified in an even less revolutionary manner. The way was open for experiments with 'market socialism' and partial acceptance of capitalist forms of

46. Zhang Chunqiao, Hongqi, 4, 1975, Peking Review, 14 (4 April 1975), pp. 5-11; Yao Wenyuan, Hongqi, 3, 1975, Peking Review, 10 (7 March 1975), pp. 5-10.

47. K. Marx, 'Critique of the Gotha Programme' (1875), in K. Marx and F. Engels, Selected Works, vol. 3 (Progress Publishers, Moscow, 1970), pp. 18-9.

48. See M. Sullivan, 'The Politics of Conflict and Compromise', in B. Brugger (ed.), China Since the 'Gang of Four' (Croom Helm, London, 1980), pp. 36-9.

organisation. In Mao's view, I am sure, such developments would have been seen as 'revisionist' and it is significant that the present leadership has decided that the term revisionist is devoid of content, having been used as a justification for fundamentalist dogmatism.

The Chinese revolution once again has indeed been interrupted. It is probable that, in the future, China will again be portrayed as an ideal type; but will it be revolutionary? In the meantime, however much one regrets the loss of revolutionary elan, one cannot but welcome the advent of a new debate on 'socialist purpose' - a debate which might eventually produce a new concept of revolution and, inevitably, new interruptions. It is probably too early to categorise the Chinese revolution as 'defunct'.

Chapter Ten

NAZI GERMANY - A DOOMED REVOLUTION

David Close

The purpose of this section is to test the claims to revolutionary status of a regime with features often thought incompatible with revolution. Besides possessing the right-wing qualities referred to in Chapter 1, it was retrograde in its worship of force, contempt for compassion, general anti-intellectualism and ambivalence towards advanced industrial society. Two interpretations of the regime have been offered that are of special interest. Wertheim implicitly includes it in his counter-revolutionary category, which he defines as being opposed to emancipation 'from the forces of nature, or from the fetters of social hierarchy and domination by man,' dedicated to the restoration of old forms of authority, and relatively weak both in popular support and in distinctive ideology.[1] Hagopian includes it in his more flexible definition of revolution, as an attempt to overturn any of the 'traditional systems of stratification (class, status, power) of a political community.'[2]

Examination of Nazism's revolutionary credentials may appropriately start with its ideals, which were in effect those of Adolf Hitler because he dominated the movement. They may be divided into primary and secondary categories. The first, which the movement pursued throughout its existence, was based on racial nationalism - the belief in the existence of races, each differing in merit, flourishing in accordance with its genetic purity, and the proper basis of a political community - and on social Darwinism - the belief in the naturalness of a constant and ubiquitous struggle for existence between individuals and communities, according to the rule of the survival of the fittest. From these ideas the Nazis derived their violent anti-semitism, their adulation of the German race, its alleged need for *Lebensraum* (living-space) east of Germany, and the *Fuhrerprinzip* (leader principle) as a general principle of social organization. The secondary category was effectively abandoned by the Nazi leaders soon after they won power.

1. *Evolution and Revolution*, pp. 128, 133.

2. *The Phenomenon of Revolution* (Harper & Row, New York, 1974), pp. 353-8.

It was embodied largely in the proposals designed to benefit the lower middle class, including farmers, at the expense of wealthy capitalists and landowners. While valuing the proposals, the Nazi leaders found that they conflicted with their primary ideals. These required a programme of rearmament, which could be carried out only by the vested interests which the secondary ideals threatened. The social reforms which Nazis remained especially attached to - even though for various reasons they did little about them - were those which contributed directly to their racial goals: examples were programmes of land settlement in conquered territories and the encouragement of larger families among racially pure Germans.

By abandoning their secondary ideals, the Nazis committed themselves to pursuing their revolution, as Hagopian remarked, by political and cultural, rather than by social and economic means.[3] Their strategy was, moreover, characterised by respect for the views and interests of large sectors of German society. Unlike most revolutionaries who win power, they inherited a political and economic order which was still largely viable, their claim to lead it having been won by the constitutional method of amassing electoral support. Their strategy was gradually to infiltrate and subvert this old order, a process which was still far from complete when their power ended in 1945. For most of their period of power they had to tolerate the existence of institutions, like the churches and the army officer corps, with values antagonistic to their own. Some respect for public opinion was for the Nazi movement partly a matter of prudence and partly of habit. That it received so much support before reaching power was due partly to the fact that many, perhaps a majority, of the German people held attitudes which made them at least partly sympathetic to Nazism. Such attitudes included belief in the special racial and cultural qualities of the German nation, desire for national leadership standing above parties, and jealousy of Jewish competition in times of economic stress.[4] For several years after winning power Hitler continued to pursue popular policies; and there seems little doubt that a majority of the people in the latter half of the 1930s approved broadly of his record.[5] Skilfully aligning himself with a national consensus, Hitler allowed his followers time in which to impress their ideas on the young and extend their control over German society. Had they completed their work, the result would have been revolutionary in the fullest sense: a society cemented by racial solidarity, permanently mobilised for war, organised throughout on the *Fuhrerprinzip* and dedicated to the Nazis' barbaric ideals.

---

3. P. 358.

4. K.D. Bracher, *The German Dictatorship. The Origins, Structure and Consequences of National Socialism* (Penguin, London, 1973), pp. 51, 66.

5. Ibid., p. 308.

Proof that the Nazis' revolutionary intentions were serious rests partly on the evidence of Hitler's character.[6] He expressed his intention during the Second World War of completing the reconstruction of German society after it - for example by suppressing the churches - and showed that he could carry out his more ambitious ideals literally. At least one project which he carried far towards completion - the extermination of the European Jews - seemed too fantastic to be conceived beforehand by his closest followers. For two years (1943-5) after even he could see that they were leading Germany to disaster, he clung rigidly and obsessively to beliefs that he had expressed at the outset of his political career, in 1919-20. He carried the nation with him along this course, and kept his followers united, by extraordinary qualities of leadership, which included personal magnetism and a messianic sense of destiny. He can then be appropriately termed a revolutionary personality.

The revolutionary nature of his intentions is also shown in the kind of political authority which he established. This was radically new. The kind of state that was traditionally respected in Germany was the _Rechtsstaat_, where powers were divided and subject to a constitution and the rule of law. Hitler by contrast made his power increasingly personal and arbitrary.[7] He interpreted the _Fuhrerprinzip_ so as to claim absolute power and complete embodiment of the general will of the people: thus he allowed no formal provision for the political representation of interest-groups, through the Nazi party or through parliamentary institutions. His followers dissolved rival sources of authority (if they were political parties or trade unions) or brought them increasingly under their own control. Authoritarianism was accompanied by confusion and duplication of functions, so that ministries and agencies multiplied and competed in a kind of 'Institutional Darwinism'.[8] One result was that Hitler's authority became enhanced as the sole source of order and cohesion. The enforcement of the law became increasingly arbitrary because of Nazi intervention in judicial decisions and wholesale arrests by the Gestapo (_Geheime Staatspolizei_, secret political police). Established values in the courts, as in all other spheres of society, were challenged by Nazi values, which had a subjective character: judges for example were told to pass judgement not according to the law, but according to their interpretation of the _Fuhrer_'s will.[9] Hitler assumed the power to introduce or amend laws by personal decrees, and tended to issue

---

6. See J.C. Fest, _Hitler_ (Weidenfeld & Nicolson, London, 1973), pp.531, 535, 673, 679-81, 746, 764.

7. Bracher, pp. 424-7, 430-1.

8. D. Schoenbaum, _Hitler's Social Revolution. Class and Status in Nazi Germany_ (Weidenfeld & Nicolson, London, 1967), p.206.

9. C.W. Cassinelli, _Total Revolution. A Comparative Study of Germany under Hitler, the Soviet Union under Stalin, and China under Mao_ (Clio Press, Santa Barbara, 1976), p. 66.

directives of various kinds impulsively and casually.[10] Meanwhile some basic political values of Nazism, such as nationalism and militarism, seem to have been effectively impressed on the young through primary schools, the Hitler Youth and universal military service.[11] A radical change in the political culture of Germany seems then to have been taking place.

The effect of Nazi rule on the general distribution of wealth and status was more gradual than its effect on political authority.[12] If, for example, we tentatively rank elites according to the degree of change in personnel and function which the Nazis brought about, we find that the largest category, including civil servants, churchmen, schoolteachers, bankers and industrialists experienced small-scale change; a much smaller one,including officers of the armed forces - and perhaps we should add academics and judges - experienced substantial change; while another small one, comprising politicians, police and those working in the media, experienced sweeping change. In general the main conflicts of interest in German society continued, although in a less overt manner: for example between bosses and workers, peasants and finance institutions, large and small retailers. In some ways Nazi rule was regressive. For example in industry it had the intentional effect, consistent with the Fuhrerprinzip, of strengthening the authority of managers over employees. Having outlawed strikes as well as trade unions, the regime stabilised wages and lengthened working hours, with the help of police measures against rebellious workers. Meanwhile profits rose steadily under the stimuli of rearmament and public works programmes.[13] (Admittedly, the living-standards of the working class as a whole were improved by the creation of jobs for nearly all of the unemployed of 1933.) Large firms were in general better placed than small ones, and some large firms better placed than others, to benefit from the regime's massive programmes of rearmament and the substitution of domestic for imported products. They were better equipped for example to bribe Nazi functionaries and carry out large-scale orders. In return they were rewarded with confiscated enterprises belonging to German Jews or foreigners in conquered territories. Thus the regime's policies encouraged industrial concentration, and - in accordance with its social Darwinism but in contradiction to its defence of the lower middle-class - the general decline of small-scale enterprise.[14]

Although certain kinds of industrialist were then much favoured by the regime, their welfare was an instrument, not an object, of its policy. Their skills were exploited by the regime for its own purposes, which - insofar as they led ultimately to national disaster - were not

---

10. W. Carr, Hitler. A Study in Personality and Politics (E. Arnold, London, 1978), p. 41.
11. Bracher, p. 330.
12. Schoenbaum is the main source for this paragraph.
13. Ibid., pp. 102-3, 116, 156.
14. Ibid., pp. 137-9, 149.

ones which any industrialist desired. The far-reaching controls which the Nazi leaders imposed on the economy, as they prepared it for war, showed that they were no respecters of private enterprise in itself. The controls covered the allocation of raw materials, labour, finance and foreign exchange, and included the compulsion of some firms to produce goods needed by the war economy.[15] The rights of bosses as well as of workers were subjected to the requirements of the Volksgemeinschaft (national community) as these were interpreted by the Nazi leaders.

There were, however, important ways in which Nazi policy eroded traditional privileges. A broad ladder to high status was offered to the small man by the Nazi party's official apparatus, which grew enormously until there eventually existed two million "leader positions", each with a share of reward and authority. Although the party as a whole had less importance than its Soviet counterpart, it provided stepping-stones to power for individuals, while one of its branches, the SS (Schutzstaffel, or guard corps) acquired great power in special areas. The Nazi leaders in most spheres, national and local, differed in origin from traditional elites such as politicians and civil servants. They tended to be younger and moulded by the experience of the First World War and its economic aftermath; while socially they tended, like Hitler, to be lower middle-class failures or drifters.[16] Another ladder for those outside the old elites was offered by the expansion of the armed forces, where, for example, the aristocratic dominance of the officer corps finally disappeared.[17] The fast transition of the economy from slump to boom, and the especially rapid growth of the technologically advanced industries like chemicals, must have increased the opportunities of the working class and lower middle class for promotion to jobs of higher status. Upward mobility was blessed by official ideology. As David Schoenbaum remarked, a social revolution took place at the verbal level, with words like bourgeois, capitalist and intellectual being treated abusively in the Nazis' all-pervasive propaganda, while the small man, especially the manual worker and farmer, was idealised. The combination of social mobility and official attitudes seems to have created a general atmosphere of expanding opportunity, and in many situations to have partly replaced old status distinctions by a feeling of national camaraderie.[18]

It should now be obvious that the regime will not fit Wertheim's definition of counter-revolution. In only one respect did it comply with the definition - in being opposed on balance to emancipation - while in all others it conflicted head-on. It enjoyed mass support; it possessed

15. Ibid., pp. 151, 154, 157; D. Landes, The Unbound Prometheus. Technological Change and Industrial Development in Western Europe from 1750 to the Present (Cambridge University Press, London, 1969), p. 405.

16. Bracher, pp. 345-6, 433.

17. Schoenbaum, p. 249

18. Ibid., pp. 46, 51-2, 61-2, 75-6, 249, 284-5.

a serious if ill-defined ideology; and it came into being not to reverse or forestall radical changes but to make them. Above all it tried to create new sources of authority, not restore old ones, and in the process might even be said (quoting Wertheim himself) to have opened 'a perspective to large social groups, that were hitherto excluded from power, of being able to realise their aspirations for a greater scope of action and greater political influence'.[19] It also appears at first glance that the regime fits without difficulty into Hagopian's definition. This allows for variation in intensity of revolution; and the Nazi movement could accordingly be ranked as one of moderate intensity, having achieved radical change in political stratification, moderate-to-substantial change in status stratification, and negligible change in class stratification.[20] But Hagopian's definition - even if his threefold division of stratification is deemed acceptable - omits an important dimension of revolution, which is its capacity for success or failure. Did the Nazi regime have the ability to perpetuate its political changes and fulfil its aspirations for change in other spheres? It will now be argued that it did not.

That it failed in a decisive sense is obvious. It ended in military catastrophe. It left a legacy of ideas and loyalties which was meagre - remarkably so considering how great its popularity had been. Admittedly, opinion polls in West Germany in the 1950s revealed a widespread respect for Hitler's achievements, and a substantial (12-13%) sympathy for neo-Nazi ideas, which at a time of economic stress in the late 1960s was translated briefly into support for the NPD (Nationaldemokratische Partei Deutschlands, or German National Democratic Party). Yet the extreme right seems never to have been strong enough to form even a potential threat to the democratic regime in West Germany, which has been based, with a fair degree of security, on revulsion against much of what the Nazis stood for.

Although the agents of Nazism's failure were invading armies, the basic causes of failure were intrinsic to it. The foreign invasions were the predictable result of Hitler's decisions to declare (or provoke) war with Britain, the USA and the USSR, and these decisions flowed almost inevitably from his long-held beliefs, and from the nature of the regime which he established. It has been shown, for example, that the process of rearmament undertaken by the Nazi leaders, in alliance with the service chiefs and big industrialists, by itself created reasons for foreign aggression which weighed heavily with Hitler. This is because it caused critical shortages of raw materials and labour, and provoked other powers to rearm in turn. Thus Hitler apparently found it necessary to undertake foreign conquests in order to satisfy Germany's economic needs, and in order to achieve his ideological goals before the international balance of power moved against him. But Germany's first round of foreign conquest, in 1938-40, merely revived the same problems in new forms: it created fresh economic needs, and

19. Ibid., p. 136.
20. Ibid., pp. 97-100.

stimulated other powers to rearm still further. With his essential aim of expansion eastward still far from realized, Hitler had brought on Germany a blockade by Britain, and provoked an arms race with the USSR which the latter had the resources to win. So he felt impelled to undertake new conquests without delay.[21] One can, then, describe his regime as impelled by an inner dynamism to self-destruction.

In addition it suffered from a serious lack of constructive ability, which revealed itself in numerous ways. The ideologically-derived goals which elicited most enthusiasm and systematic attention from the Nazi leaders were basically destructive: the elimination of the Versailles treaty, of the Soviet Union and of European Jewry. The further tasks of creating a new society and a new race of supermen remained dreams, realised only in trivial and dilettante ways. Hitler failed to give political substance to what his propagandists kept calling the 'thousand-year Reich' by making any effective provision for his own succession. Indeed by identifying the whole regime with his personality, and tolerating rivalries among his subordinates, he did what he could to make succession to himself impossible.[22] The Nazis' political incapacity was also shown in the steady deterioration in the efficiency of government at all levels, as it became more corrupt and costly, and as rivalries between overlapping agencies multiplied. The avoidance of administrative order was no symptom of the Nazi leaders' revolutionary vitality: for example a serious obstacle to the imposition of rationing in Germany during the war was the fact that they had lost their 'sacrificial devotion' and become wedded to their privileges.[23] Administrative confusion was marked in the execution of Hitler's dearest aims. For example the elite training schools set up by various of his henchmen were uncoordinated, and suffered from failure either to attract students or to place their graduates in respected positions.[24] The administration of conquered territories in the east suffered from conflict between authorities such as the SS, the army and governors-general.[25]

In such cases inefficiency was partly due to the impracticability of the Nazis' ultimate aims. A good example was the policy of winning Lebensraum and colonising it with German farmers, which was so dear to Hitler that it formed a serious reason for his attack on Russia. Yet the notion that the German people was short of space was economically primitive, as was the idea that the mass colonisation would be viable. Little serious preparation had gone into the policy. German farmers had been neglected by the regime, and were poorly represented in the Nazi party, including the SS, which was responsible for this area of policy. When the Lebensraum had been won, it emerged that there were

---

21. Carr, pp. 54, 58, 93; Bracher, p. 415.
22. Bracher, pp. 428-9.
23. Fest, p. 675.
24. Schoenbaum, pp. 277-83.
25. Fest, p. 679.

few German volunteers to colonise it.[26] Also impracticable was the policy of genocide when considered as not only a prerequisite but a permanent feature of the Nazi utopia, a mission in which the German race would unite. Relatively few Germans had the necessary cold-bloodedness to participate. The public was realistically judged to be 'not (yet) ready' to know about it; and even the top Nazi leaders found it too distasteful to mention to each other. The only one of them ever to attend a mass execution was Heinrich Himmler, who was chiefly responsible for carrying out the policy - and he had hysterics afterwards.[27] Lack of realism is a normal, and perhaps necessary, ingredient of revolutionary utopias; but the Nazi one was so crude and inhuman as well that it lacked one of their obviously essential ingredients, which is the power to inspire anyone other than hard-core fanatics. The popular support which Hitler won up to 1940 was not for his utopian aims, which few people took seriously, but for his practical achievements.

We should conclude then that the Nazis were indeed revolutionary in aspiration, but showed little sign of the constructive capacity needed to turn aspiration into lasting achievement. As Hagopian pointed out, the study of revolution affords opportunity for 'mutual aid' between 'cautious fact-finders and unabashed theorists'.[28] Hagopian's theory that the Nazi regime was revolutionary in the fullest sense needs qualification in the light of the facts.

---

26. Fest, pp. 684-5, 687; Bracher pp. 416-7.
27. Bracher, pp. 520, 532; Fest, pp. 679-81.
28. Phenomenon of Revolution, p. 364.

Chapter Eleven

GUINEA-BISSAU—REVOLUTION AND DEVELOPMENT

Cherry Gertzel

Introduction*

The purpose of this chapter is to consider how a revolutionary struggle for independence may contribute to the process of development in the situation of late twentieth-century Africa. There has been a growing disillusionment, since the late sixties, among many Africans and others, with the development process in the post-colonial state. Decolonisation after 1945 for most sub-Saharan African states was comparatively peaceful. Political and industrial protest had been crucial to the success of the nationalist movements, and the nationalist parties had certainly won their independence in the political battle.[1] Nonetheless in most cases colonial policies had allowed for political change and the major powers withdrew peacefully in the face of organised protest, leaving the nationalist leaders to take over governments with policies of reform. At the end of the first independence decade, however, the 'reformist option', to use Basil Davidson's phrase, had produced not radical structural change but a

---

* This chapter draws largely on Patrick Chabal, Amilcar Cabral; revolutionary leadership and people's war (Cambridge University Press, Cambridge, 1983); Lars Rudebeck, Guinea-Bissau, a study in political mobilization (Institute for African Studies, Uppsala, 1974); Basil Davidson, Liberation of Guinea (Penguin, London, 1969), and No Fist is Too Big to Hide the Sky (Zed Press, London, 1983); and Gerard Chaliand, Armed Struggle in Africa (Monthly Review Press, London, 1959). All four volumes have good bibliographies but see also R.H. Chilcote (ed), Emerging Nationalism in Portuguese Africa: A Bibliography of Documents of Ephemera through 1965 (Hoover Institute, Stanford, 1969) and idem 'Amilcar Cabral: a Bio-Bibliography of his Life and Thought, 1925-1973', Africana Journal vol. V, no. 4, Winter 1974-5, pp.289-307.

I would like to thank Richard DeAngelis, Andrew Mack and David Close for their constructive criticisms of an earlier draft of this chapter.

1. See especially Thomas Hodgkin, Nationalism in Colonial Africa (Muller, London, 1956).

rapid expansion of the African elites and a widening gap between rich and poor. The colonial economic structures remained more or less intact, and the African states continued for the most part as primary commodity exporters dependent upon the 'trading and producing relations' of the world market.[2] Independence appeared merely to have Africanised colonial structures, creating a 'distinctive pattern of external dependence and domestic hierarchy which served to choke off development'.[3] The resulting patterns of inequality were for many observers the antithesis of development and demonstrated a 'fair measure of failure in the performance of...state powers as a whole'.[4]

The failure of post-colonial states to achieve structural change was attributed by radicals to neo-colonialism, defined as early as 1961 at the all-African People's Conference in Cairo as 'the survival of the colonial system in spite of the formal recognition of political independence in emerging countries which become the victims of an indirect and subtle form of domination by political, economic, social, military or technical means'.[5] By the end of the sixties there was also a good deal more radical criticism of the African elites in power which endorsed Frantz Fanon's earlier, savage critique of an acquisitive ruling class. Moreover dependency theorists and Marxists had provoked a new debate about the nature of development and the constraints imposed by that ruling class on radical structural change.[6]

In this context the three Portuguese African colonies of Angola, Mozambique and Guinea-Bissau were in the early seventies of particular significance. Their revolutionary nationalism seemed to offer an alternative path to development. The scale and duration of the liberation struggle in all three states set them apart from those whose political independence had followed the road of peaceful transfer of power. It had also radicalised their ideas about development. The struggle was directed against neo-colonial solutions as well as colonial rule. Hence they were engaged in not merely 'a struggle for independence but a revolution in the making'.[7] Viewed from this perspective Guinea-Bissau attracted an attention out of proportion to its diminutive size. Guinea-Bissau is scarcely typical of African States. Its party however was the most clearly developed of the liberation movements in Portuguese Africa, and the first to win its independence through armed struggle. Observers looked to it,

---

2. John Dunn, West African States; Failure and Promise (Cambridge University Press, Cambridge, 1978), p. 4.

3. John Saul, 'Neo-Colonialism vs. Liberation Struggle: Some Lessons from Portugal's African Colonies', The Socialist Register, 1973.

4. Dunn, p. 4.

5. Quoted in Colin Leys, Underdevelopment in Kenya (Heinemann's, London, 1974), p. 26, which see for a useful, succinct discussion of the term itself.

6. Leys, Underdevelopment. Frantz Fanon, The Damned (Presence Africain, Paris 1963).

7. Saul, p. 310.

therefore, for a greater understanding of prospects of revolutionary development in the post-colonial state.[8]

The main architect of the revolution in Guinea-Bissau was Amilcar Cabral, co-founder and leader of the African Party for the Independence of Guinea and Cape Verde (PAIGC). Cabral was first and foremost an outstanding strategist and a successful practitioner. By the time of his death, in January 1973, however, he had been recognised also as a most remarkable revolutionary leader and contemporary thinker on revolution.[9] In his view, the armed struggle was essentially a prelude to development; he was therefore concerned about the relationship between the two in both theory and practice. Adamant that development required an end to imperialist domination, he was critical of the 'half way house of national independence in a majority of the African States'.[10] In the course of the war his attention was as much on the evolution of new political structures for the future, as on the military strategy.

Background to Revolution: Guinea-Bissau in the 1950s

Guinea-Bissau is a tiny enclave wedged between Senegal and Guinea on the West African coast. The population today is less than a million. In 1950 it was about 502,000, almost entirely African, divided into about twenty-five different ethnic groups which varied significantly both in size and social and political structures.[11]

By any criteria it was a poor, backward territory. The impact of colonialism upon rural society had been very limited. Education and health services were minimal; the vast majority of the people were illiterate. Among the Fula in particular traditional leaders still retained considerable power but elsewhere, too, there had been little change from the small, kinship-orientated, village societies of the

---

8. Immanuel Wallerstein, 'The Lessons of the PAIGC' in Africa Today, vol. 18, no. 3 (1971), p. 109; Chabal, Cabral, Ch. 7.

9. Chabal, Cabral, provides the first full-length biography of Cabral. See also Chaliand, 'The Legacy of Amilcar Cabral', Ramparts, vol. 11, no. 10 (April 1973), pp. 17-20; Clapham, 'Africa's Philosopher King', The Times Higher Education Supplement, 19 August 1983, p. 12. Among the most useful analyses of Cabral as a revolutionary thinker see H. Bienen, 'State and Revolution: the work of Amilcar Cabral', Journal of Modern African Studies, vol. 15, no. 4 (December 1977), pp. 555-595; R. Blackey, 'Fanon and Cabral: A Contrast in Theories of Revolution in Africa', The Journal of Modern African Studies, vol. 12, no.2 (1974), pp. 191-209. McCullough, In the Twilight of Revolution (Routledge & Kegan Paul, London, 1983) and McCollister, 'The African Revolution: Theory and Practice', Monthly Review, vol. 24 (March 1973), pp.10-21.

10. Davidson, No Fist, p. 21.

11. Cabral, 'A Brief Analysis of the Social Structure of Guinea', in Revolution in Guinea (Monthly Review Press, New York, 1969).

past.[12] Bissau the capital in the 1950s had a population variously estimated at between 17,000 and 50,000 and there was a scattering of smaller towns each with a population of about 3,000. Urban society was both socially and economically stratified. The first and fundamental distinction was that of race. A few thousand Portuguese residents, almost all of them government officials or small traders occupied the dominant, privileged stratum of colonial society. Beneath them, African society was itself divided between a tiny elite of middle-level government officials and professionals, almost all of them of Cape Verdean origins; a small group of minor officials, clerks, white-collar workers; a wage-earning labour force, mostly workers on the docks, in transport, and domestic service; and finally the unemployed and fringe dwellers of urban society. Notwithstanding Portuguese commitment to the principle of assimilation there were fewer than 1,500 assimilados in the country as a whole.

Cabral was a Cape Verdean, with strong ties with the mainland.[13] He went to Portugal for university education in 1945, where he trained in Lisbon as an agricultural engineer. On his return to West Africa in 1952, he was employed by the Guinea-Bissau government as an agronomist on the mainland. In Portugal he had been one of the small band of African students who became committed to African nationalism and independence for Portugal's African colonies. Seeking to use cultural associations to arouse support for nationalist ideas, once he returned to West Africa, he quickly ran up against the rigid opposition of the conservative Portuguese colonial administration; and after three years he withdrew back to Portugal. On a visit to Bissau in 1956, however, he founded, with five others, the PAIGC.[14]

The PAIGC was committed to the complete independence of both Guinea-Bissau and the Cape Verde islands, and to their eventual integration. The circumstances of neither colony seemed in 1956 propitious for the development of a nationalist movement. On the one hand the Portuguese refused to countenance any genuine social or political development, or to allow political organisations to function. On the other the very backwardness of both colonies had precluded the growth of the kind of nationalist sentiment that flourished elsewhere in Africa. Nevertheless, the party's first, clandestine, activity was directed at Bissau's small urban population, where between 1956 and

12. For the colonial period, see Ronald Chilcote, Portuguese Africa (Englewood Cliffs, New Jersey, Prentice-Hall, 1967); James Duffy, Portugal in Africa (Penguin, London, 1962); Basil Davidson, Africa in History (Paladin, London, 1974).

13. For the Cape Verde islands, see Chabal, Cabral, and Rudebeck, Guinea-Bissau.

14. See Chabal, Ch. 2. For the years in Portugal see Davidson, 'In the Portuguese Context', in Christopher Allen and R.W. Johnson (eds.), African Perspectives (Cambridge University Press, 1970).

1959 they attempted to influence the workers to protest against the conditions under which they lived and worked.

The limitations of such a strategy quickly became apparent. The small PAIGC leadership had some success in persuading urban wage-earners to protest but not in building the party itself. The fundamental constraints imposed by the repressive nature of the regime were finally demonstrated in August 1959 when the Portuguese used armed force to break up striking dock and harbour workers in Bissau, killing fifty and injuring more. The party now took the important decision to resort to armed force. After moving its headquarters to Conakry, in neighbouring Guine, Cabral prepared therefore to engage in direct military struggle.

Strategy for the Armed Struggle

The PAIGC strategy demonstrates Cabral's immense capacity to respond pragmatically to the actual conditions in which the struggle had to be fought. While he acknowledged there were certain 'general laws of the theory of armed struggle' he was equally convinced that national liberation and social revolution were not 'exportable commodities'.[15] They had to be home-grown, rooted in the conditions of the country. He insisted therefore that while successful revolution required a revolutionary theory that theory must grow out of practice.

Several key decisions followed from his emphasis on local conditions: first, that the struggle must be based on the countryside, not the towns. The attempt to build the party on urban support had failed because, as Cabral pointed out, there was no working class to provide a base. Guinea-Bissau was a rural society. The struggle must therefore be fought first in the rural areas, and the peasants mobilised in support of national liberation. Second, Cabral insisted upon the need for political mobilisation of rural grass-roots support behind the PAIGC before beginning the war itself.[16] The three years after the move to Conakry were spent on intense political training and active, although slow, penetration of the countryside. While this political preparation was probably the most difficult stage of the whole war, it has been acknowledged as critical to the PAIGC's subsequent success.[17] Having thus won support in certain areas, he used them as bases for attacks upon the Portuguese.

The third key decision concerned the relationship between the party and the military. Cabral insisted from the outset on the prime importance of the political aspects of the liberation struggle and therefore on party control over both the armed forces and the conduct of the war. Thus in his view there were no purely military personnel; those who dedicated themselves to the armed struggle were armed

---

15. 'The Weapon of Theory' in Unity and Struggle, p. 122. See also Return to the Source, Selected Speeches of Amilcar Cabral (Monthly Review Press, New York and London, 1973), p. 86.

16. E.g. Our People Are Our Mountains, pp. 16-17.

17. Chabal, p. 68.

militants. Not all the guerrilla groups in the field were initially willing to submit to political control. The principle was however finally accepted albeit after a hard struggle, at the party's first congress in February 1964. Control of the guerrilla forces was subsequently centralised in the small war council of which Cabral was the chairman. The guerrilla forces were reorganised into a national army, the FARP, which operated across the whole country. Within each unit, from the basic commando unit, the bi-gripo, upwards, the leadership was shared by a military commander and a political commissar.[18]

Cabral's basic strategy was to push the Portuguese out of the rural areas, to isolate them in their fortified camps, and gradually to move towards and to encircle the towns. The war developed in three successive phases, each merging into the next, but distinguished from each other by the expanding scope of PAIGC military action and territorial control. The first phase, up to 1964, was essentially the guerrilla phase, during which the PAIGC first embarked on sabotage attacks within Guinea, and established bases from which they could further operate. In the second phase Cabral welded his best guerrilla volunteers into a regular army, and shifted from localised guerrilla warfare to a coordinated military strategy as a result of which by 1968 the PAIGC controlled two-thirds of the country. A third phase developed from 1969 when the PAIGC, still extending their territorial control, now also turned increased attention to administration and development in the liberated areas of the southern region and much of the north. Cabral's assassination in January 1973 did not seriously weaken the struggle, and in September the PAIGC declared Guinea-Bissau's sovereignty.

The PAIGC did not win the war easily, and mistakes were undoubtedly made. The external support that the PAIGC received, particularly in the supply of arms, was essential to military success and to the party's ability to establish the rudiments of local services in the liberated areas. The external base in Conakry and sanctuaries in Senegal were equally vital to the prosecution of the war, although Cabral increasingly sought to reduce his dependence on that base, and to make the party inside Guinea-Bissau self-reliant. Success was ultimately dependent however not only on arms supplies but also on he political support of the local population.

Strategy for Development: Reconstruction inside the Liberated Areas

Cabral's second objective was to destroy the Portuguese colonial infrastructure and with it the villagers' dependence on the colonial system, and to replace it with new institutions that would in due course provide the basis for the independent state.[19]

As they gained a firmer hold on the military situation, the leadership therefore gave increasing attention to the development of the

---

18. Davidson, The People's Cause, pp. 177-179; Chabal, p. 99.

19. 'Destroy the economy and build our own economy', Unity and Struggle, p. 239.

party and of social and economic institutions in the areas now under their control. The objective was to change living conditions in the rural area, and thus to provide concrete benefits that would win over peasant support. It was also to lay the foundations of a new society.

The party provided the agency for mobilisation and reconstruction. Under Cabral's leadership the PAIGC became well-organised and cohesive, its success being reflected in widespread popular involvement in the liberation struggle that had been built up across the liberated areas by 1972. He found his party leadership in the tiny, urban-educated middle class, of which he was himself a part, against whom colonial society discriminated and whose resulting frustration and sense of alienation provided the stimulus for revolutionary action.[20] He found his party cadres, for the same reason, first of all, among workers and youth in the town, what he termed the 'declasses'; young people of petty bourgeois background whose failure to find employment and a place in colonial urban society made them also conscious of injustice and receptive to revolutionary ideas.[21] Later there were also recruits for both party and military from the rural areas. He placed overwhelming importance on their political training, in which he himself played the major role, at the party's training schools.

Peasant support was no more easily won than the war, especially at the beginning. Later, as the Portuguese responded to the PAIGC action with greater repression and when the PAIGC was able to provide support and protection in the liberated areas, the situation became easier. Villagers had meanwhile to be convinced of the relevance of the liberation struggle to their own lives and then persuaded to work towards its success. Cabral did not underestimate the difficulties of mobilising support among peasants who were not in his view a revolutionary force. He insisted that success depended ultimately on the capacity of party workers to identify with villagers, and to articulate nationalist objectives in local terms. His greatest asset in this respect was his intimate knowledge of Bissau's rural societies, gained in his years as agronomist and his work of agricultural survey for the Portuguese. That experience had given him an extraordinary understanding of and sensitivity to local society, which he used both to determine his basic approach and to teach party cadres a greater awareness of rural attitudes. One of the most quoted of his instructions to party workers made explicit furthermore that local interests were related above all to the material conditions under which the rural population lived. 'Always remember' he told them,

> that the people are not fighting for ideas. They are fighting for material benefits, to live better and in peace to see their lives go forward.[22]

---

20. Cabral, Revolution in Guinea, p. 38, pp. 65-66.
21. 'A Brief Analysis', p. 62.
22. Quoted in Boniface Obichere, 'Reconstruction in Guinea-Bissau. From Revolutionary and Guerrillas to Bureaucrats and

Central control of the liberated regions was maintained through the hierarchical party structure in which each party unit was responsible to the next highest level. Party leaders at regional and district level were expected to live among the people, to work closely with them and to encourage their participation.

The basic party unit on which success ultimately depended was the village committee, consisting of five members (including two women) elected by the village as a whole. These were established slowly and with difficulty, but by 1972 there were about four hundred of them. They were responsible for local participation in the war effort, including after 1970 the village militia; for the organisation and maintenance of local health and education services; and also for agricultural production. In time, they assumed other functions as well, so that by 1973 they were involved in almost every aspect of public life in their locality.[23]

By 1973, there were about five thousand party workers involved in some kind of party function from the village upwards. At the local level they were often local people from the area itself. At higher levels, the zone and the region, party cadres could be and were moved around. Working through this party structure the PAIGC gradually provided the beginnings of an economic structure, and rudimentary social services for the population. First, on the economic front, the PAIGC increased food production, and also provided a network of People's Stores that enabled villagers to exchange their produce for basic consumer goods. In 1973, the liberated areas were self-sufficient in foodstuffs and able to feed the armed forces, and at times able in addition to export small quantities of agricultural produce to Guinea. Second, they established rudimentary health, education and judicial services where there had in the past been virtually none. By 1972 there were nine hospitals, limited but functional, eight in the charge of a trained doctor, available for civilians as well as military personnel. There were also rural health workers, visiting the villages, providing the beginnings of primary health care. Cabral estimated there were 15,000 children attending 156 primary schools and five secondary schools and semi-boarding schools, and a total of 251 teachers. Several hundred young men and women had been overseas for training. Third, there was a political and administrative network that reached the smallest villages, and the rudiments of a new judicial system based on people's courts.

In the long run it was the work of the party cadres which determined the success of the achievement. They provided the backbone of the organisation for the programmes which established new links between hitherto separate communities. Guinea-Bissau's size was in this respect an asset. It is much smaller and more compact than either of the other Portuguese African colonies, and there were few serious regional inequalities to reinforce ethnic conciousness.

Politicians', A Current Bibliography of African Affairs, vol.8, no.3 (1975), pp.204-219.

23. Davidson, The People's Cause, p. 161.

Parochialism and the narrowness of village life were more fundamental constraints on the subsistence cultivator. The party had to overcome local isolation and expand the limited horizons of village society. By 1974 this process had truly begun.

Between 1969 and 1970 the PAIGC created sector committees (the level above the village) for each administrative division, and then in August 1971 decided to hold general elections for a National Assembly throughout the liberated areas. This decision reflected Cabral's concern to establish the legitimacy of the PAIGC in the eyes of the international community. He was also concerned however with the long-term problems of democratic control, which in his thinking required the separation of the institutions of party and state and the provision of popular control over them.[24]

Revolution and Development: the Transition to Independence and the Post-Colonial State

We should now ask what difference would these revolutionary changes, achieved in the course of the struggle, make to the country's development as an independent state? What kind of impact had the revolutionary struggle had on the party's developmental objectives, and how would this affect future change? Cabral himself believed that the revolution was the prelude to the long struggle for development. He was equally clear as to what constituted revolution in the context of Guinea-Bissau, and by extension of the wider African situation. For Guinea-Bissau the revolution constituted the struggle of a people to regain control of their own destiny or, in his words, 'return to history'.[25] This involved three fundamental changes: first, the end of imperialist domination; second the removal of any exploitation of man by man, and therefore of any form of class privilege or class power; and third the development of the productive forces to enable the country to overcome its basic poverty and provide all the people with a decent living standard.

Cabral did not believe that this revolution was necessarily a class struggle, since exploitation in Guinea-Bissau was a function of the colonial system rather than of indigenous social structures. He recognised the existence of inequalities between the great mass of rural cultivators and the government official, the wage earners in permanent employment and the small farmers, all of whom constituted what he termed the petty bourgeoisie. He nevertheless considered that petty bourgeoisie to be the prime revolutionary force, since they had the greatest cause to be hostile to the Portuguese, having suffered most from colonial discrimination; and he looked to it to provide the party's leadership.[26] He was conscious of the danger that this petty

---

24. 'Creation of the People's National Assembly'. Communique, 8 January 1973, in Unity and Struggle, p. 277; Davidson, West Africa, 29 January 1973.

25. Unity and Struggle, p. 130.

26. 'A Brief Analysis'.

bourgeois leadership, which would necessarily asssume responsibility for government administration in the independent state, might develop into a privileged comprador class; and that the same inequalities between rulers and ruled that existed elsewhere could emerge also in Guinea-Bissau. He had no clear solution to this problem except to hope that a truly revolutionary leadership would be born out of the struggle and with it a new national culture. The petty bourgeoisie would have to 'commit suicide as a class'.[27] While he therefore essentially avoided the problem, he nonetheless clearly identified the revolution with the emergence of a classless society. He also assumed that the peasants must change their attitudes as well as the petty bourgeoisie, if a new national society was to emerge. They also had to 'break the bonds of the village universe to integrate progressively into the country and into the world'.[28]

Whether or not Cabral saw these changes as necessarily dependent on a violent struggle is not really clear. On the one hand, he insisted that the PAIGC was forced to embark on the armed struggle only because of the violence of the colonial regime itself and the refusal of the Portuguese to respond to peaceful negotiations for political change. On the other hand he described the armed struggle as a 'painful but efficient instrument for developing the cultural level of both the leadership...and the various social groups who participate in the struggle'.[29] It is important however to bear in mind that he saw the struggle not simply as a war, but also as the beginnings of the practice of democracy and the increasing responsibility of villagers for the direction of their lives. Violence by itself therefore was not the only element of the liberation struggle that would force people to transform their lives.

So far as development was concerned, Cabral obviously thought in terms of a socialist system, although he did not often use the term, and he rejected the idea that there was any single socialist model.[30] He defined development quite simply in terms of the social and economic improvement of all the people. He was convinced that ultimately Guinea-Bissau could itself effect that improvement, although he recognised that it would take a long time.[31]

If the creation of a national entity above the village is one of the prerequisites for development then the most significant achievement was undoubtedly the transformation of the PAIGC from a tiny elite group into a nationalist movement with mass support. The party had created a new national consciousness, transcending tribal differences. This transformation was not however complete. The PAIGC still faced the problem of assimilating the Fula who had benefited more from the

---

27. Ibid., pp. 69-70.

28. 'National Liberation and Culture', Return to the Source, p.55.

29. Ibid., pp. 53, 79.

30. Chabal, p. 155; 'Weapon of Theory' in Revolution in Guinea, p. 107.

31. Chilcote, Bio-Bibliography, p. 290.

colonial economy than other groups and remained outside the nationalist movement. In addition the towns had still to be incorporated into the party, because they had remained outside its control during the liberation struggle. The sector of urban society that was hardest to assimilate consisted of the civil servants, who had enjoyed material privileges under the Portuguese, and could not be replaced.[32] Finally outside the country was a tiny political opposition operating from Dakar, which attempted an abortive 'invasion' in 1974.

The PAIGC therefore at independence faced some of the same problems of integration that had beset other nationalist movements that had not fought a war.[33] It differed from those movements however in one important respect: it had a well-organised, cohesive party structure, described as a 'toughened, effective and self-confident political machine with a clear sense of political identity, realistic, ambitious and considerable political experience'.[34] Under Cabral's leadership it had built up a band of trained and dedicated young militants and a strong local structure. The leadership remained with the original pioneers, men in their late thirties and early forties; but the party had been strengthened by a second generation who had risen through the ranks to positions of command. The same was true of the armed forces. The fact that the PAIGC survived Cabral's death demonstrated its unity. Another important factor distinguished the PAIGC from many other nationalist parties: lack of reliance on patronage. The circumstances of the struggle meant there had been virtually no way in which wealth could buy power. Indeed party leaders had no wealth.

The transformation of the party into a peacetime instrument of development was not however easy . The party organisation was extended immediately to those areas that had remained under Portuguese control in the war including Bissau. Political commissioners were appointed to both urban and rural areas, and intensive political education began. The village committees were established in those areas, until there were by 1975-76 perhaps over a thousand across the country, providing the party with its basic structure for communication and control. In December 1976 a second election was held, over the whole country, in which villages elected members to regional councils which in turn elected their deputies to the National Assembly, creating therefore a parallel structure for participation alongside the party itself. The assumption of government

---

32. Chaliand, pp. 48-49; also on the Fula Cabral, Agricultural Census in Guinea in Unity and Struggle, p. 7; Chabal, p. 95, pp. 172-73; Cabral's New Year Message, January 1973, in Unity and Struggle, p. 297; West Africa, 15 December 1980, p. 2555; Saul, p. 22.

33. See A. Zolberg, Creating Political Order: the Party-States of West Africa (Rand McNally, Chicago, 1966).

34. On the party cadres see Chaliand, Cornwall, Davidson, and Chabal, p. 211-2. On the military see Davidson in West Africa, 22 & 29 January 1973.

responsibilties meant however that the PAIGC had to transfer trained party personnel out of the former liberated areas into Bissau, thus seriously depleting the rural organisation of experienced workers, so that in August 1976 the Secretary General admitted that this had 'caused paralysis or even the dissolution of long-established structures of Party and State in areas liberated during the war'.[35] Rural party cadres moreover often appeared unable to give a lead for rural development. They were not always able to resist villagers' demands, even though those demands conflicted with the party's economic programme. They were sensitive to criticism from outsiders. Foreign experts complained of inefficiencies arising out of political intervention in projects. Participation in the party at the grass roots fell off. The party's support remained predominantly in the former liberated areas. In Bissau, the former colonial civil servants maintained their privileged living standards, which contrasted with those of many party workers, especially in the rural areas, and of the armed forces. On top of this, there were also signs of corruption appearing inside the party.[36]

These difficulties combined to slow down the revolutionary momentum of the party. They help to explain the disagreements that began to emerge within the leadership about first strategy, and second the decision taken by the 1977 congress to tighten up the recruitment and turn the PAIGC into a vanguard party. This decision seems to have precipitated disagreement within the leadership, over the role of the party in development as we shall see below.

The PAIGC had inherited a shattered economy. The war had resulted in widespread physical damage, and the destruction of much of what had been a very limited national economy. The country faced acute shortages, not only of food but of equipment, foreign exchange and trained manpower. Ninety thousand refugees who had fled into Senegal and 17,000 Africans who had fought in the Portuguese army had to be reintegrated.

Guinea-Bissau began its independence with international goodwill, and offers of very considerable external assistance by a wide range of countries including China and the USA, all of which were accepted provided no strings were attached.

The PAIGC looked to state control to enable it to direct economic development to the needs of the whole society. Private enterprise was to be integrated into a state-planned economy. A state monopoly of internal trade was set up, through the People's Stores, to effect strict price controls, and the state also took over the marketing of produce, offering farmers guaranteed prices. The key objective at the outset was to revive rice production and to restore food self-

---

35. Africa Contemporary Record 1976-77, p. B601.

36. See, e.g. Goulet, Looking at Guinea-Bissau: a New Nation's Development Strategy (Overseas Development Council, March 1978); Rudebeck, in Carl G.Rosberg and Thomas M.Callaghy (eds), Socialism in Sub-Saharan Africa (University of California Press, London, 1979).

sufficiency and some progress had been made in this respect by 1977, when rice imports were reduced to 11,000 tons. Such signs of recovery were not however sustained. In 1978 rice production fell once more, and from 1979 the economic situation became increasingly grave. By 1980 Guinea-Bissau's survival depended on foreign assistance.[37]

This crisis underlined the basic problems of underdevelopment that the revolution could not overcome. Guinea-Bissau was still small, backward and lacking in natural resources. The country remained exceptionally vulnerable to forces beyond its control, such as the weather and world oil prices. Thus the severe drought that hit West Africa in 1978 partially explained the drop in food production. Nevertheless, many of the difficulties that the party had encountered in the preceding six years must be explained in terms of its severe lack of skilled man-power. The party did not, as Pereira had recognised in 1976, have the 'means of material, technical and administrative action that national reconstruction and economic independence demand'.[38] Foreign experts provided important assistance, but the party was also dependent on former colonial civil servants who sought to use their influence to modify party policy. Other difficulties suggested that both party and government machinery were overstrained. On the one hand the network of People's Stores after some initial success began to break down. On the other hand financial, marketing and transport facilities for rice producers were inadequate with the result that many peasants gave up growing for the market. Shortages of basic commodities greatly increased. The few factories operated at a fraction of their capacity. Much of the enormous amount of foreign assistance was badly used.[39]

The fundamental constraint lay in the agricultural sector, and the party's inability to sustain the villagers' early enthusiasm for increasing production. The PAIGC had recognised from the start that Guinea-Bissau must remain an agricultural economy, and that peasant agriculture must provide the necessary increase of surplus.[40] The peasant sector was however fundamentally poor, and it could not make that effort without external support. The process of transforming village agriculture would be long and, as Cabral saw, a critical block to development.[41] Guinea-Bissau was thus caught, notwithstanding its successful struggle for independence, in the same way as other small, poor, African states: between its dependence on the one hand on the global and on the other the village economy. It was the dilemma of how to confront that dependence in the search for development that began to erode the party's unity.

---

37. Africa Contemporary Record 1974-75, 1975-76, 1979-80.
38. Davidson, No Fist, p. 175.
39. Goulet, p. 35; Chabal in West Africa, 29 January 1981.
40. See Goulet, pp. 20-36, for a useful account of Guinea-Bissau's development strategy up to 1977.
41. Davidson, Liberation of Guinea, p. 135.

Disagreement over economic strategy began to appear in 1976-7, although it was not acknowledged until the coup in November 1980 when President Luis Cabral (Amilcar's brother) was ousted from office.[42] By that time three central elements of the PAIGC's whole developmental strategy were at issue: the priority accorded to agriculture in economic planning; the question of the integration of Guinea-Bissau with Cape Verde, which had also become independent in 1975 with the PAIGC in power; and the democratic basis of the party. While the debate over those three years remains somewhat obscure, the lines along which the party leadership split were made clear by the coup; between those committed to the revolution and those prepared to adopt a more pragmatic line. On the economic front President Cabral had adopted a pragmatic approach towards development. Faced with the enormous growth of Bissau, and taking bureaucrats' rather than party advice, he had begun to shift to a more urban and industrial-orientated programme. A number of doubtful industrial projects were agreed to, while in the search for foreign exchange he emphasised ground nut production again. Agriculture otherwise was neglected.[43] On the party front he appeared to move away from the old collective leadership, to ignore the democratically elected elements of the party and to forget its mass rural support. It was these actions that aroused resentment within both the party itself, and the army.

Joao Bernardo Viera, who ousted President Cabral, was a highly respected guerrilla leader who had been trained by Amilcar Cabral himself. He represented not only the military but also the party tradition as it had been moulded by the war. He justified his actions on the grounds of Luis Cabral's departure from the revolutionary principles of the party, its commitment to egalitarian development and to rural society. He challenged the growing dominance of Bissau, and its small urban elite, that seemed to be eroding those revolutionary principles.[44] The coup therefore was intended to restore the party to the central command of the struggle for development.

In so far as Guinea-Bissau has any lessons for those concerned with the relationship between revolution and development they are limited by its size. Nevertheless its experience up to 1980 serves to highlight the problems of revolutionary development in the poor African state. The post-colonial experience, brief as it was, had demonstrated the extent to which poverty and the very under-development of the new state imposed severe constraints on the achievement of a socialist strategy for development. The armed struggle had demonstrated the capacity of a revolutionary movement to wear out the superior forces of imperalism. The creation of a

---

42. Goulet, pp. 46-47.

43. Chabal, p. 161; also idem in West Africa, 22/29 December 1980; Rudebeck in Rosberg, p. 338.

44. This conclusion is based on Chabal, Rudebeck, (1979) and on the trend of events since 1974.

socialist state however required additional skills, which had still to be learned. In this respect, in 1980, the revolution had scarcely begun.

Chapter Twelve

FRANCE, MAY 1968: A NEW KIND OF 'REVOLUTION'?

Richard DeAngelis

Introduction: the 'New Left' and 'Revolution'*

Plus c'est la même chose, plus ça change.[1]

In the late 1960s, during the long boom of the post-World War II era, the advanced-capitalist, liberal-democratic world rediscovered the spectre of 'revolution'. A variety of protests - student revolts, anti-Vietnam War movements, cultural critiques of bureaucracy and 'technocracy', and 'consciousness-raising' activities by ecologists, feminists, and 'minorities' - seemed to become more radical and, eventually, to merge into a global attack on what they loosely called 'the system'. The label 'New Left' came to be associated with these protesters against bureaucratic, materialist, 'patriarchal' capitalism, since many were also sceptical of Soviet-style regimes.

After the disillusionments of the Cold War, many 'old Left' activists and groups tried to see in the themes and efforts of the New Left the resurgence of the prospect of the 'revolution' (albeit disguised in quasi-anarchist, 'petty bourgeois' rhetoric). Despite disdain for Cold War anti-communism and lingering respect for the success of Marxist-Leninist revolutions in at least gaining power, these New Left groups, however, were ambivalent about accepting the inheritance of Great Revolutionary theory which was offered to them.[2]

---

* I would like to thank Andrew Parkin and David Close for major improvements to early drafts of this chapter.

1. 'The more it's the same thing [revolution], the more it changes'.

2. By 'classical' 'Great' revolutions, I mean those the historian emphasises: sudden, violent and major, regime changes, as occurred in 1789 in France, 1917 in Russia, etc. The Marxist-Leninist notion - of the final insurrection by the vanguard-led masses to establish a temporary 'socialist dictatorship', on the way to the classless society - is self-consciously in this tradition, whose mission it seeks to fulfil.

New Left revolutionaries also said, vaguely, they wanted 'community', 'socialism', 'emancipation', and 'participatory democracy for all in decisions affecting their daily lives'. But they were often quite sceptical whether the traditional revolutionary process would work in advanced capitalism, or even if it did, whether it would lead to these desired goals. The declining prestige of the Soviet revolutionary model made the search for a new, renovated kind of 'revolution' a major preoccupation of many in the New Left.

Some seemed to find hope in variants of the Soviet model in China, Cuba or Yugoslavia; however, these were revolutions in quite different socio-economic contexts from that of western Europe or North America, and all had also triumphed via violent insurrections and/or civil wars. Caught between the critique of the 'capitalist status quo' on the one hand and the awareness, on the other, of the democratic deficiences of existing Marxian 'revolutions', New Left activists hesitated. They hoped for history to create a positive alternative to their double rejection of capitalism and existing state socialism.

However imperfectly, the May-June 1968 explosion in France seemed, at first, to fit the bill. Here a student revolt against repressive authority and 'consumerist' capitalism triggered off a massive general strike by manual workers and white-collar employees. By its scope and intensity, this strike posed a severe threat to the regime of President de Gaulle, the Fifth French Republic. Moreover, the course of events was relatively spontaneous, bloodless, non-elitist, anti-bureaucratic, and even poetic. In these respects it seemed unprecedented. It appeared (almost) to succeed, some argued, precisely because it distrusted careful planning, organisation, and 'realistic' or cold-blooded appraisals (e.g. revolutions as a military campaign) in favour of confrontations based on courage, enthusiasm, and creativity by ordinary citizens themselves.[3]

An investigation of the May-June 1968 events, therefore, should help to shed some light on the question of whether or not 'revolution', especially of a new kind, is a possible option in advanced-capitalist societies.

---

3. See especially Richard Gombin, The Origins of Modern Leftism (Penguin, Harmondsworth, 1975). Says Gombin: for 'leftism' [e.g. 'that segment of the revolutionary movement which offers ... a radical alternative to Marxism-Leninism', p. 17, based on strands of anarchism, council communism, revolutionary reformism, etc.], 1) '... the Leninist conception of revolution as the seizure of political power at the summit bears all the marks of bourgeois thought', p. 19; 2) 'all revolutions up to now have been failures. The revolution has to be reinvented ... [as] total contestation of modern capitalism', p. 69; and/or 3) '... the hard core of the councillist viewpoint [was that] in the course of its struggle, the proletariat spontaneously creates the organisation it needs ... [in] a non-centralised form...' p. 81.

Overview of the May-June Events

Une Révolution Un Peu Fête, Une Fête Un Peu Révolution[4]

The May-June events came as a surprise, both to observers and to all but a handful of eventual participants - and even that handful could not have dared hope beforehand that the movement would go as far and as fast as it did.

In 1968, France had been at peace for six years, after the recent end of the Algerian war. For the first time in nearly thirty years no immediate external conflict threatened. The regime, itself partly the product of military insurrection in 1958, was exactly ten years old in May. It had weathered army insurrections and assassination attempts while disengaging France from Algeria (1958-1962), and it had gone on to institutionalise itself both internally and externally. Although arrogant and somewhat aloof, the regime's leaders still seemed legitimated by electoral success, political stability, economic dynamism, and international prestige.

Economic growth and standards of living had been improving, rapidly though unevenly, for over twenty years, by May 1968, enabling even many peasants and workers to acquire cars and consumer durables. French reputation abroad was the highest it had been for generations.

In April, only weeks before the May events, Le Monde's senior columnist Pierre Viansson-Ponte wrote that 'France is bored'. Despite many minor problems (which in retrospect look like premonitions of what was to happen in May), to most people France, at last, seemed stable. Of course students were protesting; some about uncertain job prospects, deplorable conditions in overcrowded faculties and outmoded dormitory restrictions separating the sexes, others, more radical, about American actions in Vietnam, repressive consumerism, and/or all forms of authority as such. But when were students not protesting? And of what consequence could their protests be? Such were the conventional replies. Of course, in many parts of France, young workers and some trade unions had recently taken more extreme, even illegal means (such as street fights, holding bosses hostage) to further traditional wage demands. But most workers seemed resignedly quiescent. The unions were still weak and divided (despite some moves toward greater unity of action); and the regime had already used its authority successfully against so many groups (army officers, peasants, workers, etc.) that it seemed little chance existed for any major gains. Of course, the Communist, Socialist and Radical Left was regaining some of its lost strength and pursuing talks of unity. But when had the French Left ever shown any capacity for effective and united political action? The regime, if not perfect, was in many eyes the best of all possible alternatives. Government leaders were haughtily complacent. Only

4. 'A Revolution a bit festival, a festival a bit revolution', quoted from Le Monde Hebdomadaire, 4-10 May, 1978.

the unpredictable and spontaneous - but not entirely accidental - coming-together of discontents from many different groups with different (and conflicting) demands could create the May movement and drive it forward.

Space prevents a detailed summary of what actually occurred in those suspenseful days.[5] However, a quick overview of the main stages of the 'revolutionary' process may be useful.

In the first stage, the Student Revolt (3-12 May), a loose coalition of old and new Left student revolutionaries, sparked by the confrontationist tactics of leaders like Daniel Cohn-Bendit, provoked university authorities to overreact by calling in police. The heavyhandedness and then vacillations of the government, ultimately responsible for the universities, radicalised many moderate students and alienated public opinion - in France traditionally hostile to the police. Streetfighting and massive demonstrations, in Paris especially, escalated into violent (but not fatal) confrontations, including a particularly bitter fight on 10-11 May over street barricades in the Latin Quarter.

Public and union outrage at governmental repression of students, even if many student demands seemed far-fetched, led to the second stage, the General sit-down Strike (May 11-25). This stage coincided with a change in government policy from repression to a policy of waït-and-see. At the high point of the strike, which spread into many white-collar areas and even to many younger professionals eager to overturn the arbitrary power of cliques of privileged 'mandarins', France was at a standstill. At least, six to seven million people were on strike for more money and more respect. Many were occupying factories and offices, some were even talking of running their factory themselves. Most, though not all, were voluntary protestors.[6] When frantic attempts to negotiate a compromise settlement of the strikes was rejected by militant workers nearly everywhere, after de Gaulle's own

---

5. The best short and accessible account in English is Patrick Seale and Maureen McConville, French Revolution 1968 (Penguin, Harmondsworth, 1968). See also: Eric J. Hobsbawm, 'May 1968', pp. 234-244 in his Revolutionaries (Weidenfeld and Nicolson, London, 1973); David B. Goldey, 'A Precarious Regime; the Events of May 1968', in Philip M. Williams, French Politicians and Elections: 1951-1969 (Cambridge University Press, Cambridge 1970), pp. 226-260; George Ross, 'The Events of May-June 1968', in his Workers and Communists in France: From Popular Front to Eurocommunism (University of California Press, Berkeley, 1982), pp. 168-211; and Laurence Wylie et al, France: the Events of May-June 1968 - a Critical Bibliography (Center for West European Studies, Pittsburgh, 1973).

6. See Gérard Adam, 'Étude statistique des grèves de mai-juin 1968', Revue Française de Science Politique, vol. XX, no. 1 (février 1970:) 105-119; and Pierre Dubois et al, Grèves revendicatives ou grèves politiques? (Anthropos, Paris, 1971).

solution - a referendum - failed to win any support at all, the student crisis became a major political upheaval.

Stage three (25-30 May) was the regime crisis, when hesitations and doubts at the top of the government itself were met by increasingly severe power plays among the rival opposition groups, already disputing who was to take over. The crisis ended when de Gaulle regained his old zest for a fight and the Communists (previously ultra-cautious) were forced to come out into the open with their own power-bid, thus allowing the conflicts to be portrayed in traditional anti-Communist and Cold War terms. Threats of bloody civil war brought the movement to a halt.

In stage four, the mopping up (June) and the aftermath (1968 till the present), the regime renewed its control and then its legitimacy by organising its own supporters, winning early elections, and combining some moderate university and union reforms with continued police repression. De Gaulle, himself, wanted more. He rescheduled his referendum on more 'participation' in government in early 1969 to show he was still indispensable. He lost, however, then resigned - ultimately a casualty of the May events. But the regime survived his departure, and with moderate conservatives in charge for another thirteen years. Only in May 1981 with the election of Francois Mitterrand as President did many of the themes of May 1968 seem to have any real chance at all, and even then in a much more traditional and less 'revolutionary' context.

Why the May-June 1968 'Events'?[7]

Any standard account makes clear how many different crises there were, each with its own logic, although each also interacted with

---

7. The French themselves have come to use the neutral euphemism 'events' in reaction to the multiplicity of contradictory labels and metaphors that flourished in the literature (e.g. revolt, nightmare, crisis, wind of folly, festival, uprising, movement, 'bedwetting' [chienlit], mutation, short-circuit, system overload, explosion, irruption, and revolution [plain, or betrayed, or elusive, or dress rehearsal for .../prelude to...]. In English, see especially Charles Posner, ed., Reflections on the Revolution in France: 1968 (Penguin, Harmondsworth, 1970); Stanley Hoffmann, 'Confrontation in May 1968', in his Decline or Renewal? France Since the 1930s (Viking, New York, 1974), pp. 145-184; Gabriel and Daniel Cohn-Bendit, Obsolete Communism: the Left-Wing Alternative (Penguin, Harmondsworth, 1969); Daniel Singer, Prelude to Revolution: France in May 1968 (J. Cape, London, 1970); Henri Lefebvre, The Explosion: Marxism and the French Upheaval (Monthly Review Press, London, 1969); Raymond Aron, The Elusive Revolution (Praegor, New York, 1969). See in French: Philippe Bénéton et Jean Touchard, 'Les interprétations de la crise de mai-juin 1968', Revue Française de Science Politique, vol.XX,

the others. Loosely following the explanatory scheme first developed by Crane Brinton in his Anatomy of Revolution we will draw eclectically on a range of causal factors often cited in the literature.[8]

Background Conditions

From the 1960s on, most advanced-industrial societies experienced turmoil over issues similar to those raised in May 1968: greater and more effective liberty, equality and fellowship, and for all, and now. However, only in France did separate group protests come together to create a major cultural and political crisis. One of the reasons for this coming together was that French life is much more centralised and state-dominated than elsewhere. Under de Gaulle, especially, power seemed distant, arbitrary, and arrogant. Of that, more later. Another reason is that the Fifth Republic acclerated the scope and pace of socio-economic change in post-World War II France.[9]

Building on such Fourth Republic foundations as the Common Market, indicative economic planning, nuclear weapons research, and the early stages of rapid economic growth and rural exodus, the Gaullist Fifth Republic went further and more effectively. It developed 'strong' and stable state institutions, centered around a quasi-monarchical President, capable of breaking the Gordian knot of disengagement from colonial war in Algeria and of forcing world-competitive industrialisation on a backward economy, via state-led industrial policy and relatively tight control of wages and social reforms.

Political parties and sectional interest groups, always relatively ineffective and divided in France, were even further weakened by the reduction in the role of Parliament and by the Gaullian style of decision-making with its reliance on a techno-bureaucratic, Parisian elite. Given the extraordinary centralisation of nearly all decisive

---

no.3 (juin 1970), 503-544; Adrien Dansette, Mai 1968 (Plon, Paris, 1971); Roger Bourderon et al, 'Les événements de mai 1968', pp. 359-393 in Histoire de la France Contemporaine, tome VII: 1947-1968 (Editions Sociales, Paris, 1981); Régis Debray, Modeste contribution aux discours et cérémonies officielles du dixième anniversaire (Maspéro, Paris, 1978); Alain Touraine, Le Mouvement de mai ou le communisme utopique (Seuil, Paris, 1968).

8. Crane Brinton, The Anatomy of Revolution (Prentice-Hall, Englewood Cliffs, 1952). See also Barrington Moore, Jr's analysis of prospects for revolution in an industrial society such as the USA, in 'Some Prospects for Predatory Democracy', pp. 150-193, in his Reflections on the Causes of Human Misery... (Beacon, Boston, 1972).

9. See John Ardagh, The New French Revolution (Harper, New York, 1968), and subsequent editions (yet another use of the term "revolution"! this time to refer to major change but through evolutionary processes). See also: W.G. Andrews and Stanley Hoffmann, eds, The Impact of the Fifth Republic (State University of New York Press, Albany, 1981).

spheres of life in Paris, and within the corridors of state ministries, the government's role was extensive indeed. Its responsibility for nearly everything that happened anywhere in France, in fact, far exceeded its effective ability to control events. At the same time, however, hyper-centralisation prevented anyone else doing much on their own about key problems.

Moreover, in the face of rapid urbanisation, the relatively self-sufficient social and familial networks of provincial France were breaking down. New forms of urban social solidarity had not yet time to grow. In its isolation and fragmentation, exacerbated by the rapid pace of change and the new urban anonymity of apartment blocks and large offices and factories, French society resembled a 'lonely crowd' in many ways.[10] One of the most striking features of the May events in many cities was how neighbors, even strangers, talked to each other for the first time. When they did so, many discovered that they had in common a dislike of governmental disdain for the concerns of ordinary people.

Ironically, the regime also increasingly fell victim to its own past successes. Its strength and stability, its indifference to petty local and sectional claims, its pursuit of long-term projects on the world scene had been justified as reactions to debilitating past weaknesses and external threats. The French in 1958 had been willing, as they had often been before, to allow extraordinary power to a saviour, de Gaulle, to clean out the Augean stables.[11] But, having done that by 1962, the regime had a harder time justifying its continued reliance on 'exceptional' measures once the immediate Algerian war was over.

Whereas de Gaulle wanted a strong state and economy as means to allow France to play a greater international role, the French were slow to accept the costs of grandeur. More concerned about their daily lives, they worried about threats to their existing livelihoods, changing social mores, or the frustrations of an increasingly mobile and competitive society. Not sharing all of de Gaulle's visions, many were reluctant to make the wrenching sacrifices that rapid industrialisation required. But the strong executive state had weakened the traditional safety valves and channels of influence that had served to lower tensions previously (e.g. parties, Parliament, interest groups, local municipalities and provincial notables), precisely because it feared a responsive state would be unable to accomplish anything at all. By solving one set of crises (Algeria, a new constitution), it made the

---

10. The expression is from David Riesman et al, The Lonely Crowd (Yale University Press, New Haven, 1950). Even de Gaulle was aware of this problem: "by contrast with the individualist existence ... of our fathers, the French today see themselves constrained ... by a mechanized and socialized life ... in a grey and anonymous crowd ...", in his L'Effort, 1961 ... (Plon, Paris, 1971), pp. 115-117.

11. See S. Hoffmann, Decline or Renewal, 'The Rulers; Heroic Leadership in Modern France', pp. 63-110.

French feel less threatened and thus less willing to support a strong state indefinitely.

Economically too, the rapid growth of industry, trade, and incomes had unintended, though forseeable consequences. Although a majority, even workers and peasants, were at least gaining access to the 'good life' (e.g. cars, television, refrigerators, long vacations, better educational opportunities), the rate of improvement was very uneven; many had to leave their local areas and previous jobs; and expectations often outran performance. High-level employees in modern industries did very well, while the aged, workers, traditional peasants, and shopkeepers and employees in inefficient, older industries did much less well. At the same time, economic modernisation and urban secularism undermined the authority of many older values and groups. The humanist intelligentsia, the Catholic church, the Communist party, the bourgeois family, the army, and the state school system, all institutions which had structured French life for a hundred years at least, were caught in deep organisational and morale problems. Their prestige and long-term viability were threatened by both a loosening of older class loyalties and traditional values and the emergence of new hedonistic, privatised, and libertarian lifestyles. On the other hand, many rising groups thirsted for that which they were likely to enjoy tomorrow but felt they deserved today. Often they were also oppressed by the continuing importance, even if much reduced, of older groups, traditions, and values. Economic change whetted the appetites of the modern elements of the bourgeoisie and the young but threatened the stability and legitimacy of older bourgeois and conservative people in all classes. The regime was seen as too backward by the former, tied as it was in origin and electoral support to Catholics, the military, the peasantry, and older women. Yet the government was seen as too radically 'modern' by the latter, even if they supported it by their votes to avoid something even worse.

Finally, the regime was also culturally constrained by what Hoffmann calls the French style of authority and pattern of change, as worked out over several centuries.[12] Given a society long bitterly divided on geographic, linguistic, religious, and ideological lines but which had also evolved a centralised state to maintain national unity and to further France's 'civilising mission' at home and abroad, the French discovered a workable solution. It was a state with limited scope but broad, quasi-'authoritarian', powers within that scope and with bureaucratically uniform and rigid rules. Thus, French people could avoid having to compromise personally with other French people (often enemies from past conflicts) but could delegate difficult decisions to an impersonal state. Bureaucracy and rules prevented individual favouritism and limited the advantages or dangers of capturing the state for any one particular group. And in reserve, the

---

12. Stanley Hoffmann, 'Paradoxes of the French Political Community', in Stanley Hoffmann <u>et al</u>, <u>In Search of France</u> (Harper, New York, 1965), pp. 1-117.

French retained the right to disobey, to remain unconcerned, and ultimately to revolt.

Such a system worked, especially from 1870 to 1940, to prevent too much change. It provided a *modus vivendi* for a people condemned to live together by history but lacking political or social consensus. In a crisis, either a saviour or a mini-revolution (or both) could, with luck, make drastic changes possible for a short time. But typically, normal life revolved around bargaining to avoid changes that would affect existing rights and ways of life. The Gaullist regime had its origins in such a (decolonisation) crisis in 1958. But de Gaulle wanted to be more than a temporary saviour. He wanted to preside over long-term changes, fostered from the top down, in the absence of consensus, in the hopes that nearly all French people would agree in the end. But the process of imposed change created its own resistance before that new consensus could be achieved.

In the meantime, the French Left's own 'revolutionary' tradition kept the opposition's hopes alive to change through revolution rather than piecemeal and uncertain reforms. It also made any reforms seem dangerous to many conservatives, only too aware that they might not preclude but instead lead on to revolution.

In Hoffmann's analysis, the key to French politics is the French ambivalence to authority. It is both feared and seen as necessary. May 1968 in one sense was a holiday from ordinary authority for many but with the expectation that such a holiday could not last. Even the anarchists in May caught some of this ambivalence with their slogan 'il est interdit d'interdire' (it is forbidden to forbid). There were elements of 'psycho-drama' in May 1968; but that is true of other revolutions too.

Immediate Causes and Precipitants

In terms of classic revolutionary criteria such as those which presumably led to the Great Revolutions of 1789 or 1917, France in May 1968 was *not* in a pre-revolutionary mood (as the Communist party emphasised to justify its prudent stance).[13]

For example, there was no major new 'desertion of the intellectuals'. So long as minor intellectuals such as provincial school teachers remained loyal and the Parisian luminaries remained aloof, the government was happy. In fact, from the late 1950s on, there was an increasing desertion of the formerly pro-Communist intellectuals from the orbit of the Communist party and Soviet Marxism. They left in favor either of 'New-Left' positions like Sartre's or Gorz's in the spirit of the May 1968 movement or of 'modernist' views such as J.J. Servan-Schreiber's or Raymond Aron's emphasis on the emergence of

---

13. See L. Salini, *Mai des prolétaires* (Éditions Sociales, Paris, 1968); Bourderon, *Histoire ...*; and Ross, *Workers ....*

post-industrialism on American lines.[14] In any event, politically committed anti-Gaullist intellectuals were few.

Nor, as we have seen already, was there any critical foreign pressure or war to undermine regime legitimacy and solvency - in fact, just the opposite.[15] Nor were there any exacerbated fiscal crises in regime finances and attendant intractable class conflicts over who was to pay for them; de Gaulle emphasised a balanced budget and had gold in reserve. What economic conflicts existed (over growing unemployment or fears of inflation),[16] were paltry by 1930s or even 1970s standards. In the narrow, everyday sense, governmental efficiency had rarely been higher. Harvests were good, perhaps overabundant, and the recession of 1966-67 was merely a decline in the rate of growth of the economy. Nor were major opposition groups objectively becoming very much stronger and more radicalised. While many minor groupuscules (grouplets) such as emerged in May were very frustrated and radical, the major political parties and unions on the Left were engaged instead in long-term and legal strategies to revive their fortunes which de Gaulle had smashed in 1958 on his return to power. The Communists especially were wary of short-run crises and 'ultra-left adventurism'. Finally, although governmental authorities wanted to avoid unnecessary bloodshed and bent over backward to do so, the regime could defend itself. It could count on police and army obedience (though not enthusiasm) in a crunch. It could - and ultimately did - also bribe the farmers into quiescence and thus use rural police and gendarme reserves to quell urban riots; elites in the Great Revolutions had no such luck.

Although classical preconditions for violent civil war and insurrection were notably absent in France in 1968, there were considerable pressures towards both a more radicalised expression of long-standing discontents, and the convergence of these discontents with new ones in a way that could lead to 'system overload' and massive crisis.[17]

---

14. J.P. Sartre, Les Communistes ont peur de la révolution (J.Didier, Paris, 1968); A. Gorz, Adieux au prolétariat (Galilée, Paris, 1980); J.J. Servan-Schreiber, The Spirit of May (McGraw-Hill, New York, 1968); Raymond Aron, Le Spectateur engagé (Julliard, Paris, 1981).

15. See Theda Skocpol, States and Social Revolutions (Cambridge University Press, Cambridge, 1979), who emphasises the role of foreign pressure on regimes.

16. Unemployment had grown by several hundred thousand in the late 1960s to almost 800,000; inflation was usually in the mid-single-figures range; see Goldey, op.cit., p. 246. In the 1970s, both figures have at least doubled.

17. See Aristide and Vera Zolberg, 'The Meanings of May (Paris, 1968)', Midway Magazine, Winter, 1969, pp. 91-109. Skocpol speculates too, 'If a social revolution were to transform an advanced industrial nation, it would ... have to take a very different form, and occur under

First, there was the student revolt, a phenomenon of the 1960s in many countries. What were relatively distinctive of France were: 1) the poor conditions of high school and university[18] (e.g. outmoded sex segregation, overcrowding, poor facilities, uncertain job prospects, distant and authoritarian teachers and decision-makers, organisational rigidity), 2) the centralised and bureaucratic state control of education, which turned student protest anywhere into challenges to state authority as such, and 3) the extremely politicised and radicalised character of university student politics. The first problem was possibly avoidable by a less rapid and more coordinated expansion and democratisation of the education system. The government, however, would have been blamed by its own voters even, for being 'elitist'! The two other difficulties were (and still are) nearly impossible to change. Virtually no one in France has been able to reform the university system established under Napoleon to make it more efficient, open, flexible, and fair. French student politics moreover, have always been characterised by excessive fragmentation, ideological infighting, and divorce from ordinary student concerns.

In fact, the conjunction of a) the breakdown of the traditional student Communist movement (provoked by the parent party's refusal to destalinise), b) the emergence of Left Catholic militancy among students, and c) the familiarity with street protest against the Algerian and Vietnam wars meant a student movement bubbling with rival groups. All were hoping to revive their influence and regain ordinary student interest by new forms of political activities, not necessarily legal or peaceful. In fact, the anarchist tactics of Cohn-Bendit and other leaders <u>required</u> radical and illegitimate forms of protests to provoke authorities; their overreactions would then allow unification of the squabbling student militant groups for even further provocations and confrontations, ultimately exposing the ugly repressive face of the regime behind the 'democratic' mask. The Gaullists' disdainful neglect and then harsh repression of the student radicals, when they did not truly want to risk a blood bath, played into the student leaders' hands. The latter wanted or did not fear a showdown; when the government's bluff was called, it either had to shoot or back down. Its public humiliation when it retreated (by withdrawing police from the Latin Quarter after the week of street fights) was the signal that the regime was weaker than it appeared. It

---

quite different international conditions, from the great historical social revolutions. ... a modern social revolution would probably have to flow gradually, not cataclysmically, out of a long series of "non-reformist reforms", accomplished by mass-based political movements struggling to democratize every major institution...', <u>States and Social Revolutions</u>, pp. 292-3.

18. These conditions were much less frustrating in the 'great schools' such as the <u>Polytechnique</u>; however, students even in such elite institutions felt some fo the same feelings as their university comrades.

was the moment for everyone else with a grievance to attempt to do what the students had done.

The second stream of protest came from workers, technicians, and employees. By comparison with the amount of writing on students and their views, much less is known, even today, about what happened in May among workers, especially in the provinces.[19] Nor were all workers likely to have the same feelings and demands. As the Communist party and its affiliated union the General Confederation of Work (CGT) alleged then and later, the majority of workers had no conscious wish to overturn the whole social order or to risk civil war. They mostly wanted material demands met on a much larger scale, or often simply more consideration from distant company bosses.[20] But younger workers, workers in new factories, declining areas or anti-union environments, and many politicised technicians were often more radical.

Since the mid-1960s, especially after a mini-recession and anti-inflationary economic policy in the few years just before 1968, workers and unions were under considerable pressure to maintain their standard of living, meagre political influence, and past social reforms. Both government and employers were seeking by restrictive incomes policies (without real consultations) to restrict the growth of welfare costs and wages to meet international competition, especially in the Common Market. Many workers, however saw other social classes getting richer more quickly and resented such restrictions as unfair. As well, industrialisation and economic concentrations meant the emergence of more intensive assembly-line work in many factories. 'Modernisation' meant disruptions to traditional routines, for which workers and unions wanted at least monetary compensations. Coupled with continuing frustrations on the part of the more Leftist unions at being frozen out of the political process, the mood in the factories was one of readiness for determined protest at the first sign of hesitation on the part of the government.

Even so, it was a surprise to everyone involved that the movement spread so widely and so rapidly, even into areas and industries previously unaffected by unions such as women workers in textile factories in small villages. Whether or not the workers were consciously revolutionary in _intent_, the _methods_ used (often illegal and requiring troops to break if worker morale remained high), the _scope_ of the strike (nearly all public and private services and goods, including utilities occasionally as a show of strength), and the _spontaneous, mass-origin_ of many of the strikes (despite the unions' initial caution) meant

19. See Adam, _Étude_; Ross, _Workers_; and Richard DeAngelis, _Blue-collar Workers and Politics: a French Paradox_ (Croom Helm, London, 1982).

20. Salini, _Mai_ and Ross, _Workers_ '... the necessary unity of the French Left to propose any alternative to Gaullism in May was not present... [thus] it was vastly preferable to allow the regime to stay in power...', pp. 210-211.

a severe crisis for the regime.

Union rivalries in the face of these mass pressures also made compromise difficult. For fear of being outrun on the far Left by student groups, the largest union (the pro-Communist CGT) took over the strike and generalised it after the first few days. They did so too because the formerly-Catholic but now socialist-leaning French Democratic Confederation of Work (CFDT) union, which was sympathetic to the student radicals, was pushing the strike for all it was worth. Both the CFDT and the students wanted to show to the workers that the CGT was simply a conservative appendage to the ossified Communist party. Accused by the far-left of 'betraying' the revolution, the CGT and the Communists (PCF) could not publicly disown the strike, however much they feared provoking bloody repression against themselves. They could only hope to limit the strike to negotiable, non-'revolutionary', material demands.[21]

The government under Prime Minister Pompidou knew this and counted on the CGT to help bring the conflict to an end by bargaining. However, the (reluctant) Communist leading role in the strike gave it an ominous tone in the eyes of the anti-Communist middle classes and the peasantry, who feared ulterior motives and a Soviet-style push for power. Unfortunately for the PCF and CGT, this fear could not be assuaged, nor a bargain struck with Pompidou without appearing to confirm the charges of 'betrayal' of the revolution laid by union and student rivals. Caught between a romantic belief in ultimate revolution and cautious appraisal of the limits to change in the present, both Communist party and union followed more than they led their troops. They were compelled to fan the flames of the strike at first but then could not end it when they wanted to, after negotiations, (27 May) when radical workers rejected the agreed protocols.[22] This failure left the government leaders with no policy other than civil war or abdication - a choice none dared make for several days until de Gaulle did so for them all. It also left the Communists and CGT out on a limb, which they could escape from only by becoming more radical themselves - just the move that Gaulle needed, however, as we shall see.

The strike, then, was a complex affair and a mix of anti-authority, anti-industrial discipline, anti-government, and anti-austerity themes. It did not really harmonise with the student radicals' ideology, except on the negative position of opposition to the Gaullist authorities. The strikers' desires were for 'materialist', wage-and-conditions improvements or a state-socialist, Popular Front strategy - which were anathema to the student leaders.

The key link between the student revolt and the sit-down strike and between the limited aims of many strikers and the crisis-induced radicalisation of the strike movement was political: the partisan struggle for power, exacerbated by the isolation, errors and arrogance

---

21. Ross, Workers, p. 201.
22. Ibid.

of the Gaullists we have already mentioned. If the origins of the May movement were largely socio-economic and the mood was influenced by cultural and psychological factors, the immediate causes of the spontaneous combustion of these different elements were political and personal.

It would take several books to describe and analyse the French political scene as it stood in 1968. For our purposes let us mention only a couple of main points.

First, in the late 1960s all French political parties were to some degree in crisis. This weakness encouraged and allowed the growth and politicisation of other groups (such as students, unions, environmentalists, feminists),[23] - while at the same time it made government policy hesitant and contradictory.

Second, the rivalries within the government camp (since the demise of the aging de Gaulle was inevitable very soon) were growing worse, as the regime had to find ways to outlive its charismatic founder.

Third, the (Socialist, Communist, and Radical) Lefts had begun 1) to recover from their drubbing by the Gaullists in elections in 1958 and 1962 and 2) to seek more unified methods of attaining power, despite still considerable fear and distrust by their 'allies' of the Communists who had been so slow to destalinise.[24] Moreover, in the 1965 presidential and 1967 legislative elections, the more unified Left forces seemed to be on the way back to power. In 1967, the government coalition won by only one seat. The government began to feel desperate and was liable to overreact.

Given these rivalries between Left and Right and within each camp and given the long-term strategies both coalitions were pursuing in virtual isolation from the concerns of many ordinary French people, there were few effective channels available to detect the rumblings which were to lead to May or to find adequate means for controlling the events once they started. And once the mishandling of the student revolt had made a sit-down strike occur, the government lost heart and hope rapidly (though briefly), while the Left fell too quickly for the dream that the regime would simply collapse.

The Right had placed itself in orbit around de Gaulle. When he stumbled, they found it hard to improvise and had to wait for him to regain his decisiveness. The Left meanwhile, was caught with three different strategies: 1) a Popular Front strategy, which only the Communists wanted any longer if power were really in the street where they were dominant; 2) an electoral and parliamentary reform strategy which was in-appropriate in the chaos of May; and 3) a student radical

---

23. Significantly, by comparison with the Great Revolutions, <u>not</u> the peasantry, which, despite some violent protests in the early 1960s, on the whole, had been coopted by the regime.

24. The Communists, of course, had reason to distrust <u>their</u> potential 'allies'. But as things turned out, the non-communists' <u>fears</u> were more important in May, since they had more options.

strategy of confrontations everywhere until something happened, which was too frightening for all the established Left parties. The Communists, while helpless to impose their strategy on others, were strong enough to prevent others' strategies from being imposed upon them.

This stalemate allowed the May cauldron to boil for several weeks. Ultimately, however, the initiative passed back into the hands of de Gaulle when the Communists had to bid for power for themselves simply to ward off rivals. This bid turned moderate public opinion against them as fears of a coup were fanned by Gaullist propaganda. The Left as a whole was hostage to the Communists, who seemed indispensable to them. When de Gaulle turned on the Communists themselves, the entire Left foundered.

All of this may have been inevitable. Certainly the success of a Popular Front strategy along the lines preferred by the Communists seems to have been unlikely given the way the party had failed to reform itself prior to 1968, thus making its allies very nervous indeed. Certainly too, the peaceful, legal transfer of power to a Socialist-led government (with only a few Communist ministers) via an accommodating abdication by the Gaullist ministry seems even more implausible.

However, the continuation of the student-led confrontationist strategy might have produced more results. A nebulous and multifarious, cultural and participatory revolutionary festival was, in de Gaulle's own words, '<u>insaisissable</u>' (ungraspable, elusive). Even if it too had to raise the question of state power and a return to normalcy some time, such a bloodless, non-insurrectionary movement could have undermined the existing regime even more.

On the other hand, when, late in May, the student radicals tried to gain state power by quasi-insurrectionary demonstrations (burning the Stock Market, calls to take over the Presidential palace), and the Communists were in the streets demanding 'popular government', de Gaulle had just the situation he understood and could handle. Whereas before, de Gaulle admitted, he felt like resigning because he understood so little of what happened, now he was determined not to be pushed aside by his traditional enemies.

Whether the May movement might have 'succeeded' is unanswerable. It did come close to inducing a very strong regime to crumble. But one thing is clear. The movement had no chance and ended abruptly when it tried to force the pace by imitating past insurrections. A new kind of revolution cannot use the methods of classical revolutions without imperiling its own integrity and chances.

Interpretation: A New Kind of Revolution?

> It is not a revolution; it cannot be a revolution. No one is being killed. For it to be a revolution it is necessary to kill. But here it

is students in the street. They call the police 'SS', but these 'SS' kill no one; it is not serious...[25]

Despite the desires and predictions of Karl Marx, the last century of capitalist society in western Europe, North America and Australasia has not been characterised by mass, revolutionary insurrections leading to rapid, fundamental changes in political and socio-economic regimes. Instead, the major locus for 'classical'-style revolutions in this period has been either 1) in early industrialising, 'agrarian bureaucracies' such as Russia and China,[26] or 2) in colonies and former colonies of European empires such as Cuba, Algeria, Vietnam, and Guinea-Bissau.[27]

While advanced-capitalist 'polyarchies'[28] have undergone enormous changes, these improvements (e.g. the provision of social security, medical, family, and educational services and financial support on the basis of need) have been more the result of either 1) the accumulation of gradual minor struggles and changes or 2) relatively consensual compromises resulting from wartime crises. They have not been due to a revolutionary process. And however qualitatively better than the early capitalist period the present situation may be, it is not usually seen as a revolutionary outcome either. In this period, in these kinds of societies, the only socio-political change that might be considered 'revolutionary' is, interestingly, not from the Left but from the Right.[29]

Fascism and Nazism, as argued by David Close above,[30] do incorporate authentically '(counter)-revolutionary' elements. By their very emergence they demonstrated that industrial capitalist society and liberal democracy were no necessary guarantees of governmental effectiveness or societal stability. However, both of these historical phenomena proved to be much less revolutionary in practice and effect than in theory or intent.

Thus, while advanced-capitalist societies have not proved immune to economic and political crises, they have found ways to assure long-run survival. Interestingly, industrialised, state-socialist

---

25. Aron's friend, the Eastern European emigré philosopher Kojeve, in telephone calls to Aron, cited in Aron, Le Spectateur, p. 254.

26. See Barrington Moore, Jr., Social Origins of Dictatorship and Democracy (Beacon, Boston, 1966).

27. C.Gertzel and other chapters in this volume.

28. Robert Dahl, Polyarchy (Yale University Press, New Haven, 1971).

29. There have been, of course, a number of interesting 'failed revolutions' on the Left, such as the German one of 1918-20, which is the closest to a true 'proletarian' armed insurrection in any industrial society; see Barrington Moore, Jr., Chapters 8-11, pp. 275-397, in his Injustice..., (Macmillan, London, 1978).

30. See David Close's chapter on Nazism in this volume.

societies of the Soviet model have also been able, for a variety of reasons (including the Red Army), to ensure regime maintenance, despite enormous internal and external constraints and contradictions.

Given these phenomena, most political activists and analysts after World War II thought that classic revolutions similar to 1789 or 1917 were no longer possible in any complex, industrial society. Established elites retained the minimum of necessary control over the state bureaucracy and the means of repression - or were included in the sphere of influence of a foreign power with both access to such means and the will to use them. In addition, a number of phenomena of the post war boom such as rapid economic growth and rising private affluence, increased social mobility, rising levels of education and knowledge coupled with the relatively open, 'pluralistic' patterns of political decision-making,[31] tended in 'western' societies to deprive potential revolutions of either mass support or of a plausible ethical case for revolutionary violence.

The most compelling case for looking at the May-June 'events' of 1968 in France is they seem to contradict this line of analysis. If many of the accepted beliefs of the 1950s and 60s had been true, these ambiguous, simultaneously frightening and exhilarating 'evenements' should not have taken place at all. However, many of the participants in the 'events' as well as many sympathetic observers claim that revolution is no longer impossible in advanced-capitalist, liberal democracies.[32] This claim comes in two basic forms, which are partially contradictory and partially complementary.

According to one line of argument, a relatively classical revolution almost did, or could have occurred in France in 1968. Even if the movement ultimately 'failed' or was 'betrayed' in the short-run, it is merely a 'prelude' to the successful revolution that is still, and soon, to come, just as 1905 was the precursor of 1917 in Russia.[33]

The relatively more radical, *gauchiste*, or 'New Left' view is that the May events marked the first full-scale emergence of a *new kind* of revolution, as both process and goal. This new revolution rejects the 'classical' model as either irrelevant or dangerous in its overemphasis on a worked-out ideology and program, on vanguard parties and professional leaders, and on state power as an instrument to be captured and turned to different purposes. This new revolution sees means and ends as inextricably linked, violence as counterproductive, bureaucratic hierarchy and materialist affluence as avoidable evils, and self-management (*autogestion*) and cultural creativity as both the way

---

31. Dahl, *Polyarchy*. Interestingly, most sophisticated power elite and/or ruling-class models of power agree that most ordinary, day-to-day decision-making in complex societies is the monopoly of no single, clear, cohesive group; while the capitalist system may be hegemonic, it is not easy to agree on *who* is hegemonic *within it*.

32. See Seale and McConville, *French Revolution*, p. 94.

33. See Singer, *Prelude*; and A. Barjonet, *La Révolution trahie* (J. Didier, Paris, 1968).

forward and the ends to be achieved.[34] What makes May 1968 so fascinating, but also so complex and ambiguous, is the intricate mix of both kinds of revolutionary phenomena (as well as more traditional, non-revolutionary, interest-group demands) all happening together and influencing each other.

It is easy to forget how differently the world appeared to people, including ourselves, fifteen years ago. Between then and now lies an abyss. The world economic crisis since 1974 has exploded the myth of permanent affluence and growth. The USA's defeat in Vietnam and then Watergate officially ended an era of arrogant American Empire, while the deaths of Mao and Tito, the 'routinisation' of the Cuban revolution, and, last but not least, the incomprehensible genocide of the Khmer Rouge in Kampuchea - all served to create doubt and ideological confusion on the Left, where before there had been hope and certainty, or anger and determination. If ever there was a decade of rising expectations then it must have been the 1960s era of decolonisation, Third World development, test-ban treaties, Kennedy rhetoric, the Peace Corps, civil-rights movements, student protests, and the Prague Spring. In an era of declining expectations, however, the mood surrounding the May-June explosion is lost and the very idea that it might have been in any sense 'revolutionary' seems incongruous.

If this chapter had been written ten years ago in the immediate aftermath of 1968, it would have been hard to choose between these two arguments. Writing fifteen years after the 'events', however, one must conclude that the analysis of May as a failed or rehearsal form of classical revolution by workers and students seems increasingly implausible. However, it is much more difficult to discount the second line of argument, which redefines the 'essence' of revolution in modern industrial societies.[35]

Revolution may best be seen today as a decisive shift in the balance of social forces and values, a change in the basic rules of the socio-political game. If so, it can occur over a several-year period, in fits and starts, through crises and mass mobilisations but relatively non-violently. A revolutionary result may happen, but without armed insurrection, civil war or conquered state bastions. Just as 'hot' war is increasingly replaced by 'cold war' in international relations, 'hot' revolutions may be increasingly replaced by 'cold' (or 'cultural'?) revolutions in the age of urban, information-based, bureaucratic authority.[36]

If such a change in the character of revolution were plausible, it might help account not only for May-June 1968 in France but also for the emergence of the Solidarity movement in Poland after August 1980 (and its relative persistence despite martial-law repression after

34. R.Gombin, Origins.

35. Ibid., and Skocpol, States.

36. The metaphor is borrowed from Le Monde columnist Andre Fontaine, who has likened French politics to 'cold civil war'.

1981). In both France 1968 and Poland 1980, a crisis of political and economic legitimacy led to a surprising and spontaneous but also self-controlled mobilisation of a wide range of social groups (including workers, students, technicians). Not always coherently, these social forces aimed not to take over state power for themselves but rather to confront state authorities and force them to concede reforms. These reforms were to allow civil society more scope for autonomous development and to create conditions for a more equal dialogue between the state and ordinary citizens, using both direct and representative democratic procedures. In both cases (but of course to a qualitatively higher degree in Poland), foreign armed forces prevented classical, violent conflict as a reasonable strategy, especially since in both cases internal police and army forces were still loyal to established authority. However, despite such constraints, the revolutionary radicalisation of diverse and previously cowed social groups took place. While it is still much too soon to be certain, the long-term results of both struggles too are linked to quite new struggles and rules of the game.

Moreover, the emergence in France in 1981 of the Mitterrand Socialist-led government, although in many ways a much more traditional, old-Left experiment, also owes much to the themes, values and personnel of May 1968. This can be seen in the Mitterrand government's occasional emphasis on culture for all,shorter hours, work-sharing, decentralisation and greater democratisation of industry and in its social base, constructed on an alliance of workers, intellectuals, and urban employees.

In any event, permanent mass quiescence, governmental stability, and an 'end to ideology' seem definitely outdated phenomena.[37] Advanced-industrial society may still be immune to conquest from the street by armed revolutionaries. But it is also exceptionally vulnerable to determined opposition from below. It is dependent on the cooperation of civil society.[38] A revolution among the citizenry may ultimately matter more than a takeover of the state apparatus.

Analysis of the May-June events of 1968 in France, then, may be of some relevance not only for an understanding of French society and politics but also for that of revolution itself in the modern age.

---

37. S.M. Lipset, Political Man (Doubleday Anchor, New York, 1963), Ch. 13, pp. 439-456.

38. See B. Moore, 'Some Prospects'.

INDEX